CRYSTALS
for PSYCHIC
SELF-DEFENSE

"*Crystals for Psychic Self-Defense* will become the go-to guide for anyone wanting to care for and protect their energy body using crystals. Insightful and empowering, this is another outstanding book by Nicholas Pearson, an author who always seeks to expand the reader's knowledge and understanding of the crystal kingdom."

GEMMA PETHERBRIDGE, FOUNDER OF
CONSCIENCE CRYSTALS AND AUTHOR OF
YOUR CRYSTAL PLAN

"Nicholas Pearson thoroughly addresses the all-too-common query of how to protect oneself from psychic, energetic, and mental assaults. He details well-researched and proven protocols, selecting from 145 historically common and arcane crystals known to amplify esoteric knowledge to safeguard your well-being. He cuts through this foggy subject and illustrates clear ways you can free yourself from a wide range of problems, from unfocused emotional afflictions to geopathic stress to outright psychic attacks. We highly recommend this book, which can benefit both novice and advanced crystal practitioners."

HAPI HARA AND JOHNDENNIS GOVERT, AUTHORS OF
THE CHINTAMANI CRYSTAL MATRIX

"It is obvious that Nicholas Pearson has a deep and practical understanding of magic, making the book kind to beginners and detailed enough for those with a developed understanding of crystal magic. This makes *Crystals for Psychic Self-Defense* a fabulous addition to any metaphysical library. I love how the author stresses the importance of forming relationships with our stones, emphasizing that crystals are spiritual allies that work as catalysts that strengthen and enhance the effectiveness of our magic!"

SALICROW, WITCH, DRUID,
NATURAL PSYCHIC MEDIUM, AND AUTHOR OF
THE PATH OF ELEMENTAL WITCHCRAFT
AND *SPIRIT SPEAKER*

"An integral aspect of self-care is knowing how to defend oneself, but what if you don't realize you're even being attacked? In *Crystals for Psychic Self-Defense*, celebrated author Nicholas Pearson warns us of the various types of attacks and, more importantly, what we can do about them. The best offense is often a solid defense, and in this practical and in-depth guide, Pearson introduces us to the defensive attributes of stones from across the planet while also offering rituals and exercises to engage with these defensive qualities specifically. A powerful addition to your gemstone library, this book will easily complement other defensive practices."

BEN STIMPSON, AUTHOR OF
ANCESTRAL WHISPERS

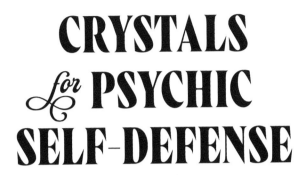

CRYSTALS for PSYCHIC SELF-DEFENSE

145 Gemstones
for Banishing, Binding, and Magickal Protection

NICHOLAS PEARSON

Destiny Books
Rochester, Vermont

Destiny Books
One Park Street
Rochester, Vermont 05767
www.DestinyBooks.com

Destiny Books is a division of Inner Traditions International

Note to the reader: *This book is intended to be an informational guide. The remedies, approaches, and techniques described herein are meant to supplement, and not to be a substitute for, professional medical care or treatment. They should not be used to treat a serious ailment without prior consultation with a qualified health care professional.*

Cataloging-in-Publication Data for this title is available from the Library of Congress

ISBN 978-1-64411-671-5 (print)
ISBN 978-1-64411-672-2 (ebook)

Printed and bound in India by Nutech Print Services

10 9 8 7 6 5 4 3 2 1

Text design and layout by Virginia Scott Bowman
This book was typeset in Garamond Premier Pro, Gill Sans, and Stone Sans with Minion and Wayfinder used as display typefaces.
Photographs and illustrations by S. T. Pearson-Walsh

To send correspondence to the author of this book, mail a first-class letter to the author c/o Inner Traditions • Bear & Company, One Park Street, Rochester, VT 05767, and we will forward the communication, or contact the author directly at **TheLuminousPearl.com**.

Scan the QR code and save 25% at InnerTraditions.com. Browse over 2,000 titles on spirituality, the occult, ancient mysteries, new science, holistic health, and natural medicine.

◆

*To the sensitive people of the world—all those
challenged by the hustle and bustle of cities,
uncomfortable with crowded spaces,
and overwhelmed by emotions and energies
flying all around—may the tools and techniques
in this book bring you strength,
protection, and comfort.*

Contents

Aegirine • Agate (*Blue Lace Agate* • *Botswana Agate* • *Dulcote Agate* • *Fire Agate* • *Pigeon's Blood Agate* • *Shiva Eye Agate*) • Amazonite • Amber • Amethyst (*Chevron Amethyst* • *Smoky Amethyst*) • Ammonite • Aquamarine • Aragonite • Arfvedsonite • Astrophyllite • Aventurine • Axinite • Barite • Basalt • Bloodstone • Boji Stones • Bronzite • Brucite • Calcite • Carnelian • Cassiterite • Catlinite • Cat's Eye • Celestite • Chalcedony • Chalk • Charoite • Chiastolite • Chlorite • Citrine • Clinoptilolite • Covellite • Danburite • Diamond • Dolomite • Emerald • Epidote • Ferberite • Flint • Fluorite • Galaxyite • Galena • Garnet • Granite (*Graphic Granite*) • Halite • Hanksite • Healer's Gold • Hematite • Herkimer Diamond • Holey Stone • Hübnerite • Hypersthene • Ilvaite • Isua Stone • Jade • Jasper (*Bumblebee "Jasper"* • *Judy's Jasper* • *Red Jasper*) • Jet • Kyanite • Labradorite • Lakelandite • Lapis Lace Onyx • Lapis Lazuli • Larvikite • Lepidolite • Luxullianite • Magnetite • Malachite

• Marble (*Isla Rose Marble* • *Highland Marble)* • Mohawkite • Moonstone • Muscovite • Novaculite • Nunderite • Nuummite • Obsidian • Onyx • Opal • Orpiment • Peridot • Petrified Wood • Pietersite • Pinolith • Preseli Bluestone • Psilomelane • Purpurite • Pyrite • Pyrolusite • Quantum Quattro • Quartz (*Faden Quartz* • *Phantom Quartz* • *Rutilated Quartz* • *Sulfur Quartz* • *Tibetan Quartz* • *Tourmalinated Quartz*) • Rhodonite • Rose Quartz • Ruby • Sardonyx • Sarsen Stone • Schalenblende • Selenite • Septarian Nodule • Serpentine • Shungite • Siderite • Slate • Smoky Quartz (*Smoky Elestial Quartz* • *Smoky Quartz with Hematite*) • Sodalite • Sphalerite • Staurolite • Stibnite • Sugilite • Sulfur • Sunstone • Tantalite • Tektite • Tiger's Eye • Tiger Iron • Topaz • Tourmaline (*Black Tourmaline* • *Brown Tourmaline* • *Pink Tourmaline*) • Tugtupite • Turquoise • Unakite • Vivianite • Zircon

Understanding Psychic Harm

Safety, both personal and communal, underpins much of the human experience. Take an honest look around you and you'll likely find that you live in a world that both helps and harms. Very real dangers exist in all reaches of the globe. This might not be the sort of sentiment that you'd expect to find in a book about crystals, but that makes it no less real. That's not to say that our world is bereft of safety, comfort, joy, and healing. Rather, I mean that achieving these states requires real work. It also takes a willingness to embrace chaos so we can learn to be less susceptible to those forces that otherwise challenge our growth.

Ideas behind protection via magickal or spiritual means can be traced back to our earliest ancestors. Far back in prehistory, people recognized that the world around them was fraught with danger in the form of accidents, injuries, illness, physical attacks, and even spiritual harm. Nature itself could be either a blessing or a bane from one moment to the next. Early humans began to collect items of power that were imbued with naturally protective energies such as stones, bones, shells, and seeds. These sacred items were believed to keep malefic influences at bay, and they were used in tandem with more conventional, mundane forms of protection. The tradition of magickal protection continues today, and you can find protective amulets and apotropaic charms the world over.

This book is born from a place that recognizes our intrinsic need for safety. All humans deserve peace, safety, and love in order to grow. Despite this, the world doesn't always show up for us in this way. Therefore it is necessary to cultivate the resources that help us create a secure place in the world, a safe and sacred space in which to live and grow and heal.

Over all my years of working with crystals (that'll be more than three decades by the time this book is in print), the number one topic I'm asked about is crystals for protection. Which crystals ward off negative energy? Which stone will prevent a nosy coworker from spoiling my day? Which gems can my kids wear to keep them safe at school? These are just a few examples of the questions I am asked on a daily basis. Clearly the desire to protect ourselves and our loved ones persists to this day.

On a personal note, as a young man I was overly sensitive, easily knocked off-kilter by outside energies. Crowds often proved hard to navigate, as the sea of other people's vibes left me anxious, exhausted, and sometimes confused. It was hard to sort out what belonged to me and what didn't. Before long, my local spiritual community identified me as an empath. I didn't exactly know what that meant at first, but I came to wear that title like a badge of honor. At the same time I knew I needed to learn how to be less psychically vulnerable when interacting with the world at large. It took years of practice, a lot of trial and error, and a fair amount of help from people (and crystals) older, wiser, and more experienced than me. Thankfully, as an adult this is rarely something I struggle with today. I realized that being sensitive can be a superpower when used effectively, but back in the day, letting it control my identity led me to have really poor boundaries—psychically, socially, and otherwise.

Although I've learned a lot of different methods for psychic self-defense over the years, I find myself returning to the basics of grounding, cleansing, and using simple shields (more on these subjects throughout the book) on a daily basis. I also look to the world of rocks and gemstones for support everywhere I go; you'd be hard-pressed to find me in public without some of my most beloved protection stones, like labradorite, rhodonite, and Preseli bluestone. However, the most important thing I've learned has been how to take control of the narrative and not let my hypersensitivity rule my life.

SOURCES OF PSYCHIC HARM

I genuinely believe in a beneficent universe, one that is populated with kindness, love, and beauty. Nevertheless, there are sources of harm everywhere if we know where to look. Here are some of the most common sources of psychic harm and disruptive energy:

- Your own thoughts and emotions
- Thoughts and emotions coming from other people
- Judgment, envy, jealousy, hatred, and malicious emotions either generated by or directed at you
- Unintentional psychic attack
- Formal psychic attack
- The evil eye
- Etheric cords and psychic vampirism
- Geopathic stress and disharmonious environmental energy
- Offended spirits or broken vows
- Malicious spiritual entities
- Ritual curse and other forms of magickal attack
- Karmic and ancestral patterns

In most cases the disrupting energies we encounter represent a cross-section of the above list. Some of the harmful patterns in your life might be the result of psychic attacks or malicious entities, but the majority of disruptive energies have much more mundane sources. The environmental energy of the spaces where you spend your time has a huge impact on your physical and spiritual well-being. The emotions of people around you can help or hinder your own state of mind. Most importantly, your own thoughts, emotions, and actions make up the largest source of psychic harm and disruptive energy that you are likely to encounter.

Many books covering the topic of energy protection and psychic self-defense focus on psychic attack, energy vampires, supernatural beings, and malefic magick such as curses and hexes. These are genuine sources of harm, but they are appreciably less common, particularly formal curses and evil spirits. The world around us is absolutely inspirited, but most spirits are rather indifferent to the human condition, just as we are relatively unobservant and unattached to the ins and outs of insects in the garden; occasionally we might take notice, but most of their existence goes undetected. Formal psychic attack and true curses are also relatively rare. Most people have neither the training nor the willpower to effect these kinds of harms. Instead, the kind of psychic attack you'll typically encounter is the unconscious variety: ill-wishing, gossip, and bad attitudes—by yourself or by others—can creep their way past our normal defenses to take root in us and cause harm over time.

Notice that the sources of psychic harm listed above aren't labeled "negative energy." The more I practice the healing arts and engage with my daily spiritual practice, the less attached I am to words like *positive* and *negative* to describe energy. Energies themselves are rarely good or bad—it's the effects they produce in our lives that we perceive as being positive or negative. A better way to look at it is through the lens of energies (situations, people, etc.) that are helpful or harmful. No one is truly all good or all bad, but their influence can be overwhelmingly positive or negative from your perspective. For this reason, throughout this book I've favored terms like *disruptive, intrusive, disharmonious,* and *harmful* when it comes to speaking about energy. Electricity isn't morally positive or negative, but when applied at the wrong time or in the wrong place it can do a whole lot of harm. Likewise, when used effectively it provides comfort and safety to all.

It's helpful to know where disruptive and harmful energies originate, as this can help you choose the most effective path of remediation. If your own negative self-talk is causing psychic harm, you probably don't need to focus on cutting cords or warding off intrusive entities from your home; instead you'll want to focus on techniques that help you reprogram your mind and select crystals that support a healthy mindset. By the same token, when harmful thoughts and energies are intentionally sent your way, you can create shields that specifically deflect, neutralize, or otherwise overcome them.

Try not to assume the worst when evaluating the possible sources of harm in your life. We all experience most of the sources of harm in the list above at different times in our lives. The good news is that taking things too seriously won't cause any harm. Said another way, whether you are cursed or only think you are, the remedy is often the same. Use this list to help you determine which chapters in this book you'll turn to for the proper protections and remediations.

Now that we've examined where psychic harm comes from, let's look at how it affects us—and what we can do about it.

MAGICKAL PROTECTION

Throughout time and across all cultures, protective charms, amulets, and rituals have ensured peace, protection, and safety. Magickal approaches to psychic self-defense often invoke symbolic and metaphorical mechanisms of change. They speak to us through psychological, religious, spiritual, and cultural frameworks that help us tap into something greater than ourselves in order to reinforce boundaries, drive away evil, and invite healing.

Magickal protection often works on three levels: appealing or connecting to a higher power or supernatural force; drawing on a symbolic pattern or object that confers strength or protection; and fighting fire with fire by conjuring another force to face the source of the harm. In the first approach, people have historically used prayer, meditation, offerings, and other rituals to forge deeper relationships with protective spirits and forces. You might pray to a god, saint, or angel, or ask for the protection of your ancestors. Similarly, you could tap into the elemental forces to confer protection and healing in the face of harm.

The symbolic meanings of your tools, ingredients, and ritual actions may also be selected for their connection to protective actions or qualities. Stone itself is hard, durable, and resistant to outside forces, making any rock or gem a powerful ally for protection. You might also draw protective power from plants with thorns, spikes, or thick bark for the same reason. Protective symbols like the ever-popular evil eye charm confers this same kind of symbolic protection.

Protection can also be invoked magickally through the same guiding force found in homeopathy: *similia similibus curentur,* or "like heals like." To overcome a toxic person or situation you might draw power (safely, of course) from a toxic plant or mineral, or perhaps you'll ask for the assistance of an animal spirit that matches the ferocity of the situation at hand.

Magickal protection connects you to the quality, energy, or spirits that embody the kind of aid you seek. It helps you by fortifying your spirit and enchanting life to be safer. There are unseen, unmeasurable forces in the universe that can only be addressed through magickal and spiritual methods.

Each chapter of this book will introduce various magickal topics, from cleansing to curse-breaking. Rather than adhering to any single magickal, cultural, or religious framework, my goal in crafting the resources in this book is to offer a broad range of technologies and techniques, thereby allowing you to plug these into your personal practice. That means that you won't find invocations to certain gods or spirits or detailed accounts of magickal timing. Rather, you can adapt the magick in this book to your own style and form of practice.

THE AURA

Like all matter, the human body is enveloped by a field of energy called the *aura*. This field of energy includes both measurable frequencies, like those on the electromagnetic spectrum, and subtle energies that cannot be measured (yet) by scientific methods. Science and medicine have evidenced the correlation between our physical and emotional health and the health of the body's electromagnetic field. Mystics, healers, and mages have known for eons that our subtle anatomy is just as important to our well-being as our physical anatomy.

The aura itself is both around and within the body; it weaves its influence through every part of the physical, psychological, and spiritual makeup of the human being. Many spiritual traditions today subdivide this field into individual layers, called *subtle bodies*, that have distinct functions and spheres of influence. Different texts and teachers will number and name the subtle bodies differently; I've seen some systems using only four bodies (the physical and three subtle bodies in the aura),

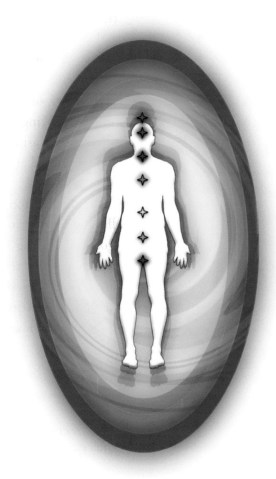

The aura is a field
of energy that
surrounds the body.

while others list more than a dozen. As well, many people make use of
the chakra system, which consists of various energy centers located in
the body and aura.

While I won't spend time subdividing the aura and enumerating
the function of each subtle body and chakra here,* it is helpful to know
that the various components of the human energy field contribute to
your ability to draw support from, process, eliminate, store, or defend
against various energies. The aura, when healthy, has natural barriers

---

*If you'd like to see the models that I use for the layers of the aura and chakras, please
consult chapter 2 of my book *Crystal Basics: the Energetic, Healing, and Spiritual Power
of 200 Gemstones* (Destiny Books, 2020).

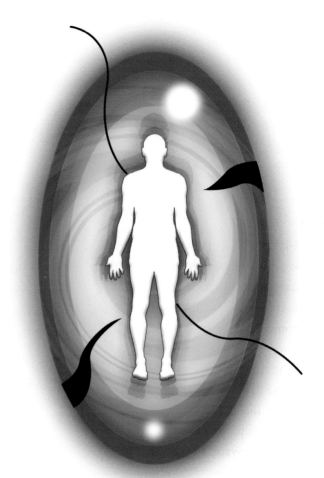

Harmful, disruptive, and deleterious energies will damage the aura over time.

against harmful and deleterious energies. These intrinsic boundaries and defense mechanisms can be rendered ineffective over time. When you are subjected to psychic, emotional, spiritual, social, and physical harm, it takes a toll on your energy body just as it does on your physical body.

Psychic harm affects the subtle anatomy in a variety of ways. It can dull your light and create pockets of stagnant energy in your aura and chakras. It might also lead to leaks, tears, and holes in the outer layers of the aura, making you more susceptible to harmful energies. Foreign energies can get lodged in the various layers of the aura and the chakras themselves and spread throughout the energy field. Cords, entities, and other attachments can also root themselves in the aura, leading to feelings of exhaustion, anxiety, fear, and more.

Ultimately, part of our approach to psychic self-defense must include an assessment of the health of the subtle anatomy. Regular cleansing and other psychic hygiene practices are the foundation of effective protection, as they help the aura perform its normal duties of filtering out unwanted energies and repairing damage incurred from harmful experiences. Let's examine how these energies interact.

THE SCIENCE OF PSYCHIC SELF-DEFENSE

Psychic self-defense can be viewed through the lens of science. To do so we must start with a discussion of energy. Energy itself is defined as the capacity to do work; it is a quality that can be measured or quantified. It is transferable from one system or object to another in order to perform some form of work. Light is energy. Heat is energy. Sound is energy. Everything around us, at one level or another, is energetic in nature. The tiniest units of matter, when divided and subdivided infinitely, will cease to behave like particles of matter with discrete mass. Instead, they move like waves and inhabit clouds of probability instead of traveling in linear paths. As well, all matter vibrates, generating energy fields that move outward at the speed of light. These energy fields are subject to predictable laws of physics that can help us understand how energies interact.

When two energy fields meet there are generally just a couple of likely outcomes. These outcomes depend on several characteristics of energy. The first is the *frequency* of the energy, or the number of cycles it makes in a given unit of measurement. The second is its *amplitude*, or the strength or volume of the signal the energy generates. These two characteristics are like the station and volume on your radio; the first determines what music you'll listen to, and the second how easy it is to hear the music.

If two energy fields that are enharmonic, or of similar frequency, meet, their goal is to harmonize with or entrain each other. Which field leads the interaction to entrain the other? The answer is always the loudest, the one with the higher amplitude. Fields that are not similar in their makeup can create interference patterns rather than syncing their frequencies; again, the higher amplitude field will successfully interfere with or distort the other.

If sources of psychic harm are energetic in nature, they will work on our energetic makeup in a similar fashion. If the amplitude of that harmful or intrusive energy is greater than the amplitude of our personal energy, it will entrain our energy and disrupt us accordingly. How can we avoid this? We have to resonate more loudly than the harm itself. To do this requires a level of coherence that is greater than the disorder or entropy of the harmful field. The body's energy field is naturally self-organizing, and it is able to repair and rebalance itself to a certain extent, but when it is taxed it may need outside help to overcome psychic harm.

Essentially, when described in the language of physics, all psychic self-defense involves generating a higher amplitude field of energy that is more coherent than the disruptive forces in our lives. Many tools can help us accomplish this, but in my opinion none are better than crystals.

HOW CRYSTALS HELP

To understand how crystals help with psychic self-defense, we first have to understand what crystals really are. A crystal is a solid substance with a regular composition (the same ingredients throughout) and a repeating, symmetrical structure (those ingredients are arranged in a symmetrical shape that repeats throughout). These repeating structures are called *crystal lattices*, and they reflect the immense order and coherence that crystals demonstrate at the molecular level. Given enough time and space, crystals form into beautiful geometric forms bound by regular faces and angles. These external shapes, called *crystal habits*, are a result of the makeup and structure that crystals have at the most fundamental level.

Crystals are everywhere around us and even inside us. There are crystals in every cell of your body, and there are probably crystals in the walls of your house, too. Naturally occurring inorganic crystals are known as *minerals*. I'm sure you could name a number of different minerals, like quartz, barite, charoite, or pyrite. Some minerals have varieties that bear their own names, like citrine, amethyst, agate, and jasper, which are all varieties of quartz. When minerals aggregate they become rocks. Rocks have variable compositions, colors, and textures because their mineral content can vary from one specimen to the next. Marble, granite, limestone, and even lapis lazuli are a handful of rocks you may already know. A few popular stones are neither rocks nor minerals—they are mineraloids, which fail to meet some of the criteria that define minerals. Some examples of mineraloids include opal, obsidian, and moldavite, all of which lack a crystal structure, as well as amber and pearl, which are organic substances.

For the most part crystals embody coherence and integrity from the inside out. Because the physical makeup of matter influences its inherent energy field, crystal energy is necessarily more organized or coherent than most other kinds of energy. Crystals are effective for psychic self-defense because they encourage us to embody the same level of crystallinity and coherence in our auras. As we are entrained by or harmonize with crystals to achieve greater order and amplitude, we become less permeable to outside influences, less susceptible to psychic harm. Crystals of all kinds therefore naturally promote protection.

Crystals also work symbolically to invoke protective qualities. The beauty and perfection of gemstones has long led to their association with divine forces. In some cultures that means that gems, crystals, and other precious mineral resources are gifts from the gods or emissaries of the angels. In others they are thought of as perfected spirits, perhaps as the embodiment of one's ancestors. Their perfection, rarity, and value translate to their spiritual qualities, which are perceived as equally perfect and rare.

Because stone is so durable it has long represented protection, strength, and victory over evil. Stone shelters and caves may have been among the first fortresses to defend early humans. Castles, forts, and cathedrals of stone endure for centuries or even millennia, signifying the power of stone to outlast the erosive nature of time and the evils of the world. Across the globe, stones have been carried, worn, and used in ritual to harness these same strengths of eternity and endurance, providing spiritual protection to all who petition them for help. Cultural symbols and meanings have been attributed to different rocks, minerals, fossils, and gems. In some cultures the color of a stone renders it protective, while in another time or place the pattern or shape of a stone imbues it with symbolic power. Even today we find new meaning in crystals and gems, many of which extend their apotropaic powers to us now.

Crystals are excellent tools for protection that have been used for hundreds of thousands of years. When you select a crystal for healing, protection, or any other purpose, you are tapping into a timeless tradition; the energy of the ages will support your work, and your magick will draw strength from all those before you who have connected to the mineral realm. The crystal or crystals will strengthen, harmonize, and amplify your energy field while also linking you to a sophisticated tradition of symbols and meaning to bring your goals into reality.

MAKING THE MOST OF THIS BOOK

Mastering the art of psychic self-defense can take a lifetime, so I've broken this book down into distinct sections to help you learn the different concepts and techniques in each chapter. Each chapter details the most helpful crystals relevant to its themes, in addition to providing detailed instructions for working with grids, elixirs, meditations, rituals, and other tools for mitigating psychic harm. Let's take a closer look at the topics covered in this book.

- Chapter 1 opens with a review of essential crystal wisdom, covering everything from cleansing and charging crystals to methods for safely storing them when not in use. We are also introduced to techniques like activating crystal grids and creating gem elixirs.
- Chapter 2 translates the cleansing practices for crystals that you learned in chapter 1 to the various areas of your life. It focuses on cleansing yourself and your space, as well as how to create dynamic grids and layouts for spiritual hygiene. This chapter concludes with one of my favorite techniques: a banishing ritual inspired by high magick traditions and magickal orders. It can be

used to cleanse and protect yourself and your space, and it comes in handy when you want to banish other energies, entities, and influences.

- Turning to chapter 3 we will find a cornucopia of techniques centered on personal protection. From carrying crystals and wearing crystal jewelry, to learning to craft psychic shields with the support of rocks and gems, this chapter has a multitude of techniques that will support you in your everyday life. Use them rigorously alongside the spiritual hygiene discussed in chapter 2 as preventive care, and you may never have a need for the advanced techniques described in later chapters.

- Chapter 4 widens your sphere of protection to teach you how to ward off harmful and disruptive energies in your home, office, and other spaces. You'll learn how to grid your home to fortify it against unwanted energies and will discover a variety of rituals that enhance the safety and security of your space.

- Chapter 5 explores the underlying activities of environmental energies like electromagnetic pollution and geopathic stress, which is basically harmful or disruptive earth energies. Many people can be sensitive to these invisible forces, so I've covered a wide range of techniques to help detox and protect against their influence.

- Chapter 6 provides resources for what to do when you suspect you've been the victim of a psychic attack. You'll discover the most common signs of psychic attack and learn how to mitigate its effects.

- Chapter 7 discusses what to do when ordinary protection fails. It covers techniques of countermagick that employs crystals, such as binding, banishing, and reversing spells. You'll learn how to return harmful energies to their source and how to remove heavy and hard-hitting sources of harm from your life.

- Chapter 8 explores techniques for dealing with spirits. The grids and rituals in this part of the book will show you how to handle hauntings, attachments, possession, and other paranormal phenomena. If you practice regular cleansing and warding techniques, the tools presented here may not be necessary, but if you're ever called on to help someone dealing with spirits, you'll be armed with the knowledge to succeed.

• Finally, chapter 9 is a directory of 145 crystals, rocks, minerals, fossils, and gems that offer protective qualities. The lineup is a mix of traditional and nontraditional tools, some known in the ancient world and some that have never appeared in print before. Consult the directory to find the best crystal to help you with everyday protection, deflect curses, neutralize psychic attack, and cleanse and defend your space.

My hope is that with the techniques in this book you'll be prepared for whatever harmful, disruptive, or unpleasant energies you encounter. From the psychic noise of crowded places to discarnate entities, there's a technique that will address almost anything you can think of.

Essential Crystal Wisdom

Before jumping into the mechanics of psychic self-defense and using crystals for protection, we'll need a firm foundation in crystal energy and how to harness it. Throughout this chapter we will explore essential crystal wisdom to build the skills necessary for effective healing, protection, and more.

CRYSTAL ENERGY EXPLAINED

As discussed in the introduction, crystals are defined by their highly ordered makeup, which in turn yields an orderly energy field. Crystals exhibit special arrays of their constituent molecules, known as *lattices*. These are the geometrical building blocks of crystallinity; they demonstrate the repeating, symmetrical patterns that are responsible for the dazzling crystal forms we see in our favorite minerals, from the six-sided prisms of quartz to the perfect cubes of minerals like pyrite and fluorite.

Like all matter, the molecules of crystals (and the atoms and ions that comprise them) are in a state of constant motion, the ecstatic dance of the entire cosmos contained in microcosmic form. The movement of the most fundamental units of matter contributes to the energy emanated by all things, from crystals to computers to cardboard boxes to cats. In the case of crystals, the innate order of their structure results in a similarly ordered, coherent energy field. This field is able to entrain or harmonize with other energies to become similarly organized. Thus crystals influence the energies around them, including our own, thereby superseding disorder and entropy with crystalline clarity.

When the human energy field demonstrates high levels of coherence, particularly when the energy fields of the heart and brain are synchronized, we tend to experience greater balance, harmony, and health. At the opposite end of the spectrum, when the human energy field is incoherent or disorganized, we tend to experience imbalance, discomfort, and disease. This level of disorder is an invitation for intrusive energies to take root in our energy field, leading to further concerns. Crystals can help us achieve energetic health by entraining a coherent state of being while simultaneously warding off harmful and intrusive energies.

The inherent order of crystals leads to some interesting ways by which they interact with energy in general. First, crystals are *harmonizers* that entrain or cohere with other energies to be more organized. A side effect of this kind of entrainment is that crystals *amplify* energy; organized systems have a higher-amplitude energy field, which is akin to a louder volume. Crystals also act as antennas that *transmit and receive*, oscillating at precise rates to broadcast energies to and fro. Their optical properties suggest that they are also masters of *reflection* and *refraction*, adjusting our awareness, focus, and mental state in the same ways that they bend light and other forms of electromagnetism. The lattices in crystals always demonstrate tiny, virtually imperceptible imperfections that enable them to *record* energy or information, rather like a tape recorder that captures sound. Finally, crystals can translate energy from one state to another via a process called *transduction*, which serves to convert thoughts, emotions, and intentions into the vibrational language of the cosmos.

Beyond this, crystals also convey symbolic meaning and magickal correspondence, speaking to us on the psychological and spiritual levels. Humankind has collected, revered, and collaborated with the world of rocks and gems long before recorded history, often relying on the symbolic and spiritual virtues of stones to obtain results from those human-mineral relationships. The perfection of the mineral realm underscores a hidden order in the cosmos, often pointing us toward an experience of the Divine. Working with such beacons of order and divinity has fueled spiritual, magickal, and religious practice for eons.

With so many traditions woven together to create crystal healing as we know it today, there are myriad ways to choose, cleanse, and cultivate relationships with your crystal allies. Rather than being overwhelmed with the endless possibilities open to you, let's start with the first steps: how to choose, store, and get to know your crystals.

SELECTING CRYSTALS

Thanks to the staggering variety of rocks, minerals, and fossils that are available to us, it can be hard to know where to start. Even long-time collectors and seasoned healers and magicians may occasionally be overwhelmed when tasked with choosing stones from their own collections or adding new tools to their magickal tool kit. Let's examine some easy ways to decide which crystal is the right tool for you.

- *Examine what you're drawn to.* You might fall in love with a gemstone for its color or clarity, a mineral specimen for its unusual habit, or a certain rock for the patterns and textures on its surface. Perhaps it's the feeling of the stone in your hand—something tactile or something subtle. You could also just have an inner knowing, a magnetic attraction to something for no reason other than your intuition. Those stones to which we are strongly attracted are often very timely and meaningful when we peruse their properties in a crystal encyclopedia.
- *Feel them out.* Pick up a stone and see how it feels in your hand. Does it feel comfortable? Is there a barely palpable pulse of energy? Does it just feel right? Your tactile senses, both mundane and metaphysical, can help you narrow down your choice of crystal by attuning to its energy.
- *Dowse or muscle test for the right stone.* If you are skilled in the use of a pendulum or dowsing rods or various forms of applied kinesiology, you can ask a yes-or-no question to determine whether a particular stone is the best partner for the task at hand.
- *Get prescriptive.* Consult a crystal book or go to online crystal sources and look up the condition or scenario you are experiencing

and find the crystals that match it. Always seek the underlying cause. It's rarely as simple as looking for any old stone for healing, protection, or abundance—effective crystal magick comes from seeing what drives your need for support and partnering with the stones that best match that need. And remember not to put all your faith in only the books or other resources you consult; temper what you find there with your personal experience and intuition.

- *Pay attention to the stones that you don't like.* There is valuable medicine in the stones that might feel uncomfortable, challenging, or otherwise unpleasant. This doesn't always mean they are the answer to your problems, but in many instances the gems that seemingly repel us can provide deep lessons and catalyze profound healing.

- *Ask for help.* The absolute best way to find the right stone when you feel overwhelmed or indecisive is to simply ask. You can ask a more experienced friend or mentor, a knowledgeable person in the local crystal store, or—perhaps most importantly—ask the stones themselves to show you what to work with.

SAFE STORAGE

I would be remiss to not discuss safe storage of your crystals in a book about protection. Just as you might be turning to your crystals to feel safe and sound, we should look after the safety of our stones. In this there are two main considerations: the physical safety of your stones, and the energetic effects of how you store them.

Let's begin with the mundane side of storage. Put plainly, many minerals are delicate and will damage or break if stored improperly. Some, like amethyst and kunzite, fade significantly when exposed to sunlight, while others, like halite and pyrite, are sensitive to moisture. Be sure to store delicate, sharp, or expensive crystals away from others. You can display them on shelves, wrap them carefully in a box or drawer, or keep them on an altar where they can be appreciated regularly. When storing your stones in boxes, trays, or other containers, choose softer

Safely storing your crystals ensures they
will be available to help you whenever you need them.

materials like wood or plastic over glass or ceramic. It's a good idea to sort stones by hardness; you can consult a good reference book (like my book *Crystal Basics Pocket Encyclopedia*) in order to avoid scratching the softer stones in your collection with harder ones.

From an energetic perspective, storing your crystals effectively can minimize the energetic background noise coming from your crystal collection. Sorting by species, color, hardness, or similar approaches will allow you to group your stones in ways that make them easy to find and result in cohesive energy pairings.

I like to use plastic boxes with lots of little compartments for smaller rocks and minerals, tumbled stones, and other small shapes. The separate compartments enable me to group things together so they are easy to find and won't be damaged. I have some larger plastic drawers where I can store larger specimens, carefully wrapped or placed in small boxes so they won't come to any harm. Special crystals adorn my altars and household shrines, while others are ensconced in glass cases for display. Chances are that at any moment you'll find crystals on almost every horizontal surface of my home, from the desk in my office to the dresser in my bedroom. This affords me a chance to connect to crystal energy in every room of the house.

CULTIVATING A RELATIONSHIP

It's easy to get drawn into a materialistic view of crystals as inert tools that can be used as a means to an end. However, the more you spend time with crystals, the more apparent it is that there is an animating force or spark in them. This inner spirit is actually what we collaborate with when we work with our crystals; it's not just the mechanics of their electromagnetic fields, but the indwelling consciousness that propels our work forward, whether we are seeking protection, healing, abundance, or anything else. To get the most from your work with crystals, treat them as friends and allies rather than simply as tools. Partner with them as spirits with whom you're building a conscious and conscientious relationship.

One of the best ways to approach this is to get to know each rock, mineral, fossil, and gem in your collection. I love to spend time looking at every detail of a new stone, observing every face and each inclusion, peering into the heart of the stone if it's transparent or translucent so I can see the landscape within it. It's imperative we find a sense of wonder in these beautiful gifts from the earth. As the conscious mind is engaged with the material form of the crystal, the subconscious is free to connect more deeply with the spirit within that stone.

You can also cultivate relationships with your crystals through meditation, perhaps by simply sitting with the stone and observing what feelings, energies, ideas, or symbols arise for you. Try visualizing the energy within the crystal and draw it into your body with the breath. Observe where it goes and how it feels. Alternatively, you might take a more passive route to getting to know your crystals by carrying them or wearing them throughout the day with no firm goal or intention—just to see how it feels with their presence.

However you cultivate a relationship with your crystals, doing so will ultimately help you become a more sensitive and successful practitioner. Knowing how a crystal shows up for you personally is far better than merely relying on its description in a book (even this one!), as an intimate crystal ally may be willing to offer support outside its classical description.

Form and Function

As you build your collection and assemble a crystal tool kit, you'll find a large variety of crystal forms, both natural and polished, available to you. From simple tumbled gems to exquisite crystal clusters, each shape, size, and form can offer its healing and protective virtues to you. Let's take a look at some of the commonly available shapes, especially those that can be helpful for psychic self-defense.

Crystals are available in an array of forms that
can support your psychic self-defense.

- ▶ **Single-terminated:** Crystals with a single point (either natural or polished) are excellent for directing energy, and they are essential for making grids, healing layouts, and for carrying or wearing to bolster your energy.
- ▶ **Double-terminated:** As their name suggests, these crystals have a point at each end. Double-terminated crystals are adept at

forging deeper connections, and they send and receive energies simultaneously.

▶ **Cluster:** When many crystals attached to the same matrix* pack close together, you get a crystal cluster. These formations broadcast energy throughout a room to clear away stagnation, improve the energy of a space, and instill group harmony.

▶ **Rough:** Unpolished or uncut stones are often called "rough," and they may feel slightly less refined than other crystal shapes. Many people find them extra-supportive for grounding, and the rough surface can be thought of as abrading unwanted or intrusive energy.

▶ **Geode:** Round nodules of rock lined with druzy crystals or other mineral formations are called *geodes*. These formations enhance the aura's natural shields and improve focus and imagination.

▶ **Tumbled:** Irregular rounded stones polished by a rock tumbler, these formations are excellent additions to grids, layouts, or as companions carried in a pocket or purse.

▶ **Tower, obelisk, and generator:** These related shapes share something in common: they stand upright on a flat, polished base. In these shapes, crystals act like beacons of light, beaming energy through your space and out into the heavens.

▶ **Egg:** Polished gemstone eggs are symbols of healing, fertility, creativity, and abundance. They also remind us to tend to our aura, the egglike body of light around us, thereby helping us maintain healthy boundaries.

▶ **Sphere:** The sphere represents perfection, unity, and centeredness. Crystal spheres are balancing and unifying, and they emit a gentle, even energy in all directions.

▶ **Pyramid:** The pyramid is a stabilizing form, and crystal pyramids confer stability, protection, and power to your work. They also enhance manifestation and align the human energy field.

▶ **Wand:** Whether natural or polished, crystal wands are powerful

---

*The word *matrix* describes the material in which something forms or is embedded. In the sense of a crystal cluster, it is the host rock to which the crystals themselves are attached.

tools for directing energy, empowering grids, crafting protection, and improving focus.

▸ **Flame:** Polished flames symbolize the fire of transformation, making them excellent choices to transmute and purify the energy of your home. Flame-shaped crystals share a beacon of energy that wards off unwanted or intrusive spirits.

▸ **Skull:** Skulls carved from crystals and gemstones are allies for expanding consciousness, ancestral healing, and communication with guides and guardian spirits. They are wonderful allies for protection, as they will watch over and guard your space.

▸ **Star tetrahedron:** This stellated geometric form occurs when two tetrahedra intersect; the shape is popularly referred to as a *merkaba*, a reference to the energy field or light body. These crystal shapes powerfully stimulate the aura, eliminate stagnant energies, and draw in light that can be used for psychic shields.

In addition to these there are also palm stones, worry stones, cabochons, faceted gemstones, and many other shapes available to practitioners today. As well, a large variety of specialty carvings abound in the marketplace, from stars and moons to cartoon characters. You can easily find crystals carved in the countenance of angels, dragons, animals, deities, and other forms that symbolize protection, support, and harmony in your space.

CLEANSING YOUR CRYSTALS

No crystal book is complete without a discussion of how to safely and effectively clear them of unwanted energies. The reason why this is so important is because crystals have memory; tiny defects in their lattices retain imprints of the energy or information they experience. Though this energy typically isn't inherently good or bad in itself, if a crystal is saturated with it, it can't effectively perform the rest of its duties. Cleansing, therefore, is an essential step in working with

There are myriad ways to cleanse your crystals.

crystals, whether we use them for healing, manifestation, or psychic self-defense.

There is a popular but erroneous notion today that certain crystals are exempt from being cleansed, that they somehow don't hold on to negative energy. Some lists are short, naming only a few stones like kyanite, selenite, and citrine. Others suggest dozens of crystals that don't need to be cleansed. However, if we revisit two themes it becomes evident that this just isn't the case. First, recall that one of the fundamental properties that all crystals share is their ability to remember, to retain an imprint of the energy or information they experience. Second, energy generally is neither positive nor negative, but any energy in the wrong place can cause distraction, discomfort, or even harm. Since crystals have the ability to remember any and all energies they meet, we must cleanse them to free up their capacity to perform other functions.

Cleansing your crystals is also an opportunity to cleanse yourself.

Whenever you are genuinely engaged with your preferred cleansing technique, some portion of you receives the same benefit as your crystals. By starting with cleansing your crystals, you actually end up reducing the amount of energies that need to be cleansed in your space and your own personal energy field. Additionally, many of the cleansing methods used for crystals can be used for personal and environmental cleansing, too. A more detailed discussion of how to cleanse yourself and your space can be found in chapter 2.

Methods of Cleansing Crystals

If you asked ten crystal lovers to each share their favorite cleansing method, you'd probably end up with twenty answers. Some methods are safe for all crystals, while others require more care when it comes to delicate or otherwise sensitive stones. Here is an overview of some of the most popular tools and techniques for cleansing crystals:

- Exposing them to sunlight and moonlight
- Rinsing them with running water or saltwater
- Burying them in salt, clay, or soil for a period of time
- Clearing with sound, such as a drum, singing bowl, or the voice
- Exposing them to rain, snow, or wind
- Smudging them with cleansing herbs like cedar, frankincense, rosemary, or sage
- Immersing them in dried flower petals, uncooked brown rice, or other herbs
- Clearing with the breath, visualization, or prayer
- Placing them atop an amethyst cluster, selenite slab, or other crystals
- Clearing them with flower and gemstone essences

My favorite methods that are safe for cleansing all types of crystals use sound, smoke, and the breath. Placing your crystals in uncooked organic brown rice and dried rose petals or other cleansing herbs is also safe for most specimens. Water damages many soft, porous, soluble rocks and minerals. Others can fade in the sunlight or be damaged by salt. Cleansing with an amethyst cluster might scratch or otherwise damage softer minerals and polished gemstones. You'll find instructions for cleansing with the breath, sound, salt, and clay below, and smoke cleansing is discussed later in this chapter.

◆ Cleansing with Breath

By far the safest method of cleansing crystals harnesses the power of your breath. Humanity has recognized breath's ability to channel energy and the vital life force since antiquity. We also see words like the Latin *spiritus* and Greek *pneuma*, meaning both "breath" and "spirit," thereby underscoring this relationship. The breath is a potent vehicle for projecting intention and carrying energy, which makes it perfect for cleansing crystals.

To cleanse a crystal with your breath, select the stone and hold it between the thumb and forefinger of your dominant hand. If the stone is too large, heavy, or awkwardly shaped, instead cup it in both hands. Close your eyes and take several deep breaths to relax your mind and body. Once you feel settled, shift your focus to your breath and picture that every in-breath fills you with cleansing energy. You might like to couple this with imagery that represents cleansing to you, such as a fresh breeze, a cool mountain stream, or pure, white light. When you feel saturated with this energy, mentally and visually connect to the stone, fill your lungs with this cleansing breath, and release the air in a short, sharp pulse through the nose. Intend for that out-breath to carry cleansing energy to the crystal and wipe away any energy that no longer serves. You can repeat the breath as needed, as some crystals will take two to three breaths to be fully cleared.

◆ Cleansing with Sound

Sound is a safe, easy, and universally effective way to cleanse your crystals. You can use just about anything that makes noise: drums, rattles, singing bowls, bells, chimes, orchestral instruments, the voice, or even clapping hands. Cleansing with sound is useful for purifying many crystals at once, and it has the added effect of clearing the energy of the room, too.

Gather your crystals together and choose your instrument. Whatever you choose to produce your sound, hold it in your hands (unless of course you're using toning/singing or clapping), and think of that instrument as becoming an extension of you, of your true will. Now set the intention to cleanse your crystals with sound and begin to play the instrument of your choice. If you're using a drum, rattle, or clapping your hands, start with a slow beat and increase the tempo and volume until the energy has palpably shifted. Chimes, bells, singing bowls, and similar instruments can be played continuously until the same shift is perceived. If you use your voice, try toning a sacred mantra or using whatever sound feels right. Be sure to direct sound toward all the crystals in the room as well as the room itself—I always play into the four corners, as well as above, below, and in the center of the room. This gives me a thorough space-clearing in addition to cleansing my crystals.

◈ Cleansing with Salt

Cleansing with salt is an ancient practice, as salt has been revered across the globe for millennia for its ability to clear energy, avert evil spirits, and offer benedictions. If your stone has a hardness of 4 or greater, is nonporous, and does not contain a significant amount of water in its chemical formula, you can use salt to purify it. There are several easy ways to cleanse crystals with salt, including burying the stone in a dish or bowl of salt or placing it on a salt slab or salt lamp. You can also fill a small dish with salt and place a paper towel or thin, natural-fiber cloth atop the salt to prevent softer stones from being scratched.

Cleansing with salt is a slower process than cleansing with the breath or sound, but it offers much deeper, longer-lasting effects. If a crystal or other object feels as though it has been contaminated or compromised by unpleasant energies, a salt cleanse is one of the best ways to bring it back into balance. I recommend leaving a stone in salt to cleanse for at least eight hours, and up to three days for crystals in need of deeper cleansing. On rare occasions you may need to perform a salt cleanse that lasts for a week or more. If you've buried your crystal in loose salt, give it a quick rinse and dry it thoroughly. After being cleansed with salt, crystals may feel neutral or blank, so they will benefit from a short period of inactivity or a quick recharge in sunlight or moonlight.

◆ *Cleansing with Clay*

Clay baths are a technique I learned from studying gemstone therapy (sometimes called *gemstone energy medicine*), a practice that uses high-quality gemstone spheres and beads for healing. Clay baths provide the deepest purification, and they have the added benefit of not causing a crystal to feel depleted or blank like long-term salt-cleansing does. Only use a clay bath for durable, nonporous, water-safe gems. I usually use it for natural quartz crystals as well as tumbled or polished stones that do not have cracks, crevices, or etchings in which the clay can lodge itself. Clay baths are especially helpful for neutralizing the effects of electromagnetic and other forms of radiation, and they are my purification method of choice for crystals and gemstones that have experienced some kind of trauma or intense and persistent negativity.

To prepare the bath, mix together approximately one teaspoon of bentonite or kaolinite clay per half cup of water. You can optionally add a tiny pinch of salt to the mix or a few drops of a cleansing flower or gem essence (like crab apple, garlic, aquamarine, or diamond) to boost the efficacy of the clay bath. Measurements can be approximate; more clay creates a deeper cleanse, and less clay a lighter one. Soak your crystal in the clay and water mixture for fifteen to thirty minutes, then rinse thoroughly, ensuring that no clay is left on the surface or in any small crevices. Dry your crystal immediately, and it is ready to go to work.

MORE CRYSTAL BASICS: PROGRAMMING, CHARGING, AND ACTIVATING

Once your crystals have been cleansed, there are some other basic techniques that are essential for effective crystal healing and gemstone magick. These involve programming, charging, and activating, and they help instill focus, intention, and power in the tools you work with, simultaneously offering the same benefits to you as the practitioner.

Programming and *charging* are terms that are sometimes used interchangeably to refer to the process of imbuing a crystal or other magickal tool with an intention or goal. Personally, I prefer the term *programming* to refer to instilling an intention, and *charging* to mean imbuing a crystal with an outside force or charge, such as charging something with a particular astrological transit or lunar phase.* I think of programming not as a mandate or an order given to a crystal, but instead as a co-creative act, an invitation to the crystal to participate in my goals. Similarly, charging is not something I force on a crystal, but rather an invitation to it to be receptive to the external energy that I'd like to harness for my goals, whether that comes from the heavens, an herb, or some other source. Because crystal lattices have memory, your stones can hold on to both your intention via programming and whatever charge you've given it. Crystals are usually charged with an energy that complements or enhances the work you'll be doing with it, such as charging a cleansing stone at the ocean or empowering a protective stone under the planetary influence of Mars or Saturn.

Activating is achieved by raising your consciousness and attuning a crystal to its highest potential. It's a bit like plugging it into your higher consciousness and all the resources available there. You might also think of it as cranking up the volume of the crystal's energy. Activated crystals can also be used to activate or sync up the components of a crystal grid. Generally speaking, crystals are activated when they are used for an active directional purpose, like cutting cords, moving energy, and activating grids. You can activate crystals and gemstones that will be used in layouts (see page 52) or for other purposes, but it isn't required.

Programming, charging, and activating are steps typically undertaken before a crystal is put to use and therefore should be repeated whenever you come back to working with it. Not every application will require these steps, but most people find that at the very least programming their stones enhances their crystal practice manifold.

_____

*Very often today one hears the expression "charging a crystal" to imply that its energy is depleted and must be recharged, much like a mobile phone or other device. A crystal's energy does not come from an outside source, so it does not need to be replenished. Most techniques described online and in other spaces as "charging" are actually cleansing techniques. True charging differs in that it doesn't seek to restore lost energy, but to complement the crystal's natural power with an additional frequency or energy.

◈ Programming Crystals

Although there are many ways to program crystals, let's learn a simple one that requires only a freshly cleansed crystal and your intention. Close your eyes and take a few deep, slow breaths to quiet your mind. Either hold your hands above the crystal or gently hold the stone between your hands. Silently connect to the crystal and invite it to receive the program. Now recite your intention or goal, silently or aloud, at least three times. As you repeat it you can visualize the vibration of that thought or sentiment traveling from your heart and mind down your arms and into the stone. When the crystal feels as though it has accepted the program, you can thank the stone, take a deep breath, and return to normal consciousness.

◈ Charging Crystals

Like cleansing and programming, more than one method for charging crystals exists. Charging methods fall loosely into active and passive categories. Rather than detail exact methodologies from different traditions, I'll outline the main points so you can devise your own charging technique.

Passive charging relies on a crystal's innate memory to retain an imprint of whatever energy it comes into contact with. Taking crystals to sacred sites, leaving them under the full moon, carrying them with you on pilgrimage—these are all passive charging techniques. Active charging techniques, on the other hand, are meditations or rituals to empower a crystal or gemstone to carry a particular energy or vibration. They often resemble programming techniques.

To passively charge a crystal with a particular energy or current, simply place a freshly cleansed crystal someplace where it will be exposed to the right vibration. You can leave it under the moonlight, place it on a sunny windowsill, place it atop dried herbs, or leave it under colored light that matches your intention. Active charging can be done in several ways, but the simplest and most effective method is to hold your freshly cleansed crystal in your dominant hand (or, if it's too large, hold your hand over the stone). Set your intention to charge your crystal with the appropriate energy such as moonlight, a color, or an astrological power or transit. Visualize yourself breathing in that energy, seeing it permeate every part of your body, mind, and spirit. When you are in a state of complete resonance with that energy, turn your focus to the stone and direct all the energy into the crystal. I prefer to do this with the same breathing technique described above in cleansing crystals with the breath.

When your crystal is fully imbued with that external energy or archetype, you can seal the energy in the stone, locking it in place until you expend the energy for ritual or healing or until you cleanse that vibration from the stone. To do this, hold the crystal in both hands and state, "The energy of _____ [the moon/violet/Venus] is sealed inside this stone," and draw an equal-armed cross over the stone to preserve the energy inside.

◈ Activating a Crystal

I use an activation technique that couples the breath with visualization, much like the Cleansing with the Breath exercise described in this chapter. Once a crystal is cleansed, programmed, and charged (if applicable), hold it between the thumb and forefinger of your dominant hand, or in any other way that is comfortable. Take a few deep breaths and imagine that you are stepping back from or detaching from your ordinary state of consciousness. Now will yourself to rise to a higher state, lifting your awareness to the next highest floor in the mansion of your mind. From this perspective, hold the intention to activate your crystal; fill yourself with this intention by breathing it in and letting it permeate your entire body, mind, and spirit. When you feel saturated with the energy of activation, release it toward the crystal with a single breath, using a short, sharp pulse of air through the nose. Now bring your awareness back to the room.

After using an activated crystal it is customary to deactivate it, thereby allowing it to resume its normal state. To do so, hold it firmly in your dominant hand and give the crystal a quick shake as you pulse your breath through the nose as before. As you couple the breath with this motion, intend that the crystal releases the state of activation.

◈ Activating a Crystal Grid

Activating a crystal grid or layout means connecting, harmonizing, and synchronizing all the components of a grid. It unifies them around a common theme or intention and expands the reach of the grid's energy. To activate a grid, you'll use a crystal wand, either natural or polished, or another crystal tool with a similarly projective or directional profile. Program your crystal wand with the intention you want the grid to convey and activate it using the previous exercise.

Now use that activated wand to link together all the crystals in the grid. You might trace the shape the crystals form or draw out a symbol that the grid may be based on or built atop. For simple grids that have a center stone I connect each of the outer crystals to the innermost one. More complex grids require a little creativity. I usually start by tracing the perimeter of the crystal grid and then move the wand in a spiral fashion toward the center, and then I'll move from the center outward in another spiral. Whatever physical motions you use, visualize energy flowing from the wand and connecting each element of the grid to every other element, and then see their collective light expanding to fill the space.

◈ Making Elixirs

Water can be charged with crystal energy to produce a dynamic gem elixir (also known as *gem water*, *crystal essence*, or *crystal infusion*) to be used for healing, protection, and more. The historical record attests to the use of

Crystal elixirs can be made using either indirect (left) or direct (right) methods.

gem-infused elixirs in many parts of the world. Today there are scores of commercially available lines of gem elixirs that you can find online and in specialty shops around the globe.

To make your own elixirs, you'll need to start with good-quality water. Because water is the medium that carries the energy of an elixir, it is important to use the best source with the least potential contaminants available to you. Spring water has been the traditional preference in elixir making, and distilled water also works well. You'll be using one or more crystals, and one or two vessels depending on whether you're using the direct or the indirect method. These should preferably be clear, unmarked glass bowls or containers. You'll want to have a bottle available in which to pour your prepared gem elixir, preferably dark glass, such as a dropper bottle or a spray bottle.

✦ Direct Method

To make an elixir from a stone via the direct method, first make sure the stone is physically clean, then place it in a container of water. Let the stone infuse its energies into the water for several hours in the sunlight, or overnight if using moonlight. Remove the stone, strain the liquid, and either use it straightaway as a gem water, or make a gem elixir by bottling with a one-to-one ratio of gem water to preservative (vodka, brandy, glycerin, or apple cider vinegar). A properly preserved elixir has a shelf life of several years or more, so long as you store it in a dark glass bottle out of direct sun. The resulting infusion, if prepared safely, can be taken internally, added to bathwater, sprayed or diffused in your space, or used topically.

✦ Indirect Method

We must take care when creating elixirs, as many rocks and minerals are either not suitable for direct contact with water and would result in damage to the stone, or in the case of minerals with toxic constituents, an elixir water made from these minerals would poison you. Therefore, to make an elixir from minerals that are either toxic to imbibe or too delicate to expose to water, you will be making an indirect infusion using the two-container method in which the crystal(s) sits in a smaller container, which is then placed in a larger vessel of water, as depicted in the image above.

This prevents contamination but still effectively transmits the stone's energy to the water. An elixir made by indirect method will infuse for a length of time comparable to one made by direct method: several hours in sunlight or overnight for moonlight.

Another method of creating an elixir from dangerous and toxic crystals like orpiment, galena, and stibnite is to create a potentiated quartz crystal wherein the quartz is charged by the energy of the toxic stone. To do this, cleanse both the quartz and the toxic stone thoroughly and place them together in an enclosed space, such as a small box or cloth pouch, away from light and other disturbances for at least twenty-four hours. Following this energetic infusion, wipe the quartz with a tissue or soft cloth to remove any particles and then use it in place of the toxic mineral to make an elixir, following the direct method.

Clear as Crystal

Though it might be a cliché, it is true that an ounce of prevention is worth a pound of cure. To maintain your physical well-being, it's easier to prevent illness by first washing your hands and avoiding pathogens rather than having to treat infections with medications. In the same way, practicing good spiritual hygiene and regular shielding is far easier than trying to remove toxic energies or avert a psychic attack once it's taken hold.

In this chapter we will look at various methods for clearing your space and cleansing yourself. You don't have to cleanse in this order—I just find that it is easier for most people to learn cleansing principles first on objects and spaces before moving on to self-cleansing. But regardless of how you engage in spiritual hygiene, if you use these techniques regularly they will help you maintain your balance and prevent psychic attacks and other kinds of psychic harm, making you feel crystal-clear.

THE IMPORTANCE OF SPIRITUAL HYGIENE

Cleansing isn't merely a matter of releasing or neutralizing negative energies. Effective spiritual cleansing removes all energies that don't belong—positive, negative, or neutral. When an energy, entity, or frequency occupies the wrong space it can impede the free flow of energies that are beneficial or otherwise helpful. By way of analogy, consider making a peanut butter and jelly sandwich: if you get peanut butter on your hands it isn't inherently bad, but since it doesn't belong there, it can impinge on anything else you may need to do with your hands. Thus cleansing removes whatever doesn't belong, not just the energies we classify as negative or harmful.

It's also good to remember that we don't just wash our hands once and expect them to stay clean forever; cleansing is an ongoing process. Likewise, spiritual hygiene isn't something we attend to once and then forget. We are perpetually exposed to sources of psychic harm and disruptive energies that can interfere with our optimal sense of balance and well-being. Regular cleansing practices, along with other fundamental psychic hygiene practices like grounding and meditation, help us return to a state of balance no matter what we are experiencing in the world around us.

Maintaining spiritual hygiene takes practice and diligence. How often should you cleanse yourself, your tools, or your home or workspace? The answers vary from one person to the next. If I'm working from my home office I generally practice cleansing less frequently—and less intensively—than when I'm on the road. A good rule of thumb is to cleanse more often than you think you need to. For the most part you can't cause any harm from cleansing too often, but cleansing too little sure is a recipe for trouble. It's worth noting that sensitive people, especially empaths, often find themselves in need of more regular cleansing than others.

I recommend daily self-cleansing and somewhere from once a month to once a week for cleansing your space. A well-fortified home is less permeable by outside influences, so you'll probably only need to cleanse once a month. Your crystal tools usually require cleansing before and after use, though this also depends on context. A gemstone bracelet that I wear all day when I'm running errands gets cleansed as soon as I take it off at night, whereas the fluorite that sits on my desk beside the computer only gets cleansed once a week or so. When you're just getting started or when you have reason to believe you are experiencing psychic harm of any kind, it's imperative that you cleanse frequently and practice effective grounding, shielding, and warding techniques.

CRYSTALS FOR ENERGY CLEANSING

Before discussing the methods for cleansing your space and yourself, let's examine which crystals are useful to employ in energy-clearing techniques. These crystals possess the ability to draw out, discharge, or transmute misplaced, discordant, and negative energies. Let's take a look at some of the most effective crystals for clearing the energy of other stones, your space, and yourself.

Amethyst	Garnet	Psilomelane
Aquamarine	Graphic granite	Pyrite
Aragonite	Halite	Quartz (clear)
Blue lace agate	Hanksite	Selenite
Chalk	Healer's gold	Shungite
Citrine	Hematite	Smoky quartz
Clinoptilolite	Herkimer diamond	Sodalite
Danburite	Ilvaite	Sugilite
Diamond	Iolite	Sulfur
Dolomite	Lepidolite	Tourmaline
Fluorite	Magnetite	

First, let's consider the cleansing powers of crystals classified as salts and halides. In chemistry, a salt is formed when a positively charged ion and a negatively charged ion come together to form a compound with a neutral charge. Halides are usually classified as mineral salts, and they form when a negatively charged halogen ion (for example, fluoride, chloride, or bromide) bonds with a positively charged ion. The most famous of salts is halite (sodium chloride), or common table salt. Many salt minerals form in arid environments as water evaporates. Some other examples of salts and halides include fluorite, selenite, and hanksite. These minerals scrub the energy field and neutralize dissonance and negativity.

Grounding stones, particularly those rich in metals like iron and manganese, are also excellent choices for cleansing. Iron minerals are sometimes described as initiating a descending flow of energy—in other words, they help discharge unwanted or harmful energies by grounding them so the earth can transmute them. Grounding stones that help purify energy fields include hematite, black tourmaline, garnet, magnetite, ilvaite, pyrite, and marcasite.

Some rocks and minerals have a porous structure that enables them to draw out harmful and stagnant energies. These include shungite, sugilite, and zeolite minerals such as clinoptilolite, stilbite, thomsonite, and natrolite. Fibrous selenite, better known as satin spar, is also adept at drawing out unwanted energies on account of its porous nature. Cyclosilicates—minerals with ringlike structures of silica in their makeup—are also great for cleansing. These include members of the beryl family (aquamarine, emerald, goshenite), iolite, and tourmaline.

Lithium-based minerals have a special affinity for the movement and flow of energy, and they also help transmute disharmony. Lepidolite, some tourmalines, sugilite, petalite, and kunzite are lithium-bearing minerals. Wearing, carrying, or gridding with lithium crystals prevents stagnation and allows you to release whatever doesn't serve. Similarly, sulfur compounds are effective scrubbers of the aura and energy field; consider partnering with native sulfur or with sulfide minerals (like pyrite, marcasite, galena, and sphalerite) or sulfate minerals (such as selenite, celestite, and barite) to clear your energy field.

Some crystals have certain unique cleansing actions. Amethyst invokes the alchemical power of transmutation to transform negativity into positive energy. Citrine vitalizes processes of elimination and unwinds the tension that holds old patterns in place, thereby allowing you to release unwanted or old patterns. Smoky quartz works a bit like an etheric vacuum cleaner to draw out dissonant or harmful energies. Aquamarine symbolizes the ebb and flow of the tides and eliminates stubborn, calcified energies.

You can use any of these crystals for cleansing to support practices of personal and environmental purification. Use them in grids, layouts, and elixirs to help transmute and clear the energies all around you. You can also wear or carry these crystals with the goal of letting the crystals slowly work toward releasing energies you might pick up throughout the day. As discussed earlier in this chapter, crystals that cleanse energies still need to be cleansed themselves—much like how you need to wash a sponge after using it to wash your dishes. Be sure to cleanse them frequently so they can better support your spiritual hygiene.

CLEANSING YOUR SPACE

Where you spend your time is one of the biggest influences on your spiritual hygiene. One's home is meant to be a safe space, a refuge from the outside world. Clear, cleansed spaces are integral to building and maintaining protective shields in your home, office, or other spaces. Cleansing is necessary prior to protective work because you don't want to build an energetic container that traps toxic, disruptive, or harmful energies inside.

Many of the methods used for cleansing crystals can be applied to cleansing your space. Sound, smoke, sprinkling saltwater, prayer, and visualization can all be used to clear a space. We'll cover some foundational practices like cleansing with smoke and elemental cleansing in this section. Regular cleansing can easily become part of your household routine. After clearing clutter, dusting, or sweeping the floors, perhaps you can try cleansing the energy of your space with smoke and refreshing your crystal grids.

◈ Cleansing with Smoke

Cultures around the world have traditionally used smoke from burning various herbs, trees, or resins to purify and consecrate a space. Common botanicals burned for purification include benzoin, cedar, copal, eucalyptus, frankincense, juniper, mugwort, myrrh, palo santo, pine, rose, rosemary, rue, sage, and many more. The best herbs to use are those that can be sourced responsibly, and locally if at all possible. Bundles of herbs such as sage or juniper are probably the most convenient, but dried botanicals or powders can also be used by placing them on a charcoal set in a fireproof censer. High-quality incense, handmade or commercially produced, can also be used with good effect.

Gather what you will need in the room you'd like to cleanse: a heat-proof container, matches or a lighter, and herbs or incense. When cleansing the entire home, start either in the social center of the home (usually the living room or kitchen) or wherever you have your sacred space like an altar set up. Ground and center yourself using one of the grounding meditations in this chapter (see page 46) and ask that the plant spirit of your chosen botanical offer its purificatory blessings. Light the herbs and allow the incense smoke to waft around you. I often begin by symbolically offering the smoke to the four directions, each symbolizing one of the archetypal elements. After that you can carry the smoke through the house, ensuring that you cleanse each room and paying special attention to doorways, windows, and corners, as these are places where stagnant energy can accumulate.

◆ Cleansing with a Crystal Wand

There are times when burning incense, herbs, or candles isn't possible or practical, so it's good to know at least one method for cleansing your space that can be performed without any smoke or fire. A crystal wand (natural or polished) or any elongated, bladelike, or otherwise pointy crystal is naturally gifted at generating, focusing, and projecting energy; you can harness these qualities for cleansing with the power of visualization and clear, focused intent. For a long time I've used similar techniques when I travel and when I teach in places away from home.

To begin, you'll need to select your crystal. Any terminated crystal will do. I have a preference for natural wandlike quartz crystals as well as blade-shaped pieces of kyanite and selenite for this exercise, but you can just as easily use any crystal or gemstone that has been cut and polished into a wand, generator, or tower. Cleanse and program the crystal with your intention to cleanse the space, and activate the wand to ready it for the work you will be doing. Next, evoke your inner power or spiritual flame; feel it growing within you. Stand in the doorway of the room you'd like to cleanse and point the crystal toward the center, willing the energy to flow through the crystal wand and radiate out into the room. Picture the energy expanding, like a flame spreading through the entire room, burning off and transmuting any disharmonious patterns. Now move into the center of the room and aim the wand into all the corners, tracing where the ceiling meets the walls. Outline the perimeter of the space with this same cleansing energy, drawing it down to where the walls meet the floor. Fill every nook and cranny with the cleansing flame of your inner power. When finished, mentally affirm that the space is clear and deactivate the crystal.

◈ *Elemental Cleansing and Consecration*

The four alchemical elements of earth, air, fire, and water symbolize the primal forces and processes responsible for everything in the world. Their archetypal qualities can be invoked for cleansing and consecrating your space as well as for clearing and blessing ritual tools and crystals. Elemental cleansing and consecration rituals can be complex or simple, like the one described here. Combining the four elements in symbolic fashion clears away accumulated negative, harmful, dissonant energies.

Gather a representation of each element: a dish of salt for earth, some water, incense for air, and a candle for fire. Cleanse these four elemental symbols by asking the spirit of the element each one embodies to cleanse and consecrate its symbol and set your intention to cleanse your space. Light the incense and candle and ready yourself for the cleansing rite. Carry the dish of salt clockwise around the perimeter of the room, building, or other space, sprinkling a little as you go, and affirm something along these lines: "I cleanse and consecrate this space with the element of earth." Repeat the process for each of the remaining elements, using the sequence of water, air, and fire (by carrying a lit candle around the space, allowing the light to penetrate the space). As you circumambulate with each elemental token, picture it clearing away negativity and imparting holy, healing energies.

Grids for Energy Clearing

Gridding your home with crystals provides round-the-clock cleansing and protection. Crystals are well-suited to maintaining spiritual hygiene, and they work best over the long term when the environment is supported with other kinds of cleansing, too. The grids themselves will need periodic cleansing and reactivation to ensure they work to the best of their ability.

◈ *Lithium Spiral Grid*

Crystals: six or more of lepidolites or another lithium-bearing mineral (such as kunzite, sugilite, petalite, amblygonite, and some varieties of tourmaline), six or more clear quartz points, and a clear quartz or amethyst cluster

You can make a simple and effective grid for purifying a space with a handful of tumbled lithium crystals such as lepidolite, an equal number of quartz crystals, and a larger crystal cluster. The effect of this grid is rather like a fountain that keeps energy circulating, allowing your space to naturally release, transmute, or purify the energies that no longer serve you.

Build a spiral as shown above, alternating your lithium stones with quartz crystals whose points trace the path of an inward-moving spiral.

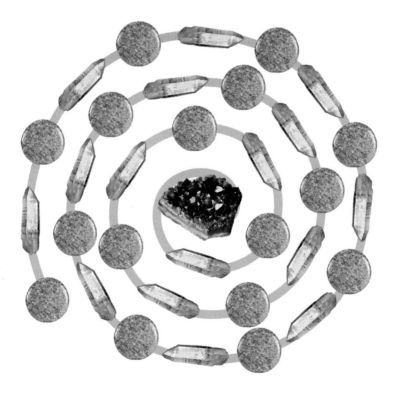

This simple grid harnesses the transformative power of
lithium minerals to rapidly cleanse and uplift the energy of
any room.

Place a quartz cluster at the center to radiate energy outward like a fountain. You can substitute a cluster with a sphere, tower, or similar shape, just so long as it projects energy outward. Activate the grid by tracing the spiral with a crystal wand three times, from the outermost part toward the center. Visualize it drawing energy from the environment along the path and radiating refreshed and balanced energy outward from the central stone. Cleanse and reactivate this grid once a month for optimum efficiency.

◈ Energy-Clearing Grid

Crystals: three clear quartz points, three smoky quartz points, and one amethyst cluster, sphere, or tower

With just seven crystals you can create a grid that circulates, purifies, and balances the energy of any space. The overall shape of this grid is that of

Three varieties of quartz come together
to create a dynamic cleansing grid.

a hexagram, sometimes called the Seal of Solomon; it has a profoundly harmonizing effect. Three smoky quartz crystals point inward to draw negative or imbalanced energy to the middle of the grid to be transmuted by the central amethyst, and three clear quartz points recycle that transmuted energy outward to bring radiant balance to the space. Small to medium-size crystals are effective for most spaces, but large crystals can also be used to make larger-than-life grids to purify the energy in a wider radius.

After cleansing the crystals, program each variety of quartz with its respective function: drawing imbalanced energy in for smoky quartz, transmuting and purifying energy for amethyst, and recycling and harmonizing energy for the clear quartz. Place the amethyst in a convenient place around the room, then lay the three smoky crystals, followed by the clear quartz to make the pattern shown above. Activate the grid with a crystal wand by tracing each triangle once, followed by tracing a spiral moving in toward the center and another spiral that moves out from the center and into the room. Cleanse this grid frequently so it can continue to purify your space.

◆ Household Cleansing and Protection Grid
Crystals: four selenites and four black tourmalines

The combination of selenite and tourmaline is a popular one for purification and protection. For many years I have placed black tourmaline in the main corners of my home to ground, transmute, and purify the energies therein, while also conferring protection. Years ago, my friend Sue Ustas of Zuzu's Healing Arts shared with me how effective placing selenite along the walls can be. Ever since then I've paired this with tourmaline in the corners for the best of both worlds. You can create one large grid for the entire home, or build a grid for a single room.

Begin by cleansing your crystals. Place one piece of black tourmaline in each corner of your home. The tourmalines can either be placed inside the home or buried just outside the four main points of the house. Their energy will anchor, transmute, and protect the home. Bars or rods of selenite (satin spar works best and is most cost-effective, but gemmy crystals are a great option, too) are then placed somewhere along the walls. I often place them

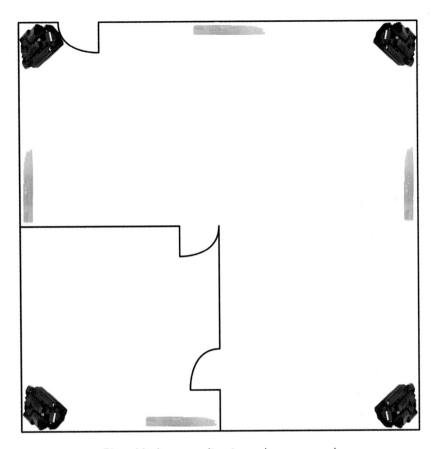

Place black tourmaline in each corner and
a selenite on each wall for cleansing and
protection for the entire home.

on windowsills or on the tops of door frames, but they can also be placed
on the floor, along the baseboards, or on a piece of furniture along the
walls. The selenites link the tourmalines and create a moving wall or stream
of white light to purify and uplift the energy of your home. To activate,
stand roughly in the center of your home and cleanse and program a crystal
or wand of your choosing for the grid activation. Aim the crystal toward a
tourmaline in any corner of your home and trace along the walls, through
the selenite, and to the next tourmaline. Repeat until you make a complete
circuit and return to the point where you started. Imagine the crystals in the
grid being connected in a line of light that flows continuously through all the

stones. Cleanse the crystals by smoke, sound, or another method of your choice once a month and reactivate as above.

CLEANSING YOURSELF AND MAINTAINING PERSONAL SPIRITUAL HYGIENE

I've saved the topic of personal spiritual hygiene for last, but not because it's less important than cleansing your tools and your space. On the contrary, it's necessary to ensure everything receives some cleansing across the board. With that said, it's much easier to cleanse yourself when your space is radiant and clear, whereas, preparing yourself first also makes it easier to cleanse your home. You (and the other residents of your home) are the single biggest influence on the energy of the space, so attending to your personal psychic hygiene ensures that everything around you benefits, too.

Maintaining your personal spiritual hygiene is about more than simply cleansing, just as your physical health requires more than an occasional shower. Your physical health requires good nutrition, exercise, a healthy environment, and recreation and relaxation, otherwise you will be susceptible to illness. Spiritual and psychic health also relies on more than just an occasional cleansing meditation. You need to practice nourishing techniques like the grounding and centering practice described below, as well as regular meditation and shielding and protection rituals. As well, and equally important: be sure to make time for joy in your life. In this chapter you'll learn some easy methods for self-cleansing that will improve your all-around spiritual hygiene.

Grounding and Centering Meditation

Regular meditation is one of the best ways to maintain good spiritual hygiene. Unplugging from the noise of the world gives your mind and spirit a chance to reset and affords you time and space where you are less likely to be bombarded by outside energies, thereby reducing the need for psychic self-defense techniques. Like the cleansing methods outlined in this chapter, meditative activities that ground and center you are powerful preventative techniques.

Grounding is the practice of connecting your energy to that of the earth. The benefits of grounding are many. It stabilizes and anchors your energy field, often bringing a sense of clarity to the mind. Grounding also gives your energy field a safe conduit for discharging and releasing whatever energies don't serve you. And grounding is also an opportunity to receive nourishment from the earth. Grounding acts like the roots of a mighty tree, rooting you safely so that you can draw the resources you need to grow tall and proud.

Centering occurs when you consciously draw any scattered, spread-too-thin parts of yourself back into the core of your being; simultaneously, centering orients your energy field to the cosmos. While centering can be practiced as a standalone meditation, most grounding techniques offer secondary benefits of centering the mind and spirit. Below you'll find two easy meditation techniques for grounding and centering. The first is a grounding cord to connect you to the earth, and the other is a variation of my favorite heaven and earth meditation, which draws nourishment from above and below to bring you into perfect balance. Try making a habit out of these techniques to promote good spiritual hygiene.

◆ *Grounding Cord*

The first grounding meditation creates a straightforward channel from your heart to the heart of the planet. The imagery is plain and easy, in the hope that it will encourage you to practice often. Make yourself comfortable in a quiet place where you won't be disturbed. Close your eyes and take several deep, rhythmic breaths. Allow the tension in your body to melt away as you relax where you're seated.

Bring your awareness to your heart chakra in the middle of your chest. See it as a brilliant green light, as luminous as a precious emerald. Imagine that a cord or ribbon of light extends from the center of this light and reaches its way through your body and into the floor beneath, continuing to travel steadily until it finds the core of Earth. As that cord of light taps into the heart of the planet, sense whatever energy doesn't serve you working its way through that cord. Let Mother Earth drink up your tension, worry, stress, agitation, frustration, and more. The immense heat and pressure in the core of Earth breaks down any feelings of imbalance and alchemizes them into beneficent, healing energies.

Now reverse the flow and receive whatever blessings Mother Earth has in store for you through that cord. Let waves of balance move through you as you draw the healing light of Earth's heart into your own. After a few moments or whenever you feel ready, you can end the meditation by releasing the image of the grounding cord and bringing your awareness back to the room around you.

◈ *Heaven and Earth Meditation*

That the human experience is situated between the celestial and terrestrial planes is a nearly universal concept. Traditions across the world, including Buddhism, Shinto, the indigenous practices of the Americas, and Western occultism all make use of meditations, visualizations, and rituals that position the practitioner between heaven and earth and invite a balance of these ouranic and telluric forces within us as a means of grounding, centering, cleansing, and strengthening the practitioner's energy field. This meditation is inspired by a range of sources and can be performed while standing or seated.

Find a quiet, comfortable place where you will be undisturbed for your meditation. Begin by closing your eyes and taking several deep, rhythmic breaths. Bring your awareness to the heavens above you. Imagine that as you inhale, a celestial light descends through the crown of your skull and collects in your heart. As you exhale, this light continues to descend through your body and deep into the earth below. On your next in-breath, visualize a brilliant light emerging from the depths of the earth and rising upward, collecting in your heart space. With the next out-breath this light continues to rise upward toward the heavens. Continue alternating the flow of energy from heaven to earth and earth to heaven for as long as you like, imagining that every breath helps you feel more grounded and centered.

When you are ready to draw the meditation to a close, draw energy in from above and below (heaven and earth) into your heart simultaneously, and as you exhale allow that energy to expand outward in a sphere of light from the middle of your chest. Feel the energy of heaven and earth merging to create a wave of clear, pure energy that nurtures and strengthens each part of your body, mind, and spirit. Repeat this final step two more times, then allow your breath to return to normal and open your eyes.

Techniques for Cleansing Yourself

I've included a mix of exercises here, some of which rely on meditation and visualization, while others make use of crystals, either singly or in combination. You'll find hands-on exercises, essences, layouts, and more to offer whatever kind of cleansing technique best suits you.

◈ Light Bathing

A simple spiritual hygiene practice that I have found in many traditions is to visualize a shower or bath of light to clean and clear the aura. In the most basic version you need only hold the intention to cleanse your aura and maintain a focused image of colored lights pouring through your aura and body. You can choose from a wide range of colors. Here are some of the best choices for cleansing:

> ▸ **White:** White is the standard color used by many people for cleansing and basic protection. It is generally cleansing, but overusing it can feel a bit stuffy or even abrasive to the aura. Try visualizing a prismatic, crystalline white rather than an opaque white light for a more effective daily cleansing.
> ▸ **Gold:** Gold or golden-white light is among the most potent for cleansing and protection. Additionally, it helps uplift, restore, and strengthen the aura.
> ▸ **Silver:** Silver light is softer than gold, and it tends to have a cooling and purging effect on the energy field. I learned early on in my magickal practice to use silver light to clean the aura and gold to restore it. Try using them in sequence for a more well-rounded cleansing effect.
> ▸ **Violet:** Visualizing violet light or violet fire is my favorite of all the variations listed here. The frequency of violet not only cleanses, it transmutes negativity into positivity. Invoke flames of violet for deep cleansing.

> ▸ **Ice blue:** Pale, icy shades of blue inspire purity and clarity in the energy field. Use it to counteract muddled or confused energy patterns.

> ▸ **Rainbow:** Much like the prismatic white light mentioned above, invoking the full spectrum of a rainbow is both cleansing and restorative. Picture all seven colors of the rainbow flowing as you cleanse, intending that the appropriate colors reach wherever they are needed.

> ▸ **Lime green:** The bright, springtime shade of lime green is both cleansing and rejuvenating. It promotes release of unwanted energies while encouraging the assimilation of helpful energies to speed recovery, healing, and inner growth.

> ▸ **Rust:** Rust-colored (brownish red) light can be used to purify the physical body. This is helpful for ameliorating the physical effects of psychic harm and for reducing the effects of electromagnetic pollution.

> ▸ **Black:** In serious cases you may find that black "light" is the only energy that can disintegrate harmful energies in the aura. Always follow a shower of black energy with gold, white, or full-spectrum light.

Begin by grounding and centering yourself, and set an intention to cleanse your entire being with light. Close your eyes and take a few deep, rhythmic breaths to quiet the mind. In your mind's eye see a cloud of light beginning to materialize a foot or two over your head. At first its color is indistinct, but as the cloud takes form the color develops into the one you've chosen for this meditation. See it growing heavy and full, just like a raincloud; before long tiny droplets of light start to descend, growing in number and intensity until you are being showered with light. Let this rain of light wash over your body, caressing every part of you. Picture it flowing through you and clearing your energy field, chakras, and all the other parts of you. Let it wash away any stagnant or unbalanced energies, replacing them with healing light. When you are ready to complete your meditation, see the rain shower coming to an end and the cloud dissipating. Take another deep breath or two, then return to the room.

Selenite Sweep

The crystalline form of the mineral gypsum is selenite; it is beloved by healers, witches, and other magickally inclined people for its ability to cleanse, align, and soothe the energy field. This technique uses selenite's cleansing power to sweep through the aura and release psychic debris and smooth away imbalances. You'll need a piece of selenite at least six inches long to perform this; satin spar selenite is easily available in longer lengths at affordable prices, and it will work perfectly. Cleanse and program your selenite first and activate it if you like.

When you are ready to perform the selenite sweep, stand upright with your feet about shoulder-width apart. Hold the selenite in your dominant hand and visualize a soft white light flowing through it. Raise the crystal over your head, holding it roughly parallel to the ground. In one slow, fluid motion sweep the stone downward, several inches from your body. Let it move at whatever pace feels natural, ensuring that you sweep all the way to your toes. Next sweep along your arms, holding the selenite in the opposite hand of the arm you are sweeping, and sweep along the sides of your body, too. If it's comfortable to reach any part of your back, you can do that as well. If there are any places where you feel resistance or imbalance, sweep over them again and let the selenite work its cleansing magick. When finished, clear the selenite with your favorite method.

◆ Energy Detox Tonic

Crystals: sugilite, bloodstone, carnelian, and smoky quartz

This crystal elixir is inspired by a combination of gems used in gemstone energy medicine (also called *gemstone therapy*) to initiate a state of deep cleansing and renewal. The stones chosen for this mixture work together to provide energetic support for physical and spiritual detoxification. Make this elixir via the indirect method outlined in chapter 1, as sugilite often contains accessory minerals that could react with water. Allow the gems to infuse for several hours in a well-lit place. Strain and bottle with a preservative. This energy detox elixir can be taken internally, a few drops in the mouth or added to some water, to support the energy field's natural ability to self-regulate. It can also be sprayed in your aura or around your space for further cleansing.

◆ Aquamarine Water

Crystal: aquamarine

Because aquamarine has a special affinity for water, it creates a powerful potion for cleansing and purification. Soak a high-quality aquamarine (ensure that it hasn't been dyed or irradiated) in water for several hours or overnight. Remove the stone and use the water immediately; it can be kept in the refrigerator for up to a day before it loses potency. This gemstone infusion helps to clear away stuck and stagnant energies in all parts of your being and reveals your inner light in the process. Drinking one or more glass of aquamarine water daily can be a potent energy detox. You can also add some to your bathwater along with a handful of sea salt for a ritual bath that removes negative energy and promotes inner balance and clarity.

Crystal Layouts

Crystal layouts—also called *arrays*, *placements*, *maps*, and *nets*—are intentional arrangements of crystals and gemstones laid on and around the body and designed to initiate healing, promote transformation, and support the manifestation of specific goals. Much like crystal grids, layouts rely on symbolism, form, and synergy to initiate lasting change by infusing the collective energy of the layout into the physical and subtle bodies simultaneously. For more on the mechanics of creating a crystal layout, see "Crystal Layouts for Protection" on page 89.

◆ Quick Cleanse Layout

Crystals: one black tourmaline, one selenite, one citrine or malachite, and two single-terminated quartz crystals

This layout is designed to shift energy quickly, helping you discharge dissonant or harmful energy with ease. It is built in a top-down movement to draw in

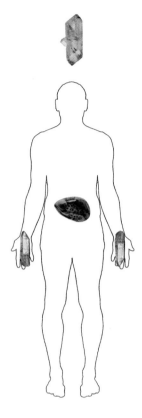

This layout of only four stones quickly shifts and clears your energy field.

spiritual energies to dislodge and loosen negative or misplaced energies so they can be grounded with ease. Note, however, that this layout may not be effective at removing longstanding energies or ameliorating serious or persistent sources of psychic harm.

Cleanse all the crystals ahead of time and find a comfortable place to lie down, then place the stones around you as shown in the figure. Place the selenite crystal over your head; if it has a natural or polished point, direct it downward through the midline of the body. Place either a citrine or malachite on the solar plexus to help reveal and loosen stagnant energies held in the body and mind. Follow that with a black tourmaline crystal placed about a foot below the feet (earth star chakra); like the selenite, direct its termination downward, following the line created by the selenite. Finally, hold a single-terminated quartz crystal in each hand, with one pointing outward in the dominant hand and the other facing inward to maximize the movement of energy in the aura and meridians. Relax and focus on your breath, and visualize drawing in purifying light from the cosmos with each in-breath, picturing it moving downward through the body and into the earth with each out-breath. After five or ten minutes have passed, remove the crystals and give them a gentle cleanse.

◈ Purification Array

Crystals: four selenites, four black tourmalines or smoky quartz, one sodalite, one aquamarine, one rainbow fluorite, two hematites, and two single-terminated quartz crystals

Oftentimes deep purification is a necessary first step in personal protection. This healing layout helps to break up and release stagnant, disharmonious, foreign energies in the energy field. Begin by laying the outer ring, consisting of four selenite and four black tourmaline or smoky quartz crystals; they may be in any form (i.e. with or without terminations). Selenite ushers in a purifying white light that helps dislodge and transform stagnant energy; it also serves to fill any voids created by releasing disharmonious energies from the aura. Both tourmaline and smoky quartz stabilize and ground the energy field and transmute harmful energy.

Next you will be placing the remaining stones starting at the head and from there descending to the hips; this sweeps discordant energy down and out of the aura. Put the sodalite on the forehead to cleanse and purify mental energies. An aquamarine takes its place at the heart to unite, balance, and purify both the emotions and the energy field as a whole. Rainbow fluorite at the solar plexus breaks up stagnation and latency, and brings a sense of order to the overall energy field. (Optionally, you can place citrine crystals on either side of the rainbow fluorite for additional support.) Two hematites are then placed on or near the hips, as their high iron content bolsters the root chakra and invites a strong downward flow of energy. Finally, two single-terminated quartz crystals are placed in the

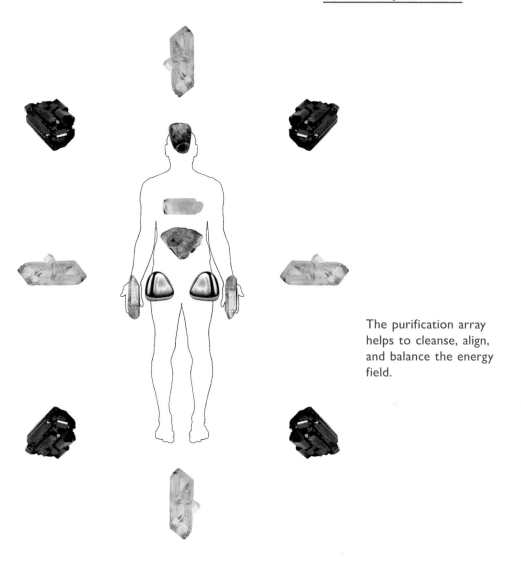

The purification array helps to cleanse, align, and balance the energy field.

hands, with the one in the dominant hand pointing outward and the other facing inward.

This layout can be used on its own, as it is subtly protective, or it can be put in place for at least five to ten minutes before removing the stones and applying another protective layout. Cleanse the space immediately after using this layout, as it is designed to discharge and release energy from the body, mind, and spirit.

Banishing Rituals

Jason Miller, who has an extensive background in magick and tantra and is the author of several books on magick, describes banishing rituals as "short daily rituals for grounding and centering, connecting with the divine, clearing away discursive spirits and forces."[1] Banishing rituals are derived from the Hermetic tradition and are designed to cleanse and clear your space of unwanted energies and terrestrial forces that do not support your highest good or that impede your true will. These kinds of practices cleanse the aura and mind of the practitioner and clear away discordant, stagnant, or harmful energies from the environment, creating sacred space.

Several years ago I made a thorough study of the Lesser Banishing Ritual of the Pentagram and adopted it into my daily practice, doing it at least once daily for approximately a year. The technique itself derives from the ceremonial magick of the Hermetic Order of the Golden Dawn, a secret society dedicated to the study of occult, Hermetic teachings. The Lesser Banishing Ritual of the Pentagram was of immense help, as I was spending a lot of time on the road teaching, doing book signings, and participating in other events. Even without burning herb bundles or using any tools, this ritual offered profound and immediate effects on the energy of whatever space I found myself in. Eventually I learned about the protocols used in other spiritual traditions and magickal orders, and I began to dream up my own version of a banishing ritual using crystals.

The banishing ritual below is called the Banishing Ritual of the Precious Stones. It consists of three stages: the *Crucem Mineralium* (Mineral Cross), the *Vigiliae Lapideis* (Sentinels of Stone), and the *Crucem Mineralium* repeated. The first and third stages, the *Crucem Mineralium*, ground and center you by drawing on heavenly and earthly forces. You'll also tap into the archetypal powers of stone and metal to be fully fortified and protected. The middle stage, or *Vigiliae Lapideis*, invokes the power of five gems—emerald, sapphire, rock crystal (quartz), ruby, and diamond—which stand as guardians or sentinels in your space/energy field. The gemstones are arranged in an order that aligns with certain angelic forces or archetypes, thereby working on both the earthly and heavenly planes simultaneously.

Banishing rituals are usually considered foundational practices in the traditions that teach them. Use the Banishing Ritual of the Precious Stones as part of a daily practice of spiritual hygiene, and you'll find that it strengthens your natural magickal abilities and psychic defenses. Because this ritual cleanses both you and your space, it can be used whenever you have need of a deep cleansing without the use of extra tools or props. I'm including the Banishing Ritual of the Precious Stones in this chapter as something you can use for psychic hygiene as part of a regular practice, but bear in mind that it can also be used to create sacred space before other rituals, or on its own to dispel or send away harmful energy coming from a psychic attack, entity attachment, and minor hexes or jinxes.

One last note: since rituals like the Banishing Ritual of the Precious Stones displace energies and spirits, some magicians follow such a banishing ritual by making simple offerings at their household shrine or to the spirits of the land as a means of building rapport with the local spiritual ecosystem (more information on this is provided in chapter 6).

◈ Banishing Ritual of the Precious Stones

✦ Part One: Crucem Mineralium (Mineral Cross)

Face east and stand upright with feet shoulder-width apart. Visualize yourself firmly rooted in the earth. Feel your feet become inseparable from the earth, as if they are part of the mineral kingdom that comprises the structure of the planet. Imagine that you are growing taller, with the crown of your head reaching out into the cosmos; picture the swirling of stars, planets, and galaxies above you. Allow yourself to feel totally connected to both the heavens above and the earth beneath you.

Extend the index and middle finger of your dominant hand, as in the sword mudra used in some Eastern traditions, and reach up high above your head. Imagine that your fingers touch the swirling cosmos above you. Intone the words "stars above," or "*super astra.*" Draw your fingers to the center of your chest, directing the light of the stars and dust of nebulas down so that they fill your heart chakra.

Sword mudra

Now point your extended fingers at the earth beneath your feet. Picture the energy of the very heart of Mother Earth connecting to your fingers. Intone the words "earth below," or "*sub terra*." Move your fingers to your heart, drawing the energy of the soul and structure of the planet to move with them and fill your heart chakra. Sense this energy blending harmoniously with the light of the heavens.

Extend your fingers out to the right and imagine that magma is drawn to them. Intone the words "by stone," or "*in lapis*." Visualize the molten rock being drawn into your heart as you move your fingers to your heart center, seeing it connect with the energies already present there.

Point your fingers out to the left, past your shoulder, and imagine molten metal being magnetized to them. Intone the words "and metal," or "*et metallum*." Draw your fingers back to your heart center, pulling the metallic energy with them and allowing this current of metal to mix harmoniously with the other energies.

Fold your hands over your heart chakra. Take several deep breaths and visualize the four streams of energy—stellar, terrestrial, stony, and metallic—connecting to your heart center. Picture these four currents expanding through your entire being and out into your aura. Feel the light of the stars and earth balance you as the energies of stone and metal congeal, becoming more crystalline and thus conferring strength, wholeness, and protection. Intone the words "I am whole," or "*ego solidum.*"* Immediately afterward, pound the fist of one hand into the palm of the other (alternately stomp one foot firmly on the ground), and picture the force of this action reverberating throughout your body and the earth. End with an "Amen."

✦ *Part Two:* Vigiliae Lapideis *(Sentinels of Stone)*

Facing east, use the index and middle finger of your dominant hand in the sword mudra to trace a large hexagram (six-pointed star) before you, visualizing it in emerald-green flame. Step forward and thrust your extended fingers into the center of the star; as you do so, imagine that it becomes a solid hexagonal cross-section of the gemstone emerald, with a flaming hexagram (six-pointed star) within it. Intone the Latin word for emerald, "*smaragdus.*" Step back to the center of your ritual space and fold your hands in prayer position at your heart and continue to visualize the emerald before you.

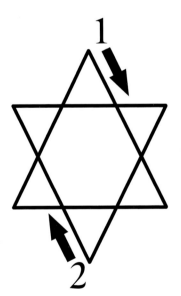

Draw the hexagram according to this diagram.

---

*The Latin translation contains a bit of wordplay. In addition to meaning "whole," *solidum* also translates as "solid," thereby connoting the process of crystallization of both stone and metal in the earth; likewise, this part of the ritual crystallizes and strengthens the energy field of the practitioner.

Extend your first two fingers toward the emerald again and trace a line of prismatic white light as you make a quarter-turn to face the south. Trace a large hexagram before you, visualizing it in sapphire-blue flame. Step forward and thrust your extended fingers into the center of the star; as you do so, imagine that it becomes a solid, hexagonal cross-section of sapphire with a fiery hexagram within it. Intone the word "*sapphirus*," Latin for sapphire. Step back to the center of your ritual space and fold your hands in prayer position at your heart and continue to visualize the sapphire before you.

Extend your first two fingers toward the sapphire again and trace a line of prismatic white light as you make a quarter-turn to face west. Trace a large hexagram before you, visualizing it in white flame. Step forward and thrust your extended fingers into the center of the star; as you do so, imagine that it becomes a solid, hexagonal cross-section of quartz crystal with a flaming hexagram (six-pointed star) within it. Intone the word "*crystallus*," which conveys the meaning of "rock crystal" or "quartz" in Latin. Step back to the center of your ritual space and fold your hands in prayer position at your heart and continue to visualize the crystal before you.

Extend your first two fingers toward the crystal again and trace a line of prismatic white light as you make a quarter-turn to face north. Trace a large hexagram before you, visualizing it in ruby-red flame. Step forward and thrust your extended fingers into the center of the star; as you do so, imagine that it becomes a solid, hexagonal cross-section of ruby with a flaming hexagram within. Intone the word "*rubeus*," meaning "ruby." Step back to the center of your ritual space and fold your hands in prayer position at your heart and continue to visualize the ruby before you. Trace the final quarter of the circle from north to east, picturing a complete ring of adamantine fire surrounding you, with the four gems at the cardinal directions.

Fold your hands as if in prayer in front of your heart, continuing to picture the four gemstones and a ring of adamantine flame around you. Raise both hands over your head and form a triangle with your fingers and thumb. Lower the triangle until it is in front of your heart and say "as above." With this motion, picture a crystalline pyramid pointing upright that has descended from the heavens into your heart chakra.

Invert the triangle and hold it over your thighs, as low as your arms will comfortably extend. Slowly raise them to the heart and say "so below." As you do so, picture an inverted pyramid rising upward from the earth into your heart chakra. Imagine that these two pyramids join to form a diamond crystal shaped like an octahedron, as shown in the figure. Hold your hands in prayer position and picture this diamond crystal spinning slowly within your heart. Intone the word "*adamas*," which means "diamond."

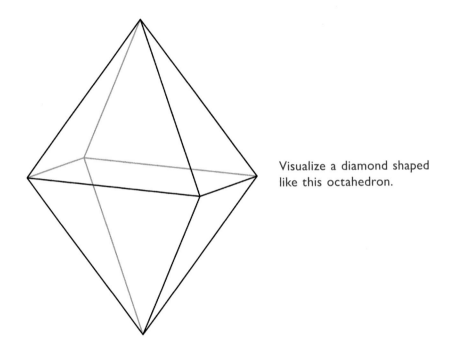

Visualize a diamond shaped like this octahedron.

Now picture the diamond within your heart connected to the *crucem mineralium* and linked to the four gemstones surrounding you to the east, south, west, and north. Picture them in your mind and recite the following:

Before me emerald
Behind me rock crystal
At my right hand sapphire
At my left hand ruby
Around me stand the precious stones
Within me shines the king of gems.

✦ *Part Three: Repeat the* Crucem Mineralium *(Mineral Cross)*

The final act of the Banishing Ritual of the Precious Stones is to repeat step one, the *Crucem Mineralium*. Doing so anchors and seals the cleansing, banishing, and protective qualities of the entire ritual, so be sure to enact it with focus and dedication for a successful and effective banishing ritual. When you've finished the third and final part of the Banishing Ritual of the Precious Stones, you can proceed with your mundane or magickal activities knowing that you have a fresh energetic slate to work with.

The Banishing Ritual of the Precious Stones is most effective when practiced regularly. Building muscle memory for the ritual actions allows you to invest more of your mental and magickal power in directing the subtle energies that underpin the ritual. Try making it a daily practice to gain the proficiency needed to reap the maximum rewards it can offer.

Personal Protection

In a world full of potential harm, the most important focus of your protective practice must be yourself. There are a multitude of options for working with crystals for psychic self-defense; they range from wearing or carrying crystals and gemstones to engaging in more active practices such as creating psychic shields and crystal grids. There are two important caveats when working with these practices, however: you must engage with your crystals regularly, and do so intentionally.

CARRYING CRYSTALS

Many of us, without even knowing why, will tuck a stone into a pocket or purse when we are first drawn to the world of crystals. Children do this intuitively when they find an otherwise ordinary rock in nature. Carrying around a piece of Mother Earth inherently feels like a natural safeguard against the dangers of the world. Since prehistory, humans have done just that, employing humble rocks and noble gems alike for defensive measures.

Carrying crystals for protection is commonplace today; even otherwise skeptical folks will keep a lucky stone tucked safely in a pocket to reap some unknown reward. Among members of the magickal and metaphysical community, pocket rocks are a common currency that offers all manner of positive results. However, many people will find that simply carrying a stone without any focused intent does not yield much in the way of measurable results. Therefore the key element for all our work with stones—in fact, with all of our spiritual life—is to develop a conscious relationship with our allies. Without this, our spiritual and magickal work is incomplete and often ineffective. We cannot expect crystals to do all the work for us. Rather, they are catalysts, and a catalyst is defined as something that lowers the amount of energy or effort required to achieve a desired outcome. Catalysts do not *do* the work (whatever the work may be), but they do make the work easier. That means that your crystals aren't a miracle cure that will solve all the problems in your life. Instead, think of them as allies and co-creators in your practice that will lead you and assist you as you grow and evolve. Remember this when you choose which crystals to carry throughout the day. Just like we humans, your crystal allies will be more effective if you give them direction, feedback, and reciprocity. This means that we should regularly cleanse and program our stones, which is an essential step in partnering with them intentionally.

When carrying crystals for protection (or for any other purpose, really), do your best to find the right mineral partner for the task ahead of you. One crystal might be better inclined to help you enforce emotional boundaries around your family rather than making you feel safe in an eerie place late at night. Especially when it comes to protective stones: it is vital that you cleanse them regularly, as the inherent memory in stones can retain imprints of the energies you are trying to ward off. I give mine a gentle cleanse each day when I empty my pockets and take off my jewelry when I get home.

Protective stones can be carried singly or combined to produce a desired result. You can tuck them away in a pocket, purse, or anywhere else that feels appropriate. Experimentation, along with trust in the wisdom of the mineral kingdom, will lead you to the right allies for the day ahead.

◆ Protective Pouches

Although crystals can be worn or carried in many different ways, when you're in need of additional protection try putting together a small parcel of stones neatly gathered in a small pouch or cloth bag. Traditionally tied-up pouches or cloths filled with magickal ingredients are known as *spell pouches,* *charm bags,* and a variety of other names. A simple version can be made containing only crystals. Try selecting a mix of darker grounding stones and brighter, more uplifting ones. It may be helpful to add something purifying to the mix, too, to ensure that no stagnant energies collect in your aura or environs. A combination such as black tourmaline, selenite, and labradorite, or smoky quartz, carnelian, and citrine offers you well-rounded energetic support throughout your day. Keep your selection of stones to a minimum, as too many different energies can lead to a chaotic effect, which will cause your protection magick to crumble. Here are some effective combinations to carry for everyday protection:

- ► Black tourmaline and selenite for general grounding, protection, and purification
- ► Lapis lazuli, jade, and hematite to thwart jealousy and avert the evil eye
- ► Labradorite, amber, and jet for more potent general protection and to prevent psychic intrusion

A cloth pouch with a few gems can provide
protection and support throughout your day.

- ▸ Bronzite, obsidian, and fire agate when you are the target of harmful magick
- ▸ Emerald, jet, and rainbow fluorite to prevent entity attachment, especially helpful when carried while visiting places where there are active hauntings
- ▸ Sugilite, shungite, and flint to protect against electromagnetic pollution and geopathic stress
- ▸ Moonstone, sodalite, and carnelian to confer protection while traveling

As with any other crystal activities you'll need to cleanse and empower/program your crystals first. Keep your intentions simple as you charge each stone individually. Place them together in a cloth bag or pouch, preferably of a color that represents protection to you, such as red or black. Finally, hold the pouch filled with stones between both hands and charge it as a whole unit, intending that your assortment of crystals works together to provide a synergistic effect. Your pouch is now charged and ready to join you no matter what your day has in store.

WEARING CRYSTALS AS JEWELRY

One of the most popular ways to employ gemstones for any use, protective or otherwise, is to wear them as jewelry. It is likely that the very first stones to adorn our earliest ancestors were chosen because they were believed to be something sacred, somehow imbued with a special quality that offered protection and power. Gemstones and crystals continue to be worn as jewelry and appreciated for their spiritual gifts today.

As with any other application of your beloved stones, the more meaningful your relationship with them the more effective they will be. Wearing crystals without being mindful or taking time for adequate preparation via cleansing and empowering them will still have some beneficial effects. However, the practice of cleansing your crystals and charging them with your intention forges a strong link between you and the spirits of the stones; it elevates you and your stones as equal co-creators. This is the quintessential step in all spiritual work with stones, and it can be as simple as spending a moment or two in silent contemplation before decking yourself out with your favorite gems.

Necklaces and Pendants

When most of us think of wearing gemstones, necklaces and pendants immediately spring to mind. Necklaces are versatile tools that can suit a variety of needs and fashions. They are available as pendants, strands of beads, and other designs. Pendants can become a focal point not only for personal protection but as talismanic reminders of our magickal and spiritual power. Wearing strands of gemstone beads allows the stones to physically encircle you, thereby providing comfort and safety in all directions. Protective gemstones are excellent when employed as beaded necklaces, such as those employed in gemstone energy medicine (gemstone therapy).

The length of your necklace will also have an impact with regard to its effects. Shorter lengths will stay close to the throat, thereby protecting your voice and means of self-expression. Those that lay near the heart are more emotionally protective. Very sensitive people

Examples of gemstone necklaces

may benefit from wearing a necklace that falls just above the heart, over the thymus gland, as this is a natural window into your energy field. A gemstone that falls over the thymus gland will shield us from unwanted intrusions. When our stones hang below the heart and toward the solar plexus they offer additional strength and support to the will and help prevent the attachment of energetic cords in the aura and chakras.

Bracelets

Bracelets allow us to wear gems in an accessible manner. Gemstone bracelets cost less than necklaces made from the same stones on account of their smaller size. Bracelets are also easily visible to the wearer, thus offering a gentle reminder about the energies at work for your protection and well-being. Another benefit of wearing gemstone bracelets is that they are in constant motion throughout your aura— as you move your arms and hands throughout the day, you are stirring the gems' energies and enlivening the whole of your aura.

Generally speaking, your dominant hand is considered more

Gemstone bracelets

projective, and your nondominant hand more receptive.* Wearing bracelets on the wrist of your receptive hand helps filter the energy that you receive from your environment. This can greatly alleviate psychic drain, especially for empaths and other naturally sensitive people. Wearing gemstones on the wrist of your dominant hand may color the energy that you send into your environment. Cloaking stones, such as larvikite and obsidian, may make you less noticeable if worn on the dominant hand. Ultimately, having a crystal or gemstone in your energy field allows it to perform its protective functions no matter where it is placed, so wear your bracelets wherever they feel most comfortable.

Rings

Jewel-bearing rings of an apotropaic nature are some of the oldest magickal tools to be found in the ruins of many an ancient city. Rings are ever-abundant on the market, and they come in a wide variety of stones and styles. They are openly displayed as a reminder for yourself as well as a signal to your surroundings that you are protected. Rings also allow you to combine the energy of your favorite stones with complementary metals. Gold, for example, is overtly solar in nature and confers success, protection, and sovereignty. Silver is a lunar metal that boosts psychic power and provides a nurturing protection. Copper is the metal of Venus, and though it is not as outright protective as gold or silver, it is a very healing metal that can assist in recovery from psychic attack.

There are esoteric systems that map out the planetary, elemental, and other spiritual correspondences of our fingers, with each finger associated with a different planet, element, meridian, and so forth. You can choose to combine the influence of a particular gemstone with the correspondences of the finger on which you wear it. The key here is to do so intentionally—if your favorite ring only fits on one finger, don't worry if that finger doesn't have the ideal elemental or astrological

*Despite popular opinion, energetically speaking we are ambidextrous, as we can send and receive with *both* hands. Although the general rules mentioned above are typically true, many people will find that the opposite hands are better suited for how they perceive and project energy. Experiment to find what works best for you.

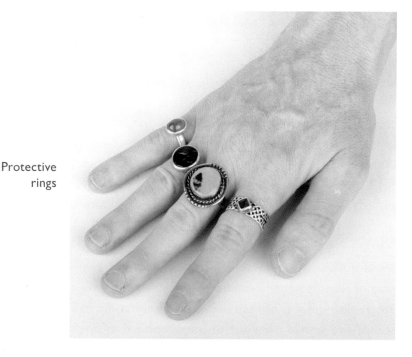

Protective rings

correspondence for your magickal working. Combining these energies should augment, not limit, your practice.

Here are a few key themes related to the planets that rule each finger to help you choose the optimal placement for protective rings:

- **Mercury** (little finger): Mercury is the planet of the mind, communication, movement, and travel. A protective gem worn on the little finger can ensure safe travels and a clear mind.
- **Sun** (ring finger): The sun represents success, identity, sovereignty, and health. A gemstone worn here infuses your entire being with its protective influences, and it may be especially helpful for safeguarding your health if you are targeted by intrusive or malicious energies.
- **Saturn** (middle finger): The middle finger is aligned with Saturn, planet of discipline, karma, banishing, and limitation. Wearing a gemstone on this finger amplifies its protective influence thanks to the virtues of Saturn.
- **Jupiter** (index finger): Jupiter is often associated with expansion,

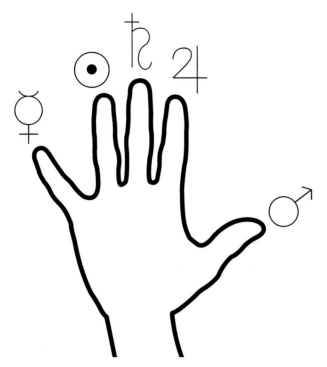

Each finger has its own planetary correspondence (from left to right): Mercury, Sun, Saturn, Jupiter, and Mars

luck, joy, and prosperity. Try coupling a protective gemstone with the influence of Jupiter to end cycles of bad luck or misfortune owed to troublesome energies or psychic harm.

- **Mars** (thumb): Mars is named for the god of war, and it bestows the qualities of protection, action, drive, and ambition. A gemstone worn on the thumb is therefore quite protective, and it can help you navigate conflict decisively.

Earrings

Crystal and gemstone earrings primarily exert their influence over the third-eye and crown chakras, making them an excellent aid for enhancing and protecting our spiritual senses. Because of the proximity of earrings to our sense organs, particularly our ears and eyes, earrings that bear protective, grounding stones can help filter out unwanted or unhelpful energies much in the same way that noise-canceling headphones filter out extraneous sound. Even though the size of the gems in your earrings may be very small, the energy of these stones is focused on sensitive areas of your physical and subtle anatomy, making them effective tools. Dangling earrings sway to and fro as you wear them, thereby further clearing and preventing stagnant energy. Gemstone earrings can alleviate some of the symptoms of psychic attack, including headaches, confusion, and communication issues. Wearing your favorite protective stones as earrings can help you maintain a clear mental picture of safety and protection, as well as promote healthy and safe decision-making in the shadow of potential harm.

Other Jewelry

Protective gems can be worn in a variety of other ways, including brooches, anklets, waist beads, crowns, and body piercings. Brooches and pins placed over the chest guard the heart against wayward emotions, while crowns, tiaras, and hair ornaments adorned with crystals can enhance your rituals and protect the uppermost chakras. You can repurpose other kinds of jewelry into protective amulets using your ingenuity and intention. For example, lockets can be filled with protective herbs, gemstone chips or shards, and a hand-drawn sigil to create a potent amulet. Miniature jars and vials can be filled with similar ingredients and strung around the neck or turned into earrings. However you choose to wear your protective stones, be sure to cleanse and empower/program them frequently in order to maintain their efficacy.

PSYCHIC SHIELDS

Psychic shields are one of the simplest and most effective ways to confer protection and bolster your personal power. There are countless ways to create and maintain psychic shields, and most of them rely on creative visualization and focused intent. Over the years I have experimented with a number of these methods, and the crystal-inspired shields described in this section are distilled from the wisdom of my teachers and from my own personal practice.

Although actual physical stones are not necessary for any of the shields described in this chapter, the effect of these shields will be greatly enhanced if you are acquainted with the energy of the crystal or gemstone being visualized or petitioned for help. Try working with the crystals that correspond to the shields for a bit before actually conjuring up a shield. The best way to do so is to connect to the stone in meditation; you may also find that wearing or carrying the stone for several days will help you attune to its energy more effectively.

When using psychic shields it is vital that you replenish their energy regularly. This typically means repeating the exercise daily for ongoing personal protection, but you may find that quickly repeating the exercise or simply holding the image of the shield in your mind periodically throughout the day will maintain the integrity of the shield, especially when you are under duress.

Psychic shields can also be effectively projected around other people, places, automobiles, and objects. Simply adapt the visualization to be centered around your desired target.

You may choose to incorporate actual physical crystals into your psychic shield meditations if you have access to the appropriate stones. There are a number of ways to do this. The simplest method is to simply hold the corresponding stone in one or both hands as you engage in the visualization. You can imagine that the crystal's energy is supporting you throughout the meditation. An alternate method is to place the crystal on a specific point on the body to help you viscerally connect with the stone and confer its protection to any weak points in your energy field. Try placing the stone at the solar plexus, heart, thymus, or brow. I like to wear the corresponding crystal in jewelry, and I often visualize the shield emerging from the stone and enfolding my aura—it's a technique I apply often to the labradorite shield described later on in this chapter. Another easy way to incorporate stones into your shielding practice is to surround yourself in a circle of the appropriate stones while conjuring the shield. This is a powerful practice, but it necessitates a fair amount of crystals in your collection. I recommend starting with four to twelve pieces of stone to start.

Use the basic instructions below for any of the psychic shields discussed throughout this chapter. Be advised that the more energy you put into your shield, the more effective it will be.

Again, I suggest getting to thoroughly know the crystal(s) you'll be using in your shield by meditating with it before casting its shield, as a sense of rapport with your stones will strengthen your casting. Basic directions for conjuring psychic shields are provided below; you can adapt these to your needs and skill set.

◆ Conjuring Psychic Shields

There are a variety of methods used by practitioners to create and maintain their psychic shields. I've chosen to focus on those that employ a crystal's symbolism and energy. Although you do not by any means need an actual crystal specimen to craft its corresponding shield, working with a sample of the stone that the shield is inspired by can augment your protection by providing a template for the energy of the shield. Working with a physical stone also improves your visualization skills, as you can copy the look and feel of the stone in your mind's eye. If you do choose to work with a stone when creating a psychic shield you can imagine that the shield itself radiates out from the stone, whether you are holding it, carrying it, or wearing it as jewelry. You may even like to have a piece of the appropriate stone reserved solely for conjuring your shield. Just be sure to cleanse and program the stone before putting it to work.

When you are ready to conjure your shield, begin by cleansing yourself (and your stone if you are using one). Ground and center yourself and close your eyes. Focus on the breath or use any technique that you are comfortable with in order to enter into a light meditative state. State your intention, silently or aloud, to build a psychic shield, and begin to visualize the shield materializing around your aura. Hold the image clearly in your mind's eye, or focus on the idea of it if you are not visually inclined.

At this point I like to use an affirmation to bolster the shield. A good example of such an affirmation or incantation is, "I charge this crystalline shield to protect me from all harm and to reflect love and compassion back on the source of the harm." Repeat the affirmation three times. When you feel as though the shield is firmly conjured, you can open your eyes.

Once you've mastered the basic technique behind creating psychic shields it's easy to adapt it to your personal needs. You can visualize pure light and energy or some other substance or symbol of protection standing as a boundary between you and the energies of the outside world. Employing different energies, crystals, and visualizations can produce highly specialized effects. It's a good idea to work with several over time, as some will fit your needs better than others depending on the situation. Try experimenting with the shields described below to find your favorites.

Crystal Prism

Of all the crystal shields I use, this one gets more mileage than any other. In my college years I began to experiment with shields because I found myself easily knocked around by the energies in my environs, and one of my favorite visualizations was to place myself inside a double-terminated crystal made of light. Years later I learned a technique with a similar outcome from my friend and teacher Christopher Penczak.[1] This latter method has become one of my daily protection practices, and I am presenting a slightly modified form below.

Crystal prism shield in rounded form

I usually use the rounded shape in my current practice, as I find it generally more effective and less restrictive on the aura itself. A double-terminated crystal shield is helpful for both protecting your energy field and aligning it with the flow of celestial and terrestrial energies, but I have found that the rounder, faceted form is more prismatic, and this helps to break up and scatter harmful energies more thoroughly. In addition to building this shield around yourself it is easy to project around your home, car, or other items in need of protection.

Although it might seem natural to picture your crystal prism as being made of quartz, you can also draw on the energy of diamond to craft this psychic shield. Diamonds are the hardest naturally occurring gemstone, and the protection that they confer is unparalleled.

Crystal Sphere

A variation on the crystal shield described above is to picture yourself in a perfectly smooth sphere of quartz crystal. Imagine that the outermost

A spherical psychic shield of polished quartz

layer of your aura crystallizes, becoming firm, smooth, and as luminous as crystal. In addition to being a general source of protection, a spherical crystal shield also helps you feel more centered, focused, and open to receiving psychic information. It manages to filter out harmful energies while allowing you to observe their source, such that you can work toward remediating the situation at hand.

A crystal sphere shield lends clarity of mind and helps to magnify your innate light. Rather than focusing solely on keeping outside energies away from you, this shield enhances your natural radiance so that external influences cannot compete with your brilliance.

Labradorite Shield

I first experimented with a psychic shield inspired by labradorite while studying other forms of magickal protection. I reasoned that if one could make a shield that resembled a crystal or prism, then one could also make them from other gemstones, too. Labradorite immediately came to mind. Labradorite is an enchanting gemstone with a beguiling

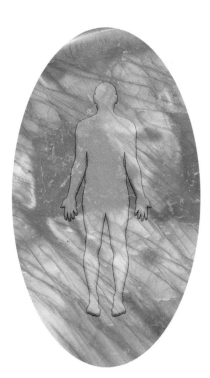

A labradorite shield to
seal and heal the aura

sheen or schiller, called *labradorescence,* which results from the inter-ference of light traveling through its microscopic layers. Just as light is broken up and made more brilliant when it passes through the stone, a shield of labradorite makes the aura more brilliant. Labradorite is praised for its relationship with auric health; it is an adept healer of holes, tears, and leaks in the aura. This gem also increases the amplitude of the aura itself. Projecting a psychic shield of this gem is perfect for ensuring a strong and healthy aura that is resistant to psychic attack. It is my favorite technique to teach empaths, highly sensitive people, and those just exploring psychic ability, as it is easy, effective, and supportive on so many levels.

I often describe the effects of a labradorite shield as spiritual Teflon; harmful energies and psychic intrusions merely fall away from your shield of labradorite light. Simultaneously it filters out all the energy that comes and goes from your aura, helping to maintain your brilliance by purifying what you send out and receive. This shield offers a refreshing, empowering energy that positively impacts your mood and gently opens your intuition. Wearing a labradorite shield can stop many forms of harmful energy and neutralize psychic attack and negative magick alike. It can offer an additional benefit when consciously directed to do so: it can be programmed to confuse your enemies or attackers. If the source of the harm is known, this defensive technique can throw them off your trail or render them unable to focus sufficiently to cause further harm.

Rose Quartz Shield

At first glance, rose quartz may seem a little incongruous among the other stones mentioned in this chapter, as it isn't particularly celebrated for being protective in the conventional sense. However, the nurturing energy of rose quartz coupled with its ability to set loving boundaries (think of the expression "tough love") makes this gemstone a capable ally in psychic self-defense. By projecting a psychic shield of rose quartz around your aura, you are able to generate a loving, peaceful enclosure free of stagnant and harmful emotional patterns. A rose quartz shield is an excellent choice for tense social environments, such as a hard day at the office or a bout of family drama.

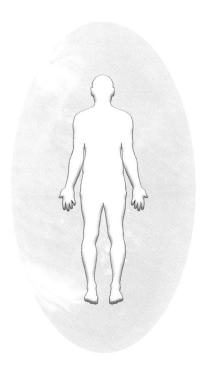

A shield of rose quartz offers a loving and gentle protective influence.

A rose quartz shield will sweeten the energy around you, thereby improving the dispositions of the people you meet. Although it's no substitute for genuine kindness and compassion, a rose quartz shield can help smooth things over when you're having a rough day. This psychic shield can also neutralize gossip and other social factors that cause spiritual harm. It helps to call on the energy of unconditional love when projecting this shield, asking that the shield transmute all energies by the power of divine love.

Garnet Shield

This shield is intended for use when you are experiencing psychic attack, physical danger, or other emergency situations. Because garnets are often associated with courage, this shield is ideal whenever you feel fear. It makes use of red garnet's fiery and earthy energies as well as its connection to the planet Mars to provide relief from psychic attack, bullying, malicious entities, harmful magick, or other sources of spiritual and mundane harm.

A glowing red shield of garnet is a potent form of protection.

When creating this shield, draw energy up from the earth and into the root chakra; visualize a brilliant red, etheric garnet crystal within your root chakra. Picture it expanding outward until the garnet surrounds and nourishes your entire aura with telluric energy. Affirm that you are grounded, protected, empowered, and filled with courage.

Obsidian Shield

Obsidian has been regarded as a protective stone for millennia, and it continues to be employed as an apotropaic tool today. As a natural glass, obsidian is highly reflective when broken or polished, a quality that lends itself well to use as a protective shield. Imagine yourself within a sphere or egg of polished black or rainbow obsidian when creating your shield. You can picture it more or less opaque as needed: more translucent for less intensive protection, and more opaque when the situation is more urgent. This shield is helpful for short-term applications, especially when psychic attack has been recognized.

Although traditionally used for protecting from harm and deflecting unwanted energies, obsidian offers additional benefits when used as a psychic shield. Boxes carved from obsidian have been employed to

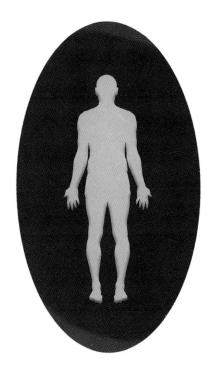

Visualize yourself within a polished obsidian shield to protect and obscure your energy field from sources of psychic harm.

psychically hide objects from people or entities. When you project a psychic shield of obsidian, you are protecting yourself against psychic intrusion. Note that this works best when there is a known case of psychic attack or psychic surveillance, as wearing a shield of obsidian full-time can be both oppressive to the wearer and ineffective for general invisibility. To conceal your aura in other cases, consider using the invisibility mist described later in this chapter.

The obsidian shield can otherwise provide a fresh perspective via its reflective qualities. Apart from deflecting external sources of psychic harm, the obsidian shield can also highlight internal causes of harm, helping you see your own thoughts and behaviors objectively such that you can make positive changes within and without.

There are a couple of easy variations on obsidian shields that are worthy of mention. For example, try working with the energy of rainbow obsidian in lieu of black obsidian; its effects feel somewhere between that of black obsidian and labradorite. This makes it better for longer durations. As an alternative to a polished sphere or egg of obsidian you can picture a raw, broken surface that is not only reflective, but also sharp and incisive. Perhaps even visualize spikes or arrowheads of obsidian protruding from your shield in every direction. This can be used to enforce the boundaries on your personal space when you feel as though someone is taking too much of your time or energy.

Hematite Shield

The hematite shield is the crystalline counterpart to the traditional mirror shield used by metaphysicians and magicians, who will project a mirrorlike sphere around their aura to not only protect themselves from harm, but also to return the harm to its source. Though there may be merits to this method, a mirror shield can also escalate problems if the harmful energy backfires or gets entangled with other people on its journey back to its source. This phenomenon, often called *blowback* or

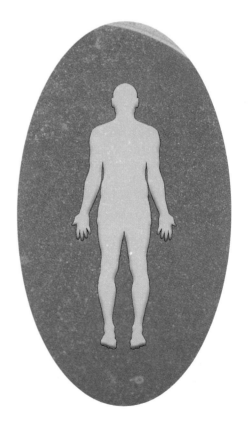

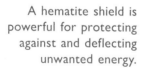

A hematite shield is powerful for protecting against and deflecting unwanted energy.

crossfire, is discussed further on page 143. For this reason such shields should be used with caution and clear intent. Ideally use them only when absolutely necessary; otherwise, employ one of the other protection shields described in this chapter.

Projecting a reflective shield of hematite around your aura breaks your connection to the source of psychic harm, often rebounding that harmful energy back to its source if you direct it to do so. Hematite lends its grounding energy to this shield, thereby discharging and releasing disharmonious energies—both inner and outer—yielding clearer thinking and better focus. This shield also draws on the iron-based composition of this stone to lend courage, stamina, and determination in the face of adversity. It can help you feel confident about getting through a tough or challenging situation or a psychic attack.

Most importantly, the hematite shield encourages the source of the harm to engage in self-reflection, hopefully inviting them to discover why they would want to engage in harmful practices, whether the attack is intentional or not. If you are using this shield because you suspect you're being targeted by psychic harm or malefic intentions of any kind, consider combining it with the techniques found in chapters 7 and 8 to neutralize the source of the harm.

Amber Bubble

Amber's bright golden color has an uplifting and empowering effect on the mind and aura. This stone imparts a sunny, cheerful energy while conferring protection. Try visualizing yourself in a bubble of amber to shield yourself from psychic intrusion and oppressive energies. Since amber is so lightweight, this shield is quite gentle in its effects. Just as this gemstone requires frequent cleansing, the amber bubble will need to be reinstated often if you find yourself in dense or oppressive energy.

Because amber is excellent at deterring unwanted psychic attention, this shield is useful when you find yourself being too open or vulnerable. Unlike heavier shields, it doesn't make you feel closed or disconnected from your surroundings. I do find that some energies can feel stuck in an amber shield, so you may decide to use it only in situations

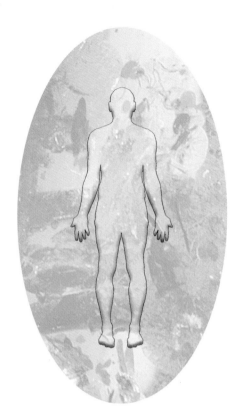

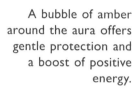

A bubble of amber around the aura offers gentle protection and a boost of positive energy.

that are generally positive. The amber bubble is perfect for using in tandem with other psychic shields to add an uplifting effect and a boost of confidence.

To conjure your amber bubble, hold a piece of amber in your dominant hand. Visualize the light of the sun above you, pouring its golden power into your crown chakra. Draw this light down into the stone to charge it with solar energy. Place the amber on your solar plexus and imagine the stone's energy as a viscous liquid, like tree sap, that gradually radiates outward until it encompasses your entire energy field. Intend that the liquid harden into a firm but transparent resinous shield, a sphere or ovoid of amber to filter and protect your personal energy.

Invisibility Mist

One of my favorite magickal tricks that I learned in my teens was disappearing. No, I couldn't turn invisible at will, but I could seemingly

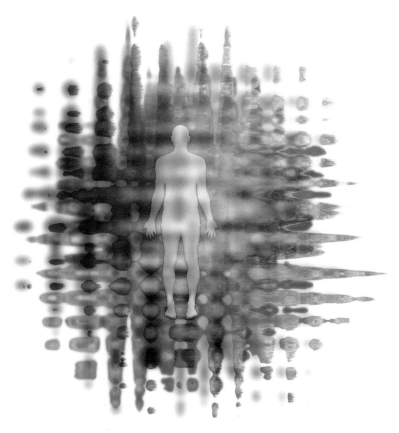

Visualize a grayish mist of larvikite to cast an
invisibility cloak around your aura.

be unidentifiable when stepping into a crowd. Despite my red hair—
practically a neon sign announcing my location—I managed to lose my
friends in the rush between classes often enough to convince me that
I'd actually mastered the art of invisibility, or at least become adept at
traveling unnoticed in a crowd.

Over the ensuing years I've learned quite a number of techniques
for casting glamours* and shields for invisibility. These days my favorite

*The terms *glamour* and *glamoury* describe the magickal art of changing your perception.
This is often done by projecting a specific energy or image into your aura, which, in turn,
is subtly perceived by those around you. A potent glamour won't change the color of your
hair, but it could make you seem more charismatic or help you disappear into a crowd.

method involves shrouding myself in a silvery mist and picturing myself as translucent. Historically, there are several stones frequently associated with conferring invisibility, including bloodstone, chrysoprase, opal, and topaz. Larvikite and septarian nodules are also used for invisibility by modern practitioners. Of these, larvikite is my first choice, as its silvery-blue sheen reminds me of an otherworldly fog—perfect for shrouding oneself from prying eyes. You can even imagine that your shield is composed of a mist that resembles this gemstone.

Use your invisibility mist when you want to avoid attention and for evading psychic attack from known or unknown sources. If you are performing a ritual at night, perhaps in a place where it might not be welcome, you can picture yourself and/or your ritual space immersed in this mist. Invisibility mist can also be helpful if you have to enter a crowded area but want to avoid making idle chatter. When faced with psychic attack, using the invisibility mist glamour in tandem with a decoy to draw the harm can diffuse dangerous situations and offer enough time to enact appropriate countermeasures.

Wall of Stone

The wall of stone is a psychic shield that aims to neutralize all incoming energy, harmful or not. This shield is supremely grounding and strengthening, and it acts like an impenetrable fortress around you. Although I generally do not recommend totally impenetrable shields, there is a time and place for every technique. This shield is best reserved for circumstances of extreme bullying, psychic attack, or when you are unsure of the motives of those around you. It can make you feel rather disconnected and appear aloof, so I do not recommend working with the wall of stone for long periods of time unless circumstances are dire enough to merit this shield.

When conjuring this shield, you can choose to hold or wear a piece of durable stone such as basalt, granite, quartzite, sarsen, slate, or any other natural stone available to you—all the better if it comes from land where you live. I like to use a piece of coquina rock, a type of limestone made from broken shells, from my hometown; it was once used by the Spanish colonists to build forts that could deflect cannonballs. Hold

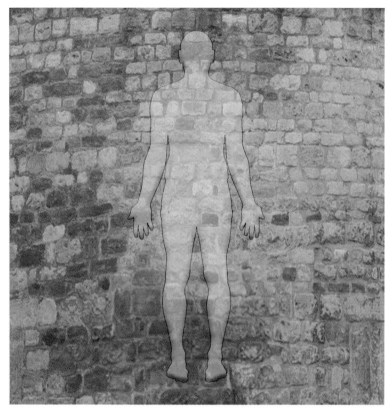

Imagine a high wall of dense, strong stone
protecting you from all sides.

the stone in your dominant hand and draw energy from the ground
below you up through your feet and into the stone. When the stone
feels saturated with this telluric energy, hold the stone at arm's length
and begin to trace a circle around yourself. Picture a circular wall of
stone rising up from the earth to completely obscure your aura from
view, protecting you from all harm. Refresh this as needed, perhaps
daily if you are in unsafe or unpleasant circumstances, and carry the
stone with you each day you use this shield.

◈ Cocoon of Light

I first wrote about the cocoon of light in my book *Crystal Basics*, and it
remains a trusted technique in my tool kit. The cocoon of light allows

you to build a psychic shield by projecting energy through a crystal and visualizing that energy as a thread or cord of light being woven through and around your aura. It becomes a breathable barrier, one that is selectively permeable, such that it permits positive vibes to enter and enables you to release what doesn't serve. This shield is a bit more kinesthetically oriented than the others mentioned above, as you must physically move the crystal around your energy field. This combination of bodily movement and mental visualization produces a magnified end result: a shield that is durable and secure.

To produce the cocoon of light, begin with a freshly cleansed and programmed crystal wand of your choice. I prefer to work with a clear quartz wand (usually natural, though sometimes polished), as they are the most versatile tools and can be employed for any color shield. Draw in light and energy with the breath and visualize it traveling from your lungs through your shoulders, arms, and hands and into the crystal. Direct this energy in any pattern that you like to wrap your aura in a protective layer of light. Be sure not to miss any large areas of your aura, as you don't want to leave yourself vulnerable. Once you've totally enveloped yourself in light, trace a lemniscate (a figure eight) in front of yourself several times, envisioning that this "ties off" the loose thread of light.

You can experiment by projecting different colors of light through the crystal you use to construct the cocoon. If possible, use a crystal wand that corresponds to the color you are projecting (such as amethyst for violet, citrine for yellow or gold, and so forth); otherwise use clear quartz and program it with a color and its correlating intention. Here are some examples:

▶ Prismatic white (crystalline or colorless light) is the best for general protection. It is gently nourishing and helps break up and scatter harmful energies.

▶ Opaque white light is strongly insulative, and it keeps out virtually all energies—even desirable ones. White light, contrary to popular belief, is not recommended for ordinary use, but it can be helpful when experiencing unknown causes of psychic harm, as it blocks everything from reaching you.

► Golden light is also strongly protective in addition to being stress-relieving and a general boost to your overall disposition, making it excellent for everyday use.

► Red is a protective color. Use red light in cases of psychic attack, as it boosts physical stamina and vital energy while defending you.

► Violet is purifying, transformational, and alchemical. It transmutes energy, both good and bad, into something helpful and healing.

CRYSTAL LAYOUTS FOR PROTECTION

To create a layout, first gather the stones required by the layout. Generally it's best to use stones that are evenly sized. Ensure that they are an adequate size and shape for laying directly on the body so they won't cause discomfort or roll off. Next, cleanse the stones you've selected; programming or charging them with your intention is recommended, too. Quiet your mind for a moment and hold the layout's purpose in your heart, perhaps even visualizing the pattern or symbolism of it. Then you are free to build the layout. This can be challenging to perform for yourself when it comes to more complex designs, so be sure to have the crystals within arm's reach, and make any adaptations necessary for your comfort.

Once erected, the layout can be left in place for anywhere from fifteen to thirty minutes. Be present with yourself or your client, as healing arrays can sometimes evoke images, memories, and energies rather unexpectedly. Some layouts are strongly purifying, too, and so they can initiate a sudden release of energies, attachments, emotions, and other patterns. Breathe comfortably and rhythmically, and allow the stones to work their magick in your energy field. End the session when it feels appropriate—and don't stick with it if the energy release is too overwhelming.

After a session in a crystal layout you may want to cleanse yourself or your space if there has been a strong release. Always cleanse and thank the stones when you've finished, as they will retain imprints of the session; cleansing allows them to be put to another use without interference.

You can treat the layouts throughout this book much like recipes. Once you have an understanding of how the crystals work individually and together, you can make substitutions or changes to suit your needs (consult the directory of protective stones in chapter 9). Feel free to be creative as long as the changes you make are aligned with the nature of the layout.

◆ Basic Protection Layout

Crystals: one labradorite, one obsidian, four or more shungites, and four or more pieces of onyx or black tourmaline

When life gets the better of us, sometimes we simply need extra support. This combination of labradorite, obsidian, shungite, and either onyx or black tourmaline aims to restore and bolster our natural defenses. It can be used regularly to build long-term defenses or when your boundaries feel depleted.

Begin by placing labradorite over the thymus gland or higher heart chakra. This point serves as an energetic window into the energy field as a whole, and labradorite seals it against harm while strengthening your light. This placement also teaches the aura discernment so that it can filter out unwanted or unhealthy energy. Obsidian at the solar plexus is strongly protective while also amplifying personal power and preventing your energy from being drained by psychic vampirism, geopathic stress, or other factors. Finally, place the outer ring of shungite and onyx or tourmaline; alternate the stones and space them evenly around the body. Begin by placing the first stone below the feet and move clockwise around the body. This combination alternates between a porous, purifying stone and a denser, more shielding stone to reinforce the aura's natural defenses while still allowing it to receive beneficial energies.

Leave the layout in place for ten to thirty minutes, then remove the stones beginning with the obsidian and labradorite. Remove the shungite and obsidian starting with the stone below the feet and move counterclockwise to remove the rest.

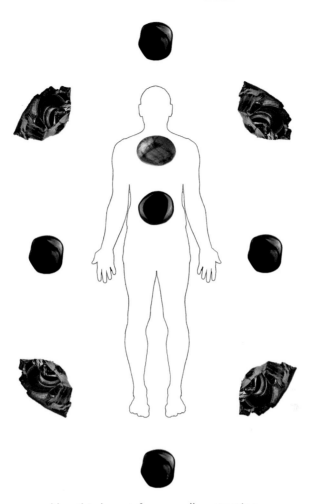

Use this layout for overall protection.

◈ Tourmaline Cross

Crystals: four black tourmalines, four brown tourmalines, and one pink, green, or watermelon tourmaline

The tourmaline family is one of the most dynamic groups of minerals in the healer's or occultist's toolbox. As cyclosilicate minerals, their structure consists of rings of silica stacked together, producing channels within their molecular structure. This allows tourmalines to siphon off unhealthy energy and infuse the empty space with nourishing, strengthening energy in its

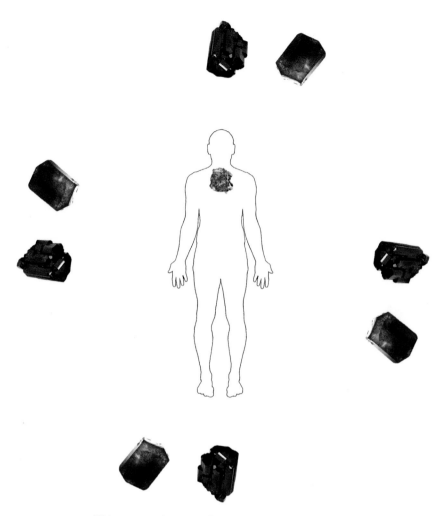

This array of tourmalines provides grounding,
protection, and comfort.

place. All tourmalines are protective, although this layout uses the most
effective tourmalines for protection.*

The tourmaline cross is built from two overlapping crosses—one

---

*My first exposure to such an array of tourmaline can be found in many of the works
of Sue and Simon Lilly, including their books *Crystal Doorways* and *The Crystal Healing
Guide*. As described in *Crystal Doorways* (p. 35), the Lillys use eight black tourmalines
for their layout, which aims to balance the physical body, alleviate pain, align with the
planet's energies, and clear and protect the aura.

centered on the body, and the other tilted slightly. This allows for a state of dynamic grounding; rather than merely rooting you to one place, it invokes healthy movement energy and realignment of the physical and subtle bodies. The first cross is made from black tourmaline. Place the brown tourmaline at oblique angles beside the black tourmaline, as depicted in the figure above. Finally, place a pink, green, or watermelon tourmaline over the heart center. The lithium content of these tourmalines is nourishing and balancing to the psyche. Both pink and green tourmalines balance the heart center, providing emotional resilience and strength.

Leave the tourmalines in place until you are ready to end the session. Note that this layout may initially heighten symptoms of pain, discomfort, or unease; however, this is usually short-lived, as the tourmalines work to rebalance quickly and effectively.

◈ Instant Protection

Crystals: four flints and three bloodstones

This layout aims to ground, center, and protect your energy field rapidly and effectively. It works by connecting your energy field directly into the earth to transmute and discharge harmful energies while simultaneously shielding you from negative thoughts and other unpleasant energies. The instant protection layout can be erected quickly and put to use for acute, emergent scenarios, or it can be left in a convenient place such as under the bed for long periods of time to provide continuous support while sleeping. A small layout can be used as a grid for warding your space, or it can be built over a photo of yourself or anyone else who needs additional protection around the clock. The inspiration for this layout comes from the work of my friend, and noted crystal expert, the late Judy Hall; a similar design can be found in her book *The Ultimate Guide to Crystal Grids*.[2] Judy recommends placing the stones beneath the body, which I find uncomfortable unless very small, flat stones are used. I've also altered the shape of the grid to evoke the image of a diamond, a powerful protective stone and symbol of invincibility.

After cleansing your crystals, hold them for a few moments and focus on the intention of creating instant protection. Once the crystals are imbued with this energy, place the four flints in a large square or diamond-shaped pattern as shown in the image above. Lie down inside this simple

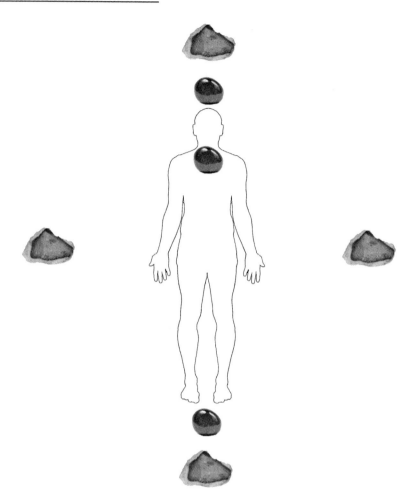

Flint and bloodstone work together for powerful,
instantaneous protection.

grid and place the three bloodstones as shown: one above the crown, another at the thymus, and the last below the feet. Mentally connect the three bloodstones from top to bottom, intending that this downward flow of energy links your entire chakra system and aura to the earth and thus offers a safe outflow for unwanted or detrimental energies. Now picture the four outer stones connecting to form a safe container around your aura, deflecting and transmuting energy from outside sources. Spend a few minutes within the grid, and when you are ready remove the bloodstone from your thymus and return to normal consciousness.

◈ Labradorite Star

Crystals: seven pieces of labradorite

Labradorite is among my favorite stones for protection because it is versatile and almost always a welcome addition to anyone's energy field. The iridescent flashes within the stone evoke images of swirling nebulas and twinkling stars, and many people find that it connects strongly to the celestial spheres. For this reason a seven-pointed star—each point representing one of the seven classical planets—draws down heavenly and planetary energies to seal, protect, and balance the aura.

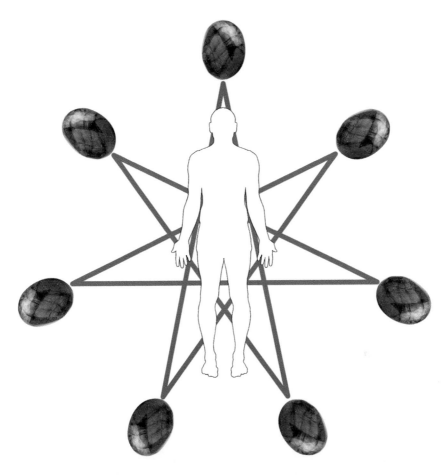

Use seven labradorites placed around the body in a seven-pointed star for this powerful layout.

If possible, choose seven labradorites with strong labradorescence or sheen. Cleanse and empower them before building the layout; if you like, you can dedicate one stone to each of the visible planets and luminaries: Sun, Moon, Mercury, Venus, Mars, Jupiter, and Saturn. Place each stone at one of the seven points of the septagram, in the sequence depicted below:

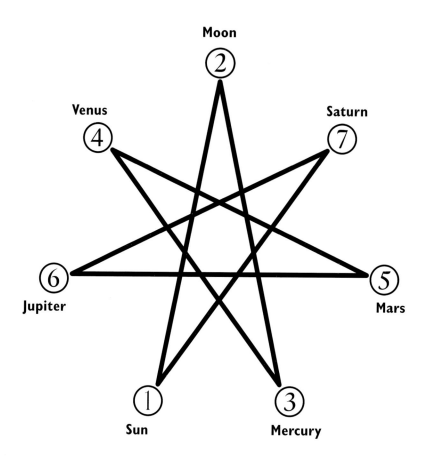

Place each stone according to this pattern.

This pattern follows the same sequence as the planetary rulers for each day of the week, starting with the Sun (Sunday), Moon (Monday), and so forth. Once the last stone is placed, use a wand, crystal point, or your fingers to trace the pattern of the septagram at least three times (though seven times is even better), silently naming the planet at each point as you go. Now lie down inside the layout for a minimum of seven minutes and allow the gems to draw down the gifts of the seven wanderers* to protect, seal, and balance your entire being. For an extra boost of protective power, add an eighth labradorite to the solar plexus as you lie within the septagram. When finished, offer a moment of gratitude to each of the seven planets and to the labradorites. This technique works best when repeated at regular intervals, either the same day each week or at the four quarters of the lunar cycle (new, first quarter, full, and last quarter).

◈ *Invisibility Layout*
Crystals: seven obsidians, two larvikites, and one chrysoprase

The invisibility layout aims to help you move unnoticed in the world. This layout combines the energies of three stones, chrysoprase, larvikite, and obsidian, which can cloak your energy in different ways. Chrysoprase has a long history of conferring invisibility; many medieval sources indicate that this gem could render its wearer invisible. Although chrysoprase doesn't literally make us unseen, it can lead our hearts and minds to the parts of the world that are ordinarily invisible. It has a long history of protecting against jealousy and greed, so it is placed at the solar plexus in this layout to prevent our will from being tampered with by others who do not have our best interests in mind. Larvikite helps the light of your aura go unnoticed, thereby keeping harmful thought forms and predatory entities at bay. Finally, obsidian offers a powerful shield that can neutralize psychic attacks and prevent unwanted psychic intrusions.

To construct the layout, place one obsidian below each foot, one beside each hip, one beside each arm, level with the heart chakra, and one above the head. Next, place one larvikite on each shoulder; if it is difficult to get the stones to stay put, simply place them on the ground as close to the shoulders as possible. Finally, add the chrysoprase to the solar plexus.

---

*The term *planet* originally meant "wanderer" since it was observed since ancient times that certain points of light "wandered," i.e., changed their position, with respect to the background stars in the sky.

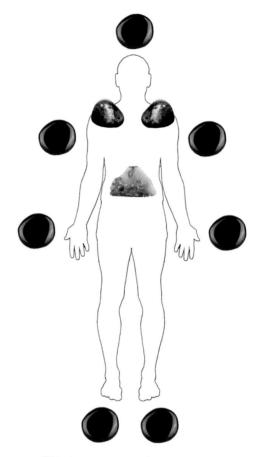

This layout can make your energy
imperceptible to others.

Mentally picture the energy of this layout infusing your aura with a haze or mist that renders you invisible. Spend at least fifteen minutes within the layout, then remove the stones. For optimum effect you can carry a small pouch with one of each type of stone from this layout; you can even use the ones from the layout itself, as they will be strongly charged to produce excellent results.

4

Warding Your Space

After learning techniques to protect your own energy field and prevent psychic attacks from reaching you on a personal level, the next step in effective psychic self-defense is protecting your home against disruptive, intrusive, or outright harmful energies. The magickal act of protecting your space is called *warding*, and throughout this chapter you'll discover a variety of techniques for warding your home.

THE MECHANICS OF WARDING

The word *ward* shares linguistic roots with a number of words that have overlapping meanings: *guard, guardian, warden, steward, aware,* and *wary.* It's etymology can be traced back to the Proto-Indo-European root *wer,* which means "to perceive" or "to watch for." We see this root change over time into the Proto-Germanic *wardon,* which means "to guard," as well as the Old English *weard,* referring to a sentry, guardian, or watcher. A ward in the magickal sense is therefore something that confers protection and watches over your space and all who reside in it.

Wards are usually anchored to a place (or perhaps a vehicle), as opposed to protection rites aimed at defending people or objects. Wards confer protection *somewhere,* be it your home, office, or sacred space. These protections can be generalized, blocking out as much discordant or intrusive energy as possible, or they can be aimed at specific kinds of defenses, like wards against harmful spirits or psychic spies. I've known people to ward against nosy neighbors or unwelcome family visits. Folk magick around the world frequently involves warding against all kinds of things, including illness, accidents, crime, the evil eye, harmful entities, and more.

Magickal wards serve several important functions. First, warding your home offers defense when you are most vulnerable, like when you are asleep. It gives your personal protections a chance to rest and recharge, as you generally won't need to maintain psychic shields within the comfort of your well-warded home. Warding also allows you to exercise some agency over the energetic state and spiritual ecosystem of your home; setting wards filters out the energies you deem unacceptable or at least unhelpful. Energetically speaking, this means fewer disturbances and distractions, which not only helps you feel safe and at peace, it improves your magickal and spiritual praxes, as they have less white noise to cut through.

Warding is achieved through ritual means, symbolic actions or objects, or by invoking gods, spirits, or other guardians to intercede. Wards create energetic or spiritual boundaries that prevent disruptive energy, psychic or magickal intrusions, and unwelcome entities from entering your home. They can be permanent or ephemeral, short-term or long-term. Simple acts of folk magick can create powerful wards, particularly when several are used in tandem. You can use spoken and written charms, amulets or talismans, sigils and symbols, chimes, plants, rocks and minerals, statues and other art, powders, and other physical tools to create the wards in and around your space. Warding spells can include simple acts of candle magick or they can take the form of crystal grids—the possibilities are endless. Wards can also be constructed such that they rely on a particular spirit or deity to guard your home, keeping watch and either blocking harmful energy or alerting you to its presence.

Always be sure to build your wards *after* cleansing your home, as you'll want to start with a blank slate, so to speak, to make sure your house is free from intrusive, harmful energies. Otherwise, you may inadvertently seal unpleasant vibes into your home. Refer to chapter 2 to review techniques for cleansing your space before laying down your wards.

Layering various wards is helpful because each works a little differently and has its own respective strengths and blind spots. In comparison to more mundane protective measures, having more than one kind of ward is a bit like locking your door, drawing the curtains, and setting the burglar alarm; together these activities are more effective than a single measure used on its own. Although genuine curses are rare, having multiple wards can make it very difficult for harmful magick, psychic attacks, and other kinds of intrusions to make their way into your personal space. On the other hand, too many wards can create a home atmosphere that feels stifled, stagnant, or even oppressive, as they will restrict the energies that come and go, including those you may want in your space.

Wards need to be refreshed periodically. This can accompany a thorough house-cleansing, which will, in part, clear away any accumulated energy gumming up the mechanics of your wards. Permanent and long-term wards such as amulets, spell pouches, and crystals can be consecrated and recharged at the same time to provide continuous protection. Temporary wards and those made from short-lived materials will need to be cleared away and replaced. Witch bottles (described later in this chapter), spirit traps (see chapter 8), and similar charms can be disposed of away from the home and replaced with a new round of apotropaic devices. Grids erected within or around your home for protection should be cleansed, reprogrammed, and returned to their location.

The question of how often to refresh your wards is an important one. I usually recommend doing so at least once each season for long-term wards, though once a month may be necessary for times when danger or disruption is imminent. You can repeat the ritual actions, however simple or complex, used in the initial construction of your wards when you refresh them, or perhaps you will simply offer a heartfelt prayer and visualization to rejuvenate their protective influence.

Finally, you need to be prepared for what you can't ward against: yourself. The state of your energy, psyche, and life can fill your home with either beneficent or baneful vibrations. Practicing spiritual hygiene and other techniques on a regular basis will reduce any psychic debris that you may inadvertently be storing. It's also difficult to ward against the energies, people, and situations that you *invite* into your home.

These may be people you live with, visitors, and the thoughts and emotions of outsiders that make their way into your home through social media and the like. Again, be sure to cleanse often to sweep away invited energies before they accumulate. Karma, fate, miasmas, and ritual pollution can't be warded off per se, though we can reduce the behaviors and circumstances that generate harmful influences. Gods and other spirit beings cannot always be warded against (in fact, I'd offer that gods can *never* be warded against), especially if we have entered into some kind of spiritual relationship with them. In these circumstances, maintaining that relationship and fulfilling agreements will bring blessings, with no need for protection against such allies.

HISTORICAL HOME PROTECTION

Throughout humanity's long time on this planet, various kinds of magickal, symbolic, and spiritual devices have been employed to confer protection on the home and other important spaces. Homes have been warded through rituals of benediction, apotropaic spells have been uttered to drive away harmful spirits, and magickal prophylactics have long ensured safety, good health, and success to the residents of countless dwellings since ancient times.

Early wards likely consisted of objects from the natural world deemed to have extraordinary characteristics: naturally perforated stones, fossils and gemstones, or unusual bits of wood. These strange pieces of the natural world are still believed by many to be imbued with some kind of exceptional quality or energy that grants protection and other boons. Over time, more complex and sophisticated systems of magick and religion developed, thereby giving rise to a host of apotropaic symbols and articles both natural and manmade that have been used for warding.

A survey of the archaeological record reveals many kinds of objects used for protecting the home. Common wards used historically in Europe have included shoes, animal remains (particularly those of cats, horses, and toads), written spells and charms, inscribed or painted marks or sigils, blades, iron implements (horseshoes, nails), stones, coins, certain household objects (spoons, tobacco pipes, buttons), dried plant matter, and more. A special class of apotropaic tools are *witch bottles*; these are stoneware or glass bottles filled with items like nails, pins, salt, thorns, effigies, bones, ochre, and the owner's hair, nails, or urine. Originally conceived as countermagick to thwart practitioners of the dark arts, witch bottles eventually became all-purpose tools for warding the home and protecting its inhabitants by acting as magickal decoys that draw harmful energy away from the person or household they are meant to protect.

Such magickal means of protection continue to be discovered thanks to modern construction projects, which usually require demolition and the occasional archaeological excavation. Wards like those mentioned above are most often found in places where they were deliberately concealed, most frequently under doorways, windows, and other liminal spaces such as chimneys and empty spaces in walls. These wards usually worked in one or more of the following ways:

- Sympathetically invoking a force, quality, or spirit that confers protection
- Acting as energy sinks or spirit traps
- Serving as spirit houses for beneficent spirits and gods
- Deflecting harmful energy or sending it back to its source
- Antagonizing sources of harm so they will rescind their magick
- Distracting or confusing spirits or other sources of harm
- Becoming decoys to draw harm away from the intended target

Choosing the right warding device has largely depended on cultural context and personal taste. In buildings with many generations of inhabitants, wards and other protections frequently accumulate such that it may be possible to find dozens, maybe hundreds of apotropaic devices in the walls or under the floor that draw from several or even all of the above methods. In a similar fashion, we too can enlist different kinds of wards when constructing the protections around our home and other spaces.

CRYSTALS FOR WARDING

Virtually any rock, mineral, crystal, or gemstone offers some level of protection to the home. By their very makeup stones are enduring, and by having them in our home and other spaces they are sharing some of their magick with us. Stone has always served to protect us, as evidenced by early shelters made in caves and lithic weapons made to defend against harm. Today we are able to fine-tune our crystal selections to include those specialized for the situations we are experiencing—or trying to prevent. In the list below, you'll find a selection of the most important home-protection stones from chapter 9.

Amethyst	Hematite	Rhodonite
Amber	Holey stone	Sardonyx
Ammonite	Jade	Selenite
Aragonite	Jasper	Serpentine
Basalt	Jet	Shungite
Bronzite	Kyanite	Slate
Calcite	Labradorite	Smoky quartz
Celestite	Lapis lazuli	Sodalite
Chalk	Malachite	Staurolite
Citrine	Moonstone	Tiger's eye
Flint	Obsidian	Tourmaline
Fluorite	Petrified wood	Unakite
Granite	Pyrite	
Halite	Quartz	

Many of the stones in this list have a tradition of protection that reaches far back in lore and legend. Some stones demonstrate their protective qualities based on their makeup and habit, while others have more poetic or symbolic means of protecting our spaces. Stones such as hematite, obsidian, and labradorite have reflective qualities that turn away harm. Other crystals, like shungite, selenite, halite, kyanite, and amethyst, transmute and transform negativity to prevent it from rooting in our spaces. Gemstones with celestial qualities such as lapis lazuli and celestite connect us to the power of the angelic sphere to ward our homes against intrusions.

Furthermore, you can marry the form of stone to the task of warding. Carvings of fierce creatures like wolves, serpents, or dragons might be placed near an entrance to ward off intrusive energies and psychic attacks. Carved crystal angels are ever popular, and you can let them alight in rooms that benefit from extra guardianship and light, like a bedroom or living room. Crystal skulls are potent guardians wherever they are placed. Revisit the discussion of form and function in chapter 1 for more inspiration.

Your selection of stones should be tailored to match your space, your lifestyle, and your spiritual needs. Don't feel limited to the crystals listed above, for they are merely starting points to inspire your team of crystal allies that will ward your space.

WHERE TO WARD

Well-crafted wards can be placed virtually anywhere in your home to obtain results. However, tailoring the kind of ward to the exact location you'll leave it in is far more effective. Certain parts of your home are more susceptible to psychic invasion, and places where you engage in activities that make you more psychically vulnerable (like sleeping, bathing, and meditating) also merit extra protection. Let's review where warding is most effective:

- Outer boundaries of your property
- Entrances and thresholds, including front, back, and side doors
- Windows
- Ceiling, walls, floor, especially when shared by neighbors in an apartment or condo.
- Chimneys
- Internal thresholds, especially the attic, basement, and bathrooms
- Bedroom
- Ritual or meditation space
- Home office

The outer boundaries of your property will benefit from simple protections, like buried pieces of quartz, tourmaline, flint, or granite, to guard them. Small stones might be hung from or buried beneath a fence at the perimeter. You could also incorporate larger stones of any variety you like—especially common rocks like granite or limestone—into your landscaping for additional strength and support in maintaining the spiritual boundaries of your space. If you live in an unsafe neighborhood or if there is any concern for possible intruders, work with stones like bronzite and sardonyx to bolster your magickal defenses.

The entrance to your home should be adequately warded. Many magickal folks set up protections at the main entrance, like the front door, but otherwise neglect the rest of the ways in and out. You can hang amulets or gemstones on, over, or near the front door for simple protection. Some of my favorite crystal wards include placing selenite atop the doorways. I also keep a reflective sentinel stone facing the main entrance; for this purpose you can use hematite, labradorite, obsidian, or pyrite to deflect intrusive energies and maintain the sanctity of your home. Protective crystals like flint or black tourmaline can also be placed on either side of a door to seal it against unwanted visitations, human and spiritual alike.

Windows, too, are easy ways into your home energetically speaking. A striking crystal on the sill can beautify your space and also keep negativity at bay. Just remember that certain crystals, like amethyst, fade in sunlight and won't be well-suited to such an application. Rods of selenite, small pieces of flint, or other protective stones can be discreetly rested atop window frames. You might also make or buy amulets, pendants, or crystal suncatchers to hang in the windows to be both decorative and protective.

Along the walls you can use rods of selenite or any other protective crystal to reinforce the boundaries they offer. Corners are prime spaces for energy to stagnate, so consider shungite, tourmaline, hematite, or quartz (clear, smoky, or amethyst) to prevent congestion and anchor a household grid. Shared walls, such as those in apartments and condominiums, and common spaces in your home are also strategic places for warding against both conflict and intrusive energies. Moonstone placed against a shared wall is said to keep peace with the neighbors, and unakite, granite, and sodalite are all helpful allies for keeping peace in common spaces. Ensure that uplifting, loving crystals are among the mix of stones you place where people gather, such as the living room, dining room, or kitchen.

Other liminal spots in your house—chimneys, attics, basements, thresholds from one room to another—may benefit from apotropaic stones. Holey stones hung in the highest point of the home such as the attic create a blanket of defense for the entire space; fossils like ammonite, petrified wood, coral, and echinoids (sea urchins) are also good choices for the attic, as there is a long tradition of employing them for defending against fire, storm damage, and accidents in the home. Basements and indoor thresholds can be treated with the crystals of your choice, though I recommend grounding stones like jasper, granite, hematite, and black tourmaline for the basement. Larger specimens of crystal clusters, polished spheres or towers, or eye-catching rough specimens are beautiful when displayed on the mantle, and they double as protectors of the chimney to prevent intrusive energies that try to make their way in that way.

Most importantly, be sure to pay attention to the spaces you spend the most time in. We are energetically more vulnerable when sleeping and bathing, so the bedroom and bathroom are effective places to defend with crystal allies. I tend to avoid too many energizing stones in the bedroom, opting for grounding, soothing crystals instead. The home office is also a good place for protective crystals, as those of us who work from home spend a fair amount of time there, and computers and other devices are a powerful, if overlooked, portal to the outside world. A chunk of shungite or polished slab of labradorite will help filter out unwanted energies in your office. Ritual and meditation spaces in your home deserve adequate protection, too, as spiritual practice can both open us to being more sensitive to outside energies while occasionally attracting attention from the astral spheres.

BEYOND THE HOME

Warding isn't limited only to where we live. You can create crystal wards for your away-from-home workspace, your vehicle, or any other place where you spend time. Let's examine a few ideas to help you stay safe and sound no matter where you are.

There are a number of crystals and gemstones historically connected to safe travel that can be tucked into the center console or the glove box of your car, or perhaps hung from the rearview mirror. Aquamarine, chiastolite, garnet, jet, lapis lazuli, moonstone, schalenblende, staurolite, tourmaline (black and pink varieties), and zircon are all examples of gems that protect when traveling and can be excellent wards to place in your vehicle or carry on a journey.

If you have a dedicated office, cubicle, desk, or other workspace you can place crystals around you to create a bubble of protection at your job. Crystals add beauty and may simply be regarded as decor by coworkers, making them excellent tools for hiding magick in plain sight. Labradorite can help you filter out unwanted psychic energy and emotions, while amethyst and rhodonite help you stay calm and centered despite others' attitudes. Try black tourmaline or arfvedsonite when faced with toxic coworkers.

CRYSTAL GRIDS FOR THE HOME

By far the most popular way to ward your home with crystals is by gridding your space with the right allies. Entire books are devoted to this subject, so I'll provide only a few more grids in addition to the Household Cleansing and Protection Grid (page 44) described in chapter 2.

When building a crystal grid, take the time needed to cleanse and program or charge all the components. Lay the stones out according to the diagrams accompanying each grid, bearing in mind that you may need to modify the shape of the grid and the number of crystals to ensure that all of your home is warded effectively. L-shaped and other nonrectangular homes can easily be covered by adding a few more crystals such that every interior corner and all the walls are defended. Grids require maintenance and good psychic hygiene to operate at peak efficiency, and you can always add, change, or otherwise amend the crystals in your home grid to provide the best energetic support to your wards.

◆ Angelic Protection

Crystals: four aragonites, four selenites, three lapis lazulis, and one danburite or celestite

When faced with heavy, dense, dark energies, invoking angelic light will uplift and ward the home against harm. This grid makes use of several crystals with angelic associations. Once your crystals are cleansed and programmed,

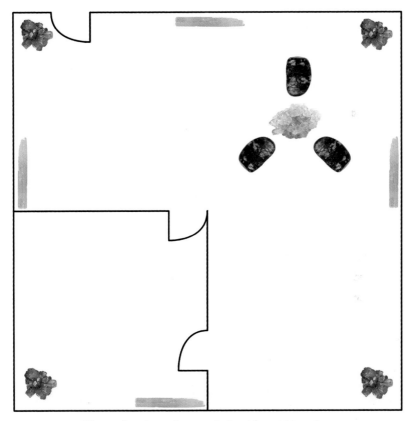

The collection of crystals in this grid invokes
protection from the angelic sphere.

place the aragonite in the corners of the home to bridge the terrestrial and celestial planes. Aragonite has the added bonus of connecting with the elementals and land spirits to invoke their aid. Selenite is placed along the walls, much like the Household Cleansing and Protection Grid described in chapter 2; this helps move energy to create a luminous barrier against harm. Finally, lay the danburite or celestite within a triangle of lapis lazuli in the center of your home. This can be either the geographical or social center; alternatively you can place this in the focal point of the main room, such as on the mantle or atop an altar.

◈ Repelling Psychic Spies

Crystals: four larvikites or granites, four obsidians, and one bloodstone per entryway and one moonstone per bed

If you suspect that psychic spying, remote viewing, or any other kind of

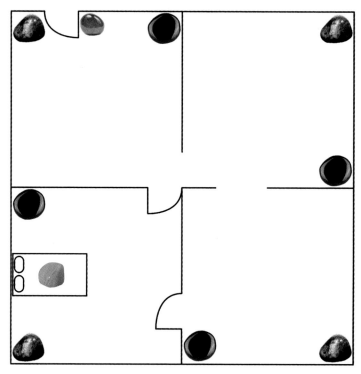

Place the crystals as shown above to cast a cloak of
psychic invisibility over your home.

prying activity is being directed at your home, this grid can neutralize the intrusion. Gather your crystals, cleanse and program them, and prepare to build your grid. Start by laying larvikite or granite at the corners of your home and obsidian at the midpoints between them. This combination helps to simultaneously insulate against and deflect psychic intrusions. Follow this with bloodstone placed at or near any entrance regularly used. Bloodstone has been worn for invisibility since at least the Medieval period, and it is a powerful defender against harm thanks to its planetary association with Mars. Finally, you can hang a piece of moonstone over each bed or tuck it away beneath the mattress to add an extra layer of protection when you are asleep and more psychically vulnerable.

◆ *Conflict Resolution*

Crystals: four black tourmalines, four blue kyanites, one rose quartz, and one or more unakite

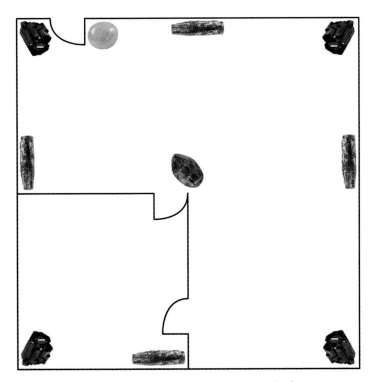

This crystal combination thwarts outside forces
from stirring up conflict and ensures peace in the home.

Conflict in the home can be a powerful source of psychic harm. It is also sometimes a sign of psychic attack. No matter its source, this crystal grid is aimed at promoting harmony in the home. With your crystals cleansed and programmed, begin to build this grid with black tourmaline in the corners and kyanite along the walls between them. The goal is to keep energy within the home moving in a healthy fashion while blocking intrusive energies. Kyanite also supports people to build meaningful connections. Rose quartz is placed near the front door (or other primary entrance) so that each time a resident of the household walks past it they are bathed in its loving energy. Finally, add unakite to any rooms where people gather to facilitate conflict resolution.

◆ Fiery Wall of Protection

Crystals: four garnets, four carnelians (or red jaspers or fire agates), two flints, and two pyrites

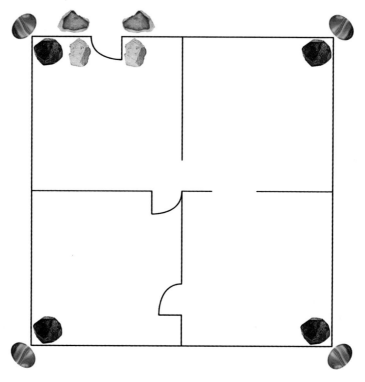

This grid invokes the power of fiery stones
for a blazing barrier against harm.

Named for a popular formula in hoodoo and American folk magick, this crystal grid invokes the fiery, martial qualities of several crystals to create a boundary against psychic vampires, curses and hexes, harmful spirits, and unwanted visitors. Place your freshly cleansed and programmed stones as shown in the diagram above, beginning with the garnets in the corners of your house to stabilize it against intrusive energy. Add four carnelians, red jaspers, or fire agates to the corners outside the home if possible; otherwise, place them at the midpoints along the walls between the garnets. On the interior of your home add two pyrites at the entrance to your home to reflect harm. Two pieces of flint on either side of the door on the exterior of your home will seal it against unwanted visitations of all kinds, and the combination of flint and pyrite sparks a divine flame that will burn away evil, envy, and other kinds of harm.

WARDING CHARMS AND RITUALS

From previous sections in this chapter that detail historical wards and home protection crystals you can already see that there is a lot of room for creativity when it comes to building spiritual defenses around your home and other spaces. Charms, amulets, and other wards can be worked into your home decor, hung in windows, discreetly hidden, or even buried to have the desired effect. That means that you have a lot of freedom in the ways you construct your wards.

As you can see in the image on the following page, amulets that ward the home can incorporate crystals, rocks, gems, and more along with other magickal materials. The best wards aren't necessarily those that use the flashiest and most expensive materials, nor do they need to be copied from centuries-old manuscripts to confidently defend your home. Rather, you'll get success from the charms and rituals that have personal meaning for you and help build sincere relationships with the indwelling spirits of the stones, the land, and any other allies you call on. Start with one or more of the warding rituals and charms below, and let your inspiration spark new and meaningful wards of your own design.

Examples of crystal amulets for warding the home (from left to right):
a cross made of quartz and black yarn, a small jar filled with chips of
shungite, and an amulet made from twigs, yarn, and a holey stone

◈ *Holey Stone Amulet*

Natural holed stones are still commonly seen as apotropaic devices in many
places today. To make a simple holey stone amulet, you need only two
items: the stone and some ribbon, yard, or cord. Red is the traditional color
to hang it on, but I've seen many a holey stone suspended on string or yarn
of many colors, as well as leather and wire, and they presumably all provide
the intended effect. A simple ritual for empowering your holey stone amulet
consists of cleansing and consecrating the stone with the elements and then
stringing and hanging it in the appropriate place.

Begin by collecting your holey stone and some red cord. Optionally, you
can select beads, charms, or other accessories to adorn and augment your
amulet. Gather tokens of the elements to use in cleansing and blessing your
holey stone: some fresh water, a candle, incense or herbs whose smoke
will signify the air element, and salt to represent earth. Ground and center
yourself, light the candle and incense, and bring your attention to the stone.
Sprinkle the stone with salt and ask that it be cleansed and consecrated
by the power of earth. Dip the stone into a vessel of water and ask that

Hang a holey stone
on red yarn or ribbon
to create a potent
protective amulet.

it be cleansed and consecrated by the power of water. Hold the stone in the smoke of the incense and ask that it be cleaned and consecrated by the power of air. Carefully pass it through the candle flame (taking care not to scorch the stone or injure yourself) and ask that it be cleansed and consecrated by the power of fire. Hold the stone to your heart with both hands and ask that it be cleansed and consecrated by the power of the quintessence—the power of spirit.

When the stone is adequately charged, string it on your red cord, adding any accompaniments you like (such as beads, metal charms, or other decorative and protective elements), and knot the cord firmly and deliberately. Imagine that you are tying all the elemental energies together and sealing them into your amulet as you knot the cord. Hold the finished amulet between your hands and draw your willpower into it, affirming that it will protect you against harm. Thank the stone, the elementals, and any other spirits that have assisted in your work, and hang the stone someplace where you'd like it to work its magick.

◈ Chalk and Slate Charm

My most recent trip to the United Kingdom afforded me a chance to deepen my appreciation for the stones of that landscape and the folk magick they are embedded in. This protective technique is inspired by two of the humble stones I spend time with: chalk and slate.

With a piece of natural chalk, draw a protective glyph on a piece of slate to create a home protection charm inspired by folk magick.

You only need two ingredients for this spell. First, a piece of slate with a nice, flat surface serves as the base for the spell. Ensure that it has at least one face that is large and smooth enough to draw on. Next, find a bit of natural chalk* to use on the slate. Cleanse the slate in water to wash it free from spiritual contaminants and render the surface smooth and clean. Cleanse the chalk with smoke from your favorite herb, resin, or incense. Hold the slate in your palms and connect to its spirit. Ask that the stone will deflect harmful and intrusive energy, keeping your home safe and sound. Turn your attention to the chalk, holding it between your palms and

---

*In a pinch, store-bought chalk will work, although it is made of dehydrated gypsum, not calcite.

sensing its buoyant energy and spirit. Ask that the chalk will dissolve harmful energies and bring happiness and joy into your home. When the stones feel sufficiently charged, use the chalk to draw any protective symbol you like on the slate. A few choices include a pentagram, daisy wheel, equal-armed cross, spiral, eye, or a personal sigil of your own design.

Once you've finished adorning your slate, gaze at the symbol inscribed on it and picture it emanating protective energy in all directions. Fill the slate with your willpower so that it will radiate an apotropaic force to stop evil from entering your home. When the stone has been sufficiently charged, place or hang it in an advantageous location, such as near the entrance of your home or on your altar. If the chalk symbol smears or fades, wash the stone and repeat the ritual by drawing a new glyph on its surface.

◆ Salt and Crystal Ward

Salt's ability to preserve against harm is a truly ancient and widespread belief. Many witches, healers, and magicians take advantage of this essential mineral's ability to cleanse energy and ward off harm. When mixed with the right ingredients, it can create a near-impenetrable barrier to defend your home, property, business, or other spaces. Mixtures like this are frequently sprinkled around your home or other space to erect a spiritual boundary, but you could also fill a decorative dish or bowl with it as a means of purifying and protecting the energy in your space. Another option is to fill a small glass bottle with the mix and hang it on or near an entrance with some ribbon or yarn, where it will act as an amulet that repels harm.

To make this salt and crystal ward you'll need several key ingredients. Find a coarse-grained salt for this spell; I like to use Himalayan rock salt, chunky sea salt, or kosher salt. About a cup of salt will do for the average home. You'll also need some small beads or chips of amethyst and hematite—about a tablespoon of each, depending on their size. A tablespoon of yarrow and a few drops of an aromatic and protective oil like frankincense round out the mix. Finally, select a large bowl and a spoon to mix the ingredients together.

Prepare your supplies with a gentle cleansing and add the salt to the bowl. Hold your hands over the salt and ask that its virtues drive out harm and seal against evil. Hold the hematite crystals in your hands and invoke

Mixing salt, crystals, and botanicals creates a
powerful boundary against ill-fated energy.

the fire and ambition of their iron-rich makeup to defend your home with warrior's strength before adding them to the bowl. Hold the amethyst and ask for its blessings of serenity, protection, and transformation, and add it to the mix. Next, call to the spirit of yarrow so that it will nourish your space and keep it safe. Add it to the bowl and select the frankincense oil. Ask that it consecrate your space such that no unclean energies can enter and add several drops to the bowl. Mix everything thoroughly, visualizing that as you stir you are mixing in your intention and willpower to create a potent ward.

When all the ingredients are incorporated, sprinkle the mixture around the outside of your home or property, moving clockwise as you go. If you live in an apartment, townhouse, or condo, sprinkle it along the doors and windows. Know that even though the salt will dissolve and the other ingredients may be swept away, their blessings of protection remain.

◈ *Stone Anchor Spell*

One of my favorite simple rituals for protection, which is inspired by the work of Christopher Penczak,[1] involves just a simple piece of stone from your landscape. Although you can use any large stone, I've found that the best results come from partnering with the same kind of rock beneath—or at the very least near—your home. A conscious relationship with that stone empowers it to draw dense energies inward and downward, carrying them into the underworld to be broken down and transmuted.

Choose a stone to be your home guardian and heavy-energy anchor. It should be somewhat large and preferably a variety that can be found in your region; if such a stone isn't available, use what you do have available to you, whether a humble rock, polished crystal, or a fine mineral specimen. Cleanse the stone and your space thoroughly and prepare for meditation. Place the stone in your lap (or if it's too large, sit beside it with your hands on it). Close your eyes and take several deep breaths as you ground and center yourself and attune to the stone's energy. In time it may feel as though the stone comes alive or wakes up; it might be accompanied by a

A piece of your local bedrock or basement rock,
such as this Floridian limestone from my locale, can anchor
and transmute dense and disruptive energy in your home.

sense of warmth, humming, or pulsing emanating from within the stone.

Greet the guardian consciousness of your anchor stone and ask for its permission to serve as the protector of your home. Once consent is granted, imagine that you are sinking deep, deep into the earth until you reach the underground realm of bedrock or basement rock far beneath you. As you descend, you become aware that you are holding a cord or stream of light that stretches from the anchor stone in your home into the bedrock. Invite this stone to guide you to the ideal location for this luminous cord. Once you find it, take the cord and bury or tie it to the location, creating a powerful, living connection to the underworld, where dense, intrusive, or harmful energy can be safely guided to be broken down and transmuted.

Allow yourself to return to normal consciousness, ascending back to your home and becoming aware of the room around you. Thank the stone for its role in the health and safety of your home. Affirm that it has a one-way connection, so energy can only be released downward to be transformed. Be sure to periodically replenish the stone at least once every few months by giving it a thorough cleansing and repeating the meditation.

◈ Witch Bottle

Witch bottles are excellent apotropaic devices, serving as magickal decoys to draw psychic harm, the evil eye, and baneful magick away from you and your home. A glass or stoneware bottle is filled with a variety of ingredients before being sealed, and then it is buried nearby. Antique witch bottles are sometimes found inside homes, but most modern practitioners opt to bury them outside the home. The idea is that they confuse and distract harmful energies since they contain a bit of hair, nails, or something else of the person they aim to protect. The sharp or thorny components snare harmful energy, evil spirits, and baneful magick, where they remain entangled and ultimately neutralized. Witch's bottles can, and frequently do, break after they have taken their fair share of harm, so they should be replaced periodically with a newly made bottle.

There is no standard recipe for crafting a witch bottle, as evidenced by the broad range of materials used by modern and historic practitioners alike. The version presented here is a modern, crystal-infused take on

Witch bottles can be filled with iron-rich minerals, sharp crystal fragments, and protective herbs to snare harmful energies before they settle into your home.

protection in keeping with the theme of this book. To start, you'll want a small to medium-size glass or stoneware bottle with a tight-fitting lid. Next, collect the ingredients that will fill it. Traditional witch bottles contain sharp objects like thorns, nails, needles, and so forth; you can use these or add sharp crystals: black kyanite, tiny blades of quartz, bits of axinite, or fragments of stones that have broken. Salt and iron are also important ingredients, and you can add a pinch of your favorite kind of salt and a bit of hematite (iron oxide) to contain and neutralize harmful energy. You can add small rough or tumbled chips of other protective crystals, too; consult the directory in chapter 9 for more inspiration. Fresh or dried botanicals can round out your list, and some of my favorite protective herbs include agrimony, basil, cedar, cloves, dill, frankincense, garlic, juniper, mullein, nettle, nightshade, oak, pine, rose, rosemary, rue, vervain, wormwood, and yew—though there are many more to choose from. Finally, you'll need a taglock to represent you (or the person you're protecting)—a bit of hair or some nail clippings, a photo, a piece of fabric you have worn, or a sample of your handwriting (such as a signature). I also like to fill my witch bottle with alcohol as a preservative, and I light a black candle to empower and seal it after it has been filled.

When all your ingredients are laid out before you, cleanse them and your working space via smoke or another method you like. As you fill the bottle, charge or consecrate each ingredient with the intention to protect you from harm; rather than a specific incantation to recite, I prefer to speak from the heart to the spirit of each component to invoke its specific virtues. After all the ingredients have been added, it's time to add the taglock. Enchant it to become a decoy, a vibrational double that will be targeted instead of you, drawing all harm away from you to be safely contained, entangled, and neutralized by the ingredients in the bottle. Optionally, you can top it off with water or alcohol, then light your candle. As the candle burns, direct its light and energy into the bottle. Use dripping wax to seal the top of the witch bottle. When the candle is spent, bury the bottle somewhere nearby, in the lawn or garden; if you don't have a green space of your own you can tuck it into the soil of a potted plant or hide it in the earth nearby where it won't be disturbed.

5

Protection from Geopathic Stress and Electromagnetic Pollution

Sensitive people, whether they identify as psychics, empaths, or just highly intuitive, often find themselves susceptible to more than just the moods and energies of the people around them. The energies all around us can affect us both positively and negatively, especially when we're exposed to them over time. These energy fields are generated by many sources—electronics, cell towers, power transformers, other man-made devices and structures; other sources of geopathic and electromagnetic stress stem from natural sources like underground water, variations in the underlying geology, and the lines of subtle energies that crisscross the planet. Shielding against and transmuting such environmental energies is an essential part of a well-rounded psychic self-defense routine.

There is growing concern about the effects of artificial electromagnetic fields on human health and well-being. Pulsed-wave radiation produced by Wi-Fi, 5G, radio waves, and other telecommunications technology is believed by some to be detrimental to our physical, emotional, and psychic well-being. Some studies indicate that these forms of electromagnetic (EM) pollution tax the body's innate ability to rest and repair, consequently lowering our resistance to illness. Humans have a natural bioeletromagnetic field; our well-being depends on the ability of this field to connect with Earth's electromagnetic field. The kinds of pulsed-wave radiation produced by Wi-Fi in particular creates artificial patterns of energy called *torsion fields*, which spiral in the opposite direction of our natural bioelectrical fields and the natural electromagnetic field of Earth.[1] The artificial EM fields all around us distort or interrupt this connection. Nowadays we are surrounded by such fields.

Another source of energetic disturbance in our environment is geopathic stress. The term *geopathic* is taken from the Greek roots *geos*, "earth," and *pathos*, "suffering" or "illness." Geopathic stress occurs when natural or artificial activities initiate energies perceived as erratic, overstimulating, or harmful to humans. It has long been recognized among indigenous and traditional cultures that certain places emit healing, balancing, and empowering energies, while other places are regarded as harmful or at the very least not especially helpful. Sources of geopathic stress include natural features like veins of ore, unusual geological formations, subterranean water, and other parts of the landscape. The movement of subtle energies such as ley lines and dragon lines and the vortices created where such lines of invisible force intersect can also contribute to geopathic stress, particularly when buildings, roads, or other structures impede the natural flow of energy through them. Though such energetic factors are natural and (when uninhibited by human activity) a normal part of Earth's energy field, they are not always conducive to restful sleep or other aspects of everyday life.

EFFECTS OF ENVIRONMENTAL ENERGIES

Exposure to electromagnetic pollution and geopathic stress causes many different symptoms, the range and intensity of which differs from one person to the next depending on the frequency and duration of exposures. Many times the effects of these energies can resemble a psychic attack. For this reason it may be necessary to first address electromagnetic pollution and geopathic stress when presented with a possible case of psychic attack.

Many people are relatively unaware of the influence of electromagnetic pollution in their everyday lives. Usually the signs and symptoms are subtle, especially at first. Vague sensations of tiredness, irritability, and a sense of being off-balance are usually what present in most people. More serious side effects can manifest as a result of the constant stress on the body due to prolonged exposures. Because you are likely to experience this invisible source of stress around the clock, your body is unable to get a break from the stress reaction. This can result in physical side effects such as headaches, digestive issues, sleep disorders, and changes in blood pressure, circulation, and metabolism. EM pollution can also trigger conditions affecting the immune system.[2]

It's worth noting that these deleterious energies don't only weaken the physical body; they also affect the mind and spirit. The additional physical stress impacts all other areas of one's being, from the emotions to one's vital energy. Overstimulation from geopathic stress can muddle your psychic and spiritual sensitivities to other kinds of harm, while erratic or harmful environmental factors can weaken your aura's natural boundaries. Overall this leads to a kind of psychic depletion that makes you more susceptible to the influence of other people's thoughts, emotions, attitudes, and energies. It also leads to weaker spiritual boundaries against foreign energies and entities of all kinds, as well as leaving you open to psychic and magickal harm. Identifying the signs of depletion by electromagnetic and geopathic stressors can be an impetus to take decisive action to maintain and sustain your vitality.

Signs of Geopathic and Electromagnetic Stress

The earliest signs of electromagnetic and geopathic stress are rather nebulous: feelings of imbalance, malaise, or depletion. At the onset it may be tough to distinguish these feelings from other stressors in your life. This vaguely off-kilter feeling in time gives way to exhaustion, headaches, insomnia, nervousness, and irritability.[3] Broadly speaking, the signs of harm by environmental energies closely resemble those of psychic attack. Some of the main things to look for include:

- Feeling stressed, anxious, nervous, irritable, and despondent
- Poor memory, reduced concentration, feeling spacey and ungrounded
- Low energy, fatigue, exhaustion
- Sleep disturbances like insomnia, poor quality of sleep, night sweats, and nightmares

- Headaches, muscle cramps or pain, numbness or tingling in the extremities
- Loss of appetite or libido
- Hypertension and accelerated heart rate
- Digestive issues or chronic illness without apparent cause
- Paranoia, insecurity, sense of not being alone

On more than one occasion someone has come to me seeking help when they believed they were the target of a psychic attack or malefic magick, only to discover that the source of harm was neither a person nor particularly magickal. Environmental factors can be checked using the same kinds of diagnostic tools used to determine psychic attack—divination with tarot, casting lots, dowsing with a pendulum, and so forth. Energetically or psychically sensitive practitioners may also be able to detect energetic imbalances when visiting the space in question. Some practitioners find muscle testing or applied kinesiology to be a helpful tool in disambiguating environmental factors from genuine psychic attack.

Effects on Spiritual Ecosystems

One topic I haven't seen discussed much anywhere is the influence that geopathic stress and electromagnetic pollution have on nonphysical residents of the affected place. These residents include land spirits, elementals, nature spirits, devas, and other kinds of spirits. If these deleterious energies affect our human spirits, it stands to reason that they can influence other spirits, too.

In my experience most household electromagnetic pollution does little to disturb the average spirit. In fact, as an animist I believe—and experience—appliances, electronic devices, and other sources of electromagnetic pollution as having their own animating spiritual forces. These are often quite different from the spirits or souls in rocks, trees, lakes, and flowers, but they are no less a part of the energetic landscape. However, the kinds of energy produced by larger, louder sources like power lines, radio and television transmitters, cell phone towers, and so forth can disturb or irritate some nature spirits. Land spirits such as wights or *genii locorum*, the protective spirits of a place, are usually not bothered by small sources of energy pollution, but they can be strongly affected by geopathic stress caused by human activity like mining, construction, urban development, and the like.

When parts of the local spirit population are distressed or affected by environmental stressors it can affect the balance of the entire local spiritual ecosystem. This might instigate paranormal phenomena that superficially resembles hauntings, as well as initiating imbalance in the local human and animal populations, perhaps even leading to "sick building syndrome," wherein the occupants of a building or structure experience acute health- and comfort-related effects that are linked to the time spent in the building. In these cases, no specific illness or individual cause can be identified. Removing human infrastructures responsible for such energetic imbalances is probably impossible in nearly all such circumstances, so there are other options we can explore.

Crystals alone are unlikely to mitigate any harm experienced by nonphysical members of the landscape, but they can still bring some relief. If human activity is creating the imbalance, simple grids of clear quartz or other gems like those explored later in this chapter can be helpful. I also like to leave offerings of rocks that match the local geology. A large piece of crystalline limestone graces my living room to harmonize our space with the underlying bedrock and honor and appease the spirits of the land. You can research your local geology to find the right rock or stone to add to your space to help discharge deleterious energies and anchor telluric forces for the benefit of all beings.

The most important tool for remediating the effects of geopathic stress and electromagnetic pollution on the spiritual ecosystem is the practice of making offerings to the spirits of the land, a subject that will be further explored later in this chapter.

CRYSTALS FOR COUNTERING ENVIRONMENTAL ENERGIES

Similar to warding against psychic and spiritual sources of harm, crystals are wonderful tools for negating the harmful effects of electromagnetic pollution and geopathic stress. They do this through their inner and outer symmetry, their coherent crystalline structure. The highly ordered nature of crystals produces highly ordered energy fields that exert a harmonizing influence on the energies all around them. For this reason, all rocks and minerals theoretically have the power to counteract electromagnetic pollution and geopathic stress because their inner crystallinity invites order to emerge from chaos. Moreover, being that they are part and parcel of the body of Earth, rocks and minerals have an affinity for balancing the energies within and around our planet and grounding and discharging unwanted or unhealthy energies.

The list of crystals and gems that deflect, discharge, and transmute deleterious environmental energies is lengthy and diverse. Most crystals that are generally grounding or protective will work effectively against electromagnetic pollution and geopathic stress. Several categories of rocks and minerals are more effective than others, however, for several reasons. First, let's address mineral content. Carbon-rich minerals exert an absorptive, neutralizing influence on harmful energies while resetting the balance of the human body. Consider working with carbon minerals like aragonite, calcite, chalk, diamond, dolomite, graphite, jet, and shungite for this application. Iron-bearing stones offer a descending action, being both grounding and energizing. Some iron minerals to consider include hematite, magnetite, marcasite, pyrite, and siderite; other stones have smaller or trace amounts of iron that are still helpful, such as bloodstone, bronzite, carnelian, epidote, red jasper, and tiger's eye. Boron-rich stones are especially neutralizing to geopathic stress and electromagnetic pollution, and these include danburite, howlite, and the tourmaline group. Minerals containing silica generally support and strengthen the energy field, so they, too, are helpful; look to the quartz family (including agate, amethyst, aventurine, flint, jasper, rose quartz, and smoky quartz) and all silicate minerals for a general tonic against environmental energies.

Certain crystal structures are also effective against harmful environmental energies. For example, the fullerene molecules in shungite absorb and transmute harmful energies, making it one of the best stones for neutralizing electromagnetic pollution. The zeolite group of minerals is microscopically porous, which makes them a bit like molecular filters, lending to their uses in medicine and industry. Energetically these minerals work in a similar fashion to filter out harmful energies, storing them in their lattice until they can be effectively cleansed. Clinoptilolite (klinoptilolith) is the only zeolite included in the crystal directory in chapter 9, but other zeolites (like heulandite, natrolite, pectolite, scolecite, stellerite, stilbite, and thomsonite) are equally effective when it comes to filtering out and neutralizing environmental harm. In addition, the spongiform cyclosilicates such as sugilite and chrysocolla absorb excess energy from the environment—just be sure to cleanse them often.

Lots of other crystals and gems are also effective for shielding, discharging, and transmuting geopathic stress and electromagnetic pollution. The stones listed below are my favorites for countering harmful environmental energies.

Amazonite	Hanksite	Quartz
Ammonite	Healer's gold	Red jasper
Aragonite	Hematite	Sarsen stone
Aventurine	Lakelandite	Selenite
Chalk	Luxullianite	Shungite
Clinoptilolite	Magnetite	Smoky quartz
Dolomite	Malachite	Sodalite
Flint	Petrified wood	Sugilite
Fluorite	Preseli bluestone	Tourmaline
Granite	Purpurite	Unakite
Halite	Obsidian	

Any of the stones listed here or described earlier can be carried, worn, or placed around your home or office to protect you from the harmful effects of disruptive environmental energies. In the next section we'll talk about some more specific applications for these and other crystals for ameliorating the effects of geopathic stress and electromagnetic pollution.

REMEDIES FOR ENVIRONMENTAL HARM

The most practical way to diminish the effects of geopathic and electro-magnetic stress with the help of the mineral kingdom is to place crystals around your space as strategically as possible. Shungite is invaluable next to computers, Wi-Fi routers, and other electronics, but any of the other stones listed in the section above will work well. When a whole room feels unsettled or like it's buzzing with unseen energies, grounding stones can be placed in the corners to calm the vibes. Crystal clusters, especially those of the quartz family, uplift the energies of any room or building and help cohere and organize the otherwise aberrant energies that cause geopathic stress. Additionally, try your hand at working with the elixirs, crystal grids, layouts, and other techniques described below.

Gem Elixirs

Gem elixirs are versatile healing tools that can be sprayed in the aura or environment, diffused in your space, or taken internally to promote inner and outer balance. Although a simple elixir of any of the gems described elsewhere in this chapter would be beneficial, here are a few easy recipes to try.

◆ Shungite Water

Shungite's first recorded therapeutic application occurred when spring water emerging from shungite rock was found to have healing properties. To make shungite water, the best method is to place several pieces of shungite weighing three to four ounces in a glass or ceramic container, then fill it with potable water and let it sit for up to three days.[4] Ensure that the shungite is clean and free of dust or visible trace minerals such as pyrite to prevent cross-contamination. Shungite water can be made using either the traditional direct method or the indirect method, as described in chapter 1.

Geobiologist and shungite expert Regina Martino recommends drinking a glass of shungite water daily (but do take a week off each month to let your system reset).[5] Doing so can revitalize your entire being and reverse many of the symptoms of geopathic stress and electromagnetic pollution. Shungite water or a traditionally prepared elixir can also be sprayed in the

Create shungite-charged water by soaking pieces of shungite for up to three days.

aura to fortify it and clear the effects of discordant environmental energies. Add some to the bath for full-body cleansing, or use some when mopping the floor for a powerful and immediate energetic reset in your space.

◆ Sodalite Elixir

Sodalite elixir can be made by direct method by placing a raw or polished piece of sodalite in a glass container of water and allowing it to soak in the sun for several hours. Alternatively, you can use the indirect method using two containers, one for the minerals and one for the water, as described in chapter 1. Remove the stone and preserve the elixir by mixing it in a one-to-one ratio with alcohol (brandy or vodka), apple cider vinegar, or vegetable glycerin. The resulting elixir can be taken orally or sprayed in your space. Another way to employ a sodalite elixir is by diffusing it in your space: fill a large glass bowl with fresh water and add a dropperful of the gem elixir to the water. Leave the bowl wherever sodalite's energy is needed. As the water slowly evaporates, it will carry the energy of the gemstone with it, permeating every part of the room.

Sodalite elixir alleviates the effects of geopathic stress and helps refresh the energy of your space. Taken internally or sprayed in the aura, it works primarily to reduce the effects of electromagnetic pollution and geopathic stress. When sprayed or diffused in a room, building, or other space, it has the added benefit of promoting a harmonious environment for everyone (human, spirit, and otherwise) who dwells or works there. When diffused, sodalite elixir can also facilitate deeper relationships with the spirits and elementals of the place where you live.

◈ EMF Protection Elixir

Crystals: carnelian, clear quartz, fluorite, lepidolite, magnetite, and tourmaline (any color tourmaline, but black or pink is best)

Using the indirect method of infusion, place the stones in a small glass container, like a cup or a jar, and place that inside a larger bowl. Fill only the larger container with water so that there is a barrier between the water and the crystals, thereby preventing contamination from any of the minerals. Leave this in a sunny place for several hours, then bottle the liquid with a preservative as described in chapter 1.

Use the indirect method to make this elixir,
as demonstrated here.

This combination elixir fortifies the body, mind, and spirit against the effects of electromagnetic pollution and geopathic stress. I prefer to spray it in my aura or dab it on my pulse points. When symptoms are more severe you can take four drops by mouth up to four times a day in addition to using it externally. Though this blend will boost all kinds of psychic boundaries, it is most effective for promoting the aura's innate resilience and resistance to environmental harm.

Grids and Layouts

The grids and layouts in this chapter aim to ameliorate the effects of electromagnetic pollution and geopathic stress. Some are intended for personal use, while others can be used to heal the energy of your home or office. If you are unable to set up a large permanent grid in your space, try gridding atop a photo, map, or blueprint of the room or building; this can even be performed remotely to improve the energies of someplace distant.

◆ EMF Detox Layout

Crystals: selenite, two aquamarines, a sodalite, an emerald, and four
   shungites

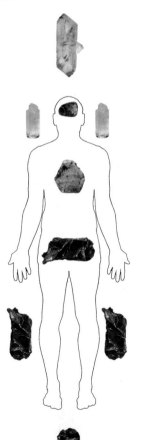

This easy layout helps clear and detox the body, mind, and spirit of the harmful effects of electromagnetic pollution.

When you feel as if you need some help releasing the effects of electromagnetic pollution, this easy grid can help you shake off those discordant and deleterious energies. The diamond or rhombus created by the shungite draws out excessive energy and establishes a firm connection to the earth. The emerald at the heart clears and exalts the heart chakra and strengthens the physical heart as the driver of your own personal electromagnetic field. The combination of aquamarine and sodalite on and around the head reduces the mental and emotional effects of electromagnetic smog, while the selenite above the head aligns the vertical axis of your energy field.

With freshly cleansed crystals, begin constructing this layout from the bottom up. Place the first shungite over the earth star chakra, about twelve inches below the feet, followed by shungites beside each knee and one just below the navel. An emerald is then placed in the center of the sternum. Next, put a small sodalite on the forehead and an aquamarine on either side of the head. Finally, a selenite crystal or piece of satin spar is placed just above the crown. Leave the crystals in place for fifteen to thirty minutes, then remove them in reverse order and cleanse them thoroughly.

◈ Elemental Balance Grid

Crystals: one serpentine, fluorite, carnelian, aquamarine, and labradorite; ten small quartz crystals; and one quartz tower or generator

To harmonize and transmute electromagnetic smog and help counteract geopathic stress you can appeal to the elementals to restore balance in the subtle realms. This grid draws together the power of the five elements of earth, air, fire, water, and spirit to stabilize the energies of your space. The stones are laid out in a pattern called the "invoking pentagram of earth." The pattern invokes or activates the archetypal qualities and energies of the earth element, thereby grounding, stabilizing, and supporting the energy of your space. Although all five elements work together in this grid, the earth element is the most important for transmuting geopathic stress. You can build this grid wherever the geopathic stress or electromagnetic pollution is felt the strongest; otherwise try placing it atop a photo, diagram, or map of your home.

Cleanse all your crystals beforehand and consecrate the tower or generator crystal with representatives of all four elements by sprinkling it

By harnessing the power of the five elements,
this grid restores balance and harmony to your office,
home, or other spaces.

with salt, rinsing it in water, passing it through incense smoke, and carefully holding it above the flame of a candle. Then hold it between your hands to charge it with vital energy, programming it to broadcast whichever elemental forces are most needed to bring balance and healing to your space. Next, arrange the crystals as shown in the diagram above, starting with the labradorite at the top, serpentine at the bottom left, fluorite at the upper right, aquamarine at the upper left, and carnelian at the bottom right. Arrange the clear quartz crystals as shown above, following the same path along the pentagram. Place the tower upright in the center of the grid and activate it by tracing the invoking pentagram of earth (i.e., following the same sequence in which the stones are laid) three times, visualizing all the stones connecting by threads of luminous energy. Leave this grid in place and cleanse all the crystals and reprogram the central tower once a month as needed.

◈ Grid for Repairing Geopathic Stress

Crystals: twelve single-terminated clear quartz crystals, twelve single-terminated smoky quartz crystals, and one grounding stone of your choice (agate, black tourmaline, flint, hematite, jasper, magnetite, or petrified wood)

Crystal grids can be used for long-term protection and repair of the earth energies of your home, office, or other space. This grid uses the symbolism of the vesica piscis, whose figure-eight infinity shape enjoins complementary or opposing forces to heal and rebalance environmental energies. The overlapping circles are created with clear quartz and smoky quartz, both excellent environmental healers in their own right. In each ring the crystals are pointing in opposing directions, thereby generating a powerful synchronizing effect on the forces and spirits of the environs. The energetic movement generated by the vesica form is anchored by the addition of a grounding stone of your choice placed in the center. A large grid can be

The vesica piscis serves as the template for this grid.

created when deep repair and balance are needed, or smaller grids can be placed somewhere safe for long-term use.

With your crystals freshly cleansed, first create the circle made from smoky quartz, with its points directed counterclockwise along the circle, as depicted above. Next, lay out the circle of clear quartz with the terminations of the crystals pointing clockwise. Finally, choose a grounding stone such as agate, black tourmaline, flint, hematite, jasper, magnetite, or petrified wood, and place it in the center. To activate the grid, trace the counterclockwise circle with a crystal wand or your fingers once, followed by the clockwise circle once; then trace a figure eight, beginning and ending with the grounding stone in the center of the grid.

Offerings to the Land and Its Spirits

One of the simplest and most profound practices for transmuting electromagnetic pollution and geopathic stress is to foster a relationship with the spirits, devas, and elementals in your surroundings. Usually the humblest offerings are all you need: a glass of fresh water and a tealight candle in your sacred space or on a household shrine are excellent for making these kinds of everyday offerings. Offerings of incense are generally well received, too. On special occasions you can make offerings of food, stones, or other gifts as you feel guided.

When making these offerings indoors, be sure to change the water (or other beverage of your choice) frequently to clear dust buildup and prevent mold from sprouting. I like to pour the water outside when I am ready to offer a fresh glass. If I make an offering of food at our household shrine I'll leave it there for a time and then compost it afterward; if it's safe to do so I'll occasionally leave food offerings outdoors for wildlife to enjoy. As well, if you make offerings outdoors, ensure that what you leave outdoors won't harm the environment by changing the soil chemistry, poisoning plants or animals, or becoming litter that won't break down.

I don't have a set prayer or script that I follow when I make offerings to the land and its spirits. Instead, I speak plainly from the heart, usually thanking the spirits and elementals for all they do. I ask them to forgive any human-led disturbances to their ecosystem and invite them to partake of the offerings and use the energy and resources for their health and well-being. Regular offerings strengthen the relationship with the spirits of your space, both your home and your surroundings, which, in turn, inclines them toward caring for you and protecting you from unwanted or harmful energies. Offerings to the land and the spirits of the land nourish and strengthen the spiritual ecosystem, potentially hastening their ability to counteract geopathic stress.

Combatting Psychic Attack

Based on trends in online spiritual forums, social media, and elsewhere, it would be easy to conclude that almost everyone is the victim of psychic attack or some other form of psychic harm. While there is a kernel of truth in this in that everyone is passively subjected to disruptive, intrusive, or harmful energies, a true psychic attack is relatively uncommon. To be successful, a psychic attack or similar malefic magick requires a strength of will and technical expertise not often attained by casual practitioners. That said, psychic intrusions, disruptions, and outright harm can come from a variety of sources, and even without a formal ritual behind them they can yield deleterious results. Throughout this chapter we'll take a deeper look at the signs of a genuine psychic attack and other forms of harm and explore some crystal-based methods for ameliorating such situations.

THE MECHANICS OF PSYCHIC ATTACK

To better understand how to mitigate the effects of a psychic attack it is helpful to know how it can happen in the first place. Rather than one specific protocol or mechanism responsible for all psychic attacks there are usually a confluence of factors. Three of the most important include the degree of openness or sensitivity in the target, the connection between the source and the target, and a disparity in power between the source and target.

Let's begin by addressing openness and sensitivity. Psychic attack is most likely to occur when someone is receptive to it. It's important to note that this is not the same as saying that psychic attack is essentially the victim's fault—far from it. Rather, what this means is that the target or recipient of psychic harm is experiencing circumstances that enhance their psychic openness or sensitivity. This might be something circumstantial, like entering a place where the psychic veil is thinner or more open than in other places, or it might be a result of coming in contact with someone who possesses a forceful personality. Psychic openness might also result from not consciously shielding oneself—which is a must if you're an empath or highly sensitive person—or from pursuing activities that naturally cultivate a sense of openness, such as meditation, psychic development, and other spiritual pursuits. Sensitivity or openness can also result from ordinary, necessary acts like sleeping, as well as from social situations in which boundaries are ordinarily somewhat lax.

A connection between the source and the target is also a key factor in psychic attack, whether it is intentional or unintentional. Rarely if ever do strangers pick random victims to send their malicious thoughts and emotions to. Most psychic attacks come from someone who knows you—or at least knows *of* you. Thanks to the power of the internet and social media, it's far easier to build connections than ever before. Connection comes in a variety of forms; it can be based on mutual support or bonding over shared trauma or other perspectives. Most unconscious, accidental psychic harm comes from the people we know and love, for their strong emotions and ideas can travel across those nodes of psychic connection into your energy field, whether they are consciously directed at you or not. Subtle energies and psychic impressions picked up from the world at large can also be spread among loved ones in much the same way that germs can spread.

A power disparity is another factor in psychic attack. This doesn't mean that the attacker is inherently stronger all around than the target. Rather, it means that psychic attack is only effective when the collective strength of the negative, intrusive, or otherwise harmful energy supersedes the strength of the target's boundaries. This can come as a result of an innate or circumstantial openness on the target's part and from the strength of will displayed by the source of harm, as in the disparities in certain social hierarchies, like a supervisor in the workplace or an elder in your community. It might also be a result of certain conditions coming together to create a perfect storm of negativity that overpowers your individual shields or natural psychic boundaries. The good news is that most ordinary, disruptive, or malicious thoughts that may be directed at you are unlikely to best your defenses. However, when they accrete from several sources you may run the risk of psychic harm.

Other factors contributing to all manner of psychic harms abound. There are cultural and religious circumstances at play in many parts of the world; an example is the strong belief in the evil eye in many parts of the world. It may be impossible to control all the variables, but addressing the three biggest—openness, connection, and power disparity—can yield good results when it comes to mitigating psychic attack. Oftentimes addressing even one of the three contributing factors alleviates psychic harm in a tangible way.

Forms of Psychic Attack

Different terms are used to describe the types of psychic and magickal harm. This is because different traditions often use their own terms or apply similar terms in unique ways. In light of this, here are some terms that describe common forms of psychic and magickal harm. Note that while these are the working definitions that I use, you may find other teachers, practitioners, books, and traditions that employ different terms. Bottom line: ultimately it may not be necessary to label the specific kind of psychic harm that you are experiencing, as the steps for remediation are generally the same. So you can rest easy if you can't identify the exact nature of a given situation by name.

▶ **Psychic attack** can refer to both formal, intentional harm actively sent from attacker to target; it can also occur when someone's harmful thoughts or emotions unintentionally affect the target. The outcome varies in each situation depending on the circumstances.

▶ **Ill-wishing** usually implies a passive form of psychic harm that results from holding negative thoughts toward someone, such as *they deserve to pay for this* or *I wish so-and-so would just drop dead*. The effects of these kinds of thought forms are usually much milder than a true psychic attack.

► **Psychic mugging** describes the effects of harmful energy left at a particular location, perhaps due to a heated argument or strong emotional reaction at that spot. The accretion of harmful thoughts and emotions at that location can subsequently be picked up by sensitive people entering that space. Depending on the nature of the thoughts and emotions, the effects of psychic mugging can range from mild to extreme.

► **Psychic spying** and **psychic intrusion** (or invasion) are related in that they both aim to gain access to your home, mind, or private life. Adept psychics but with questionable ethics may be able to breach low-level wards in your environment and penetrate personal shields that aren't maintained. In certain dramatic instances the effects of psychic invasion can resemble other forms of psychic harm or even psychic vampirism.

► **Psychic vampirism** or **emotional vampirism** can occur when someone's fundamental energetic constitution tends to be less dynamic or low in vitality. Psychic vampires draw vitality from living sources, usually fellow vampires. Some folks do this innately without ever knowing it, while others do so intentionally, with or without an ethical approach.

► **Psychic attachments** and **cords** form when thoughts, emotions, entities, or other energies take root in the aura. Attachments and cords are usually unconscious. Such connections can be severed ritually, but they often reprise unless the underlying circumstances are addressed.

► The **evil eye** is a cross-cultural belief that harmful energy can be directed with the eyes. Usually this is an unconscious action that is often motivated by jealousy or hatred. This projection of energy can disrupt the target's life in myriad ways, from incurring bad luck to impeding one's natural spiritual guidance and gifts.

► For many (but not all) practitioners, **jinxes**, **hexes**, and **curses** are separated by orders of magnitude.* Collectively they are sometimes referred to as *maleficia*, meaning "evil deeds." I consider jinxes to cause mostly minor annoyances, like bad luck and short-lived misfortune. Hexes are usually more intense and longer lived; they may run their course or dissipate when the target has changed the behavior that warranted the hex in the first place. Curses pack the most punch—some even last for generations. People, objects, and places can all be subjected to maleficia.

▶ **Crossing** refers to magickal harm intentionally cast on a target, such as a jinx, hex, or curse. Crossing magick takes its name from hoodoo, wherein dust or powder is laid down in a quincunx or X-shaped pattern in a place where the intended target will step into or walk through it. Crossed conditions can also refer to more mundane actions and energies that accumulate and cause bad luck above and beyond what is typical. Crossed conditions are not always the result of crossings or harmful magick, but they can be remediated in the same way.

▶ Finally, the topic of **blowback** or **crossfire** is worth mentioning. This occurs when the intended target of some kind of psychic harm is well-shielded, causing the harming energy to rebound. Bystanders, like the friends and family of the intended target, may be inadvertently caught in the rebounding crossfire or blowback energies.

---

*The first two terms, *jinx* and *hex*, did not originally carry the meaning of harmful magick; they instead denoted rather general types of magickal workings. *Jinx* comes from the Latin *iynx*, referring to a genus of birds known as wrynecks, which figured into certain magickal and divinatory practices. The word *hex* comes from the German *hexe*, meaning "witch." *Curse*, on the other hand, derives from an Old English root that means "to wish evil to." Because of general attitudes toward magick and witchcraft during and after the European witch hunts, all three terms became associated with malevolent magick.

SIGNS OF PSYCHIC ATTACK

Learning to recognize an authentic psychic attack requires knowledge, experience, and discernment. Though there are general symptoms common to many cases of psychic harm, they often echo the signs and symptoms of more mundane situations. It's important to assess each and every case on an individual basis, taking time to understand the background and context to ensure that the traits are indeed indicative of a psychic attack rather than physical illness, burnout, mental illness, abuse, or other nonmagickal situations.

Here is a list of the most frequently reported signs of psychic attack:

- Recurring bad luck and misfortune
- Insomnia, troubled dreams, or nightmares
- Fatigue, low vitality, poor concentration, and loss of interest in hobbies or other pursuits
- Recurring, sudden, or persistent illness or injury
- Random and severe pains, particularly headaches
- Frequent communications breakdowns and misunderstandings
- Sense of being out of step with time
- General sense of discomfort, despair, oppression, anxiety, and fear
- Inexplicable confusion, nervousness, or tension
- Sense of being followed
- Same illness shared by your family, community, or coven
- Unwanted or unusual behavior from pets and other animals in your environs
- Persistent feeling of weight on your chest, especially at night
- Repeated mishaps with magickal intention, missing the mark of your desired outcome
- Muddied, inconsistent, or absent psychic faculties
- Bruises, scrapes, and other injuries that appear inexplicably
- Unusual odors, like decay, garbage, or sulfur
- Uncharacteristic compulsions, affinities, or aversions
- Assorted supernatural phenomena such as poltergeist activity

There are several important ideas to bear in mind when reading the above list of signs. First and foremost, the signs of psychic attack will manifest beyond your ordinary experience. For example, if you are a regular insomniac or suffer from chronic pain, then you probably wouldn't consider difficulty sleeping or your body's aches to be signs of psychic attack—*unless they escalate above the normal level*. Generally it is also important to recognize that experiencing one or two or even three of the signs on this list is not cause for concern. When they begin to pile up without cause, however, you are generally experiencing some form of psychic or magickal attack.

Always take time to examine the situation in depth when considering a potential case of psychic attack. Ask when the symptoms first started to show up and see if they can be traced back to any important life events. Find out whether there are any known enemies or suspects—for example, if someone believes they are the victim of a curse but they've never interacted with any occultists or witches, a curse or hex seems the unlikeliest cause of their woes. Many of the symptoms on the list above may be indications of mental illness rather than psychic attack, and it's important to distinguish between the two. Most importantly, *it is imperative not to substitute magickal practices for medical treatment*. Consult a qualified mental health practitioner if needed, and always err on the side of caution.

When reviewing the list on the facing page, take note that the last four bullet points are typically quite rare, as most forms of psychic harm rarely if ever have the strength to produce such results. However, in cases of ritual curse, artificial servitor spirits (sometimes called *thought forms*) and other entities might be invoked, with the result that the target of such curses may experience mysterious injuries, strange odors, uncharacteristic behaviors, and other supernatural phenomena. Always rule out mundane possibilities first—for example, do things in your house mysteriously vanish because a family member or roommate is tidying up without telling you? If you still suspect maleficia, perform a divination to discern what kind of energy, entity, or presence is potentially affecting you.

Among those who teach about protection and psychic attack it is often said that whether someone actually is cursed or only believes they are, the remedy is usually the same. With the exception of cases of mental illness or other factors that might require different methods of remediation, there is generally no harm in performing the necessary steps to mitigate psychic harm or break a curse (more on this in chapter 7).

Sometimes the perceived symptoms are all derived from rather ordinary sources; but when someone really and truly feels as though they have been targeted by a hex, curse, psychic attack, or the evil eye, then they often can greatly benefit from the ritual actions of uncrossing or curse-breaking outlined in this chapter. Though harmful magick may not be the culprit, the extra support and guidance these rituals provide can help the person break out of a rut.

There is one last factor worth considering in cases of psychic attack: not every person truly wants to be healed. There are many people who identify as a victim of psychic attack and baneful magick, whether real or imagined, and no amount of healing, magick, or ritual will make the symptoms they're experiencing disappear. When someone who identifies as a victim is the target of deliberate psychic harm or magickal attack, they will call the energies right back to them as soon as the mitigating actions are finished. I've experienced this several times over with students, clients, and even friends. If you run into situations like this there is nothing you can do to solve the problem, because the signs of psychic harm will reappear in no time. These people get more attention for having a problem that can't be fixed, and they pin their identity on that. The best advice I can give you is to send them love and compassion, but do not continuously engage in advice, magickal assistance, or healing work, as you may well be taken advantage of. If the person is unwilling to look in the mirror to see the role they play in the perceived psychic harm, then no magick can make it go away.

DIAGNOSING PSYCHIC ATTACK

While we've established that a bona fide psychic attack is relatively uncommon, other kinds of psychic harm are rather frequent. Since the steps for remediation outlined in this chapter work for most kinds of psychic harm and disruptive energy, it isn't always necessary to know the precise source of the harm for minor complaints. However, in more serious cases it is imperative that you have a means of discerning genuine attack from circumstantial harm.

After carefully comparing the situation to the list of signs listed above and taking inventory of all the possible leads, you can dig a little deeper to uncover the nature of the attack. Divination is the preferred method for diagnosing these situations. While divination should never be used to obtain a medical diagnosis, it can be extraordinarily helpful in clarifying the mystical and spiritual underpinnings of a situation.

Common divination methods include astrology, tarot, oracle cards, runes, ogham, dowsing rods, pendulum, and more. If you are already skilled in a divinatory art, you can employ whatever method you are confident in using. A general reading with your favorite deck of cards can give some helpful insight into the big picture. I also like to use simple yes-or-no divination methods to discern psychic attack, as it leaves less margin for error than more subjective systems like runes or tarot. Yes-or-no divination can be accomplished by casting lots, dowsing with a pendulum, tossing a coin, or applied kinesiology, also known as muscle testing.

Whatever method of divination you use, its accuracy depends on a well-worded question. Avoid asking questions like "Is it possible that this person is experiencing psychic attack?" In theory, it is always *possible*, but you need to know if it's actually happening *now*. Effective questions to ask include:

- Is [name] currently experiencing a psychic attack?
- Has malefic magick or a curse, evil eye, or similar harm been used on [name]?
- Are the symptoms currently affecting [name] the result of psychic harm?
- Is this a case of accidental/unintentional psychic attack?
- Is the source of the attack or curse known to [name]?

Short, close-ended questions with yes-or-no answers lend themselves well to the practice of casting lots or dowsing, both of which are explained below. Open-ended questions like "Who is the source of this attack?" may be better served by more subjective means of divination, like tarot. Dowsing with a pendulum can also provide you with additional information, as you can dowse for names and for locations in the aura or environment where the attack has taken root.

No matter which method of divination you consult, two things are essential for clear and accurate readings: remain unattached to the outcome and trust the result. Impartiality is imperative; if you are expecting or hopeful of a specific outcome it is possible to influence the results or their interpretation. By the same token, act on the results that come through as long as they are obtained with clarity. If you want the answer to reveal psychic attack and you get contrary evidence from divination, there's no harm in cleansing and remediation; but to keep asking the question until you get the answer you want undermines the process. If remaining impartial or trusting the outcome is a challenge, or if you aren't competent or comfortable doing divination on your own, get a reading from a trustworthy source who can give you clear, accurate, honest answers.

◈ Casting Lots

One of the simplest divination methods is the casting of lots, sometimes called *sortition* or *cleromancy*. Casting lots is an ancient method, and there are many biblical references to divination by cleromancy. For this method

Casting lots with black and white stones is an easy
and effective form of divination.

you will need to gather ten* stones, five white and five black. The stones may be common rocks that you find in nature, or they may be store-bought riverstones such as those used in landscaping. You can also choose stones from a crystal shop such as scolecite, white quartz, or howlite for the white stones, and jet, obsidian, or tourmaline for the black. All ten stones should be of roughly even size and shape. You'll also need a pouch big enough to contain them all, with enough room to reach your hand inside.

Before using your stones for divination, cleanse, dedicate, and empower them as described in chapter 1. Formulate your question mentally first to ensure that it is clearly worded. Then holding the pouch in your hands, ask your question either aloud or silently. Shake the bag several times to shuffle the stones, and then reach one hand into the pouch without looking inside to select your stone(s) to answer the question.

Using lots can allow you to pull a single stone for a yes-or-no question, with white meaning "yes" and black meaning "no." You can also pull three stones to give you a more detailed, nuanced answer. If you ask whether or not you are under psychic attack or being subjected to harmful energies, here are the meanings of the possible outcomes of a three-stone draw:

▸ **Three white stones:** no psychic harm detected
▸ **Two white, one black:** no imminent harm detected, but regular cleansing is suggested
▸ **Two black, one white:** moderate harm is detected, more diligent cleansing and protection required
▸ **Three black:** psychic attack or other harm is likely; use more intensive cleansing and protective workings

Always be sure to cleanse your pouch of stones thoroughly between uses, and keep them in a safe place where they will not be tainted by outside energies. I like to use a red pouch for mine, as this is a protective color, and I keep them alongside my other tools for divination, such as tarot decks and pendulums.

---

*You can use more or less than ten as long as you choose an even number, with equal amounts of white and black stones. Use no fewer than six (three of each color) to obtain clear and effective results.

◆ *Pendulum Dowsing*

The use of a pendulum for dowsing can provide helpful information in diagnosing cases of psychic attack. In its simplest application the movement of a pendulum indicates a yes, no, or indeterminate answer to a question. Pendulums can also be used to select names of possible sources of psychic attack from a list, point to weak areas in the energy field, or provide other insights.

Using a pendulum can reveal the source of psychic harm.

A basic dowsing procedure begins with cleansing your pendulum and holding it suspended from the thumb and forefinger of either hand. You'll need to establish a baseline movement for both yes and no. To do this, ask a question you know the answer to, such as, "Is my name Nicholas?" Alternatively, simply ask the pendulum to show you what "yes" looks like. Repeat the process for a negative answer. For many folks, back-and-forth movement represents a "yes," while side-to-side is a "no." For others like myself, a clockwise movement indicates "yes," and counterclockwise represents "no." It's possible that either of these might show up reversed for you, so I always recommend establishing a fresh baseline before using a pendulum for divination.

Now you're ready to begin your assessment of the situation. Start with yes-or-no questions like the ones listed previously in the section "Diagnosing Psychic Attack" (page 147). Be mindful to stay open and centered, as the movement of a pendulum is easy to influence subconsciously if you're anticipating or hoping for a particular outcome.

If the pendulum indicates that the situation is indeed a genuine psychic attack, you can continue to use it to determine the source of the attack. One option is to write the names of possible sources on slips of paper and dowse each name to see if you get a positive response from the pendulum. Alternatively, work your way through the alphabet to spell out the name, waiting for a yes or no response at each letter in turn until the name comes together. You might try dowsing over a map or blueprint of the home or other space to indicate weak points in the wards, where harmful or disruptive energy has entered, or you can dowse over the target's energy field to reveal where said energies have taken root. This can give you an indication of where to perform certain kinds of healing or magick, like cord-cutting rituals.

After gathering all the necessary information, you can now move forward to combat the attack and neutralize the source of harm.

STEPS FOR REMEDIATION

The basic steps for neutralizing psychic attack are simple. In no particular order the main objectives are repairing the aura, cleansing the space, and breaking contact with the source of the harm.[1] Additionally, you'll want to fortify the home to prevent recurrence and practice effective aftercare to ensure a complete recovery.

The first step is to perform your divination. Assess the situation holistically and determine whether or not this is a case of genuine psychic harm. If possible, determine the root cause or source through divination or other investigatory method. This can help you plot the course of action you'll take to remedy the situation

Following that, the next logical step is cleansing the space. A thorough space-cleansing provides a clean slate to perform the rest of the work. Bear in mind that spiritual hygiene is an ongoing habit, not a once-and-done technique, so you'll want to cleanse thoroughly once more after all the other steps for remediation are undertaken.

Ideally, the next step is to break the connection between the source and the target. Severing this link stops the attack at its source and enables the target to recover. You might use one of the layouts or other techniques from this chapter. Simple cases of psychic harm—especially passive, unintentional cases—can be ameliorated simply with a thorough cleansing and better shielding going forward. Rituals like the Banishing Ritual of the Precious Stones, found in chapter 2, and the Lesser Banishing Ritual of the Pentagram (a technique frequently used in ceremonial magick) are also excellent for neutralizing psychic attack. More serious cases can be addressed through additional techniques of binding, banishing, and reversal, which are explored in chapter 7.

Once the source of harm is neutralized it's important to focus on repair and restoration of the target's energy field and overall vitality. This, in part, consists of adequate cleansing and personal shielding. Try some of the layouts in this chapter, or use the Labradorite Star or the Tourmaline Cross, both found in chapter 3. Repairing the energy field can also be achieved through chakra balancing layouts, soul retrieval, hands-on healing techniques like Reiki, and countless other methods. Several of the techniques in chapter 5, though described in the context of electromagnetic pollution, are also effective for balancing and repairing an energy field depleted as a result of psychic attack.

As soon as possible, refresh any and all forms of protection. You'll want to change out or bulk up the wards around your home, office, and other places where you spend time. I recommend adding or changing wards, as relying only on previous wards after experiencing psychic attack can leave you without adequate defenses. After all, intrusive energies have already made it past those wards at least once. Recharging, changing, or adding wards a few times each year is a great way to make sure that no errant psychic harm reaches you. Likewise, practice new techniques for personal protection to bolster your boundaries wherever you go.

A plethora of techniques, from reciting affirmations to having a dance party with your favorite music, can be part of post-attack aftercare. Remember to replenish your physical, emotional, and spiritual energy levels and bring joy and peace into your life. Make time for self-care and avoid places and activities that are likely to subject you to both deliberate or incidental psychic harm until you are back at full strength.

Using the above guidelines, you can prepare your own plan of attack whenever you or a loved one are faced with psychic attack or other malefic forces.

CRYSTALS FOR COMBATTING PSYCHIC ATTACK

Throughout the ages, humankind has sought out gems that dispel harmful energies, thwart unseen dangers, and help conquer evil. Today we have countless rocks, minerals, fossils, and gems to turn to when experiencing psychic attack or harmful magick. Some possible choices are rooted in antiquity, while others are the result of the experiments of modern-day mystics and healers working with newly discovered crystals. I've divided the crystals for ameliorating psychic attack into two categories: stones that combat the attack itself, and crystals that support recovery after the attack is remedied.

In cases of psychic attack we must first turn to those crystals that neutralize or mitigate the source of the attack. These crystals often work by severing ties with the attacker or source of harm, or they may reflect the energy back to its source or otherwise strengthen and defend your own energy field against attack. The following are among the most effective crystals for combatting psychic attack:

Agate	Galena	Moonstone
Amber	Garnet	Novaculite
Amethyst	Granite	Obsidian
Astrophyllite	Halite	Schalenblende
Axinite	Hematite	Staurolite
Black tourmaline	Hypersthene	Stibnite
Bloodstone	Jasper	Suglite
Bronzite	Labradorite	Sulfur
Cassiterite	Lapis lazuli	Tantalite
Cat's eye	Luxullianite	Tiger's eye
Chiastolite	Magnetite	Tiger iron
Diamond	Malachite	Turquoise
Flint	Mohawkite	Zircon

When reviewing this list of crystals we can spot several features that describe the overall mechanism of their activity. The stones commonly used to combat psychic attack include agate, cat's eye, chiastolite, lapis lazuli, staurolite, tiger's eye, and turquoise. Some of these crystals carry symbolic meanings that have been recognized for millennia. Gems such as agate, cat's eye, and tiger's eye are connected to the eyes, symbolizing their ability to watch over you to prevent attacks from taking hold. Others, like turquoise and lapis, are celebrated for their connection to the sky, the abode of the gods, who will watch over you and protect you. Staurolite and chiastolite both exhibit cruciform twinning, wherein two crystals grow together to form the shape of a cross, which has long been thought to exert a powerful protective influence.

Gems associated with strength and power are excellent stones for defense against psychic attack. Some fortify the aura to prevent the intrusive energies from taking hold of your field, while others dispel or repel harm on account of their solidity and power. These crystals include bloodstone, carnelian, cassiterite, diamond, hematite, garnet, granite, hypersthene, jasper, tantalite, tiger iron, and zircon.

Sharp stones cut through attacks and sever the connection with the source of harm. For this try axinite, flint, or obsidian. Other stones are known to reflect harm and return it to its source; these crystals often display reflective surfaces or other unusual optical phenomena. Some of the best reflective stones are fire agate, bronzite, cassiterite, hematite, and magnetite.

Toxic minerals can be powerful tools for thwarting psychic attack, though they should be handled with care. Good examples include stibnite, schalenblende, galena, and sulfur—though all toxic minerals combat toxic energies when employed sensibly.

Recovery from Psychic Attack

The next category of crystals consists of gems that support recovery after an attack or other source of harm has been neutralized. These stones are generally nourishing, fortifying, and regenerative in nature.

Aegirine	Fluorite	Psilomelane
Agate	Hematite	Purpurite
Aragonite	Jade	Rhodonite
Aventurine	Jet	Rose quartz
Bloodstone	Labradorite	Ruby
Calcite	Lepidolite	Serpentine
Carnelian	Magnetite	Shungite
Chlorite	Magnetite	Siderite
Citrine	Malachite	Sodalite
Covellite	Moonstone	Sunstone
Danburite	Opal	Tantalite
Diamond	Pinolith	Tugtupite
Emerald	Preseli bluestone	Unakite

Certain crystals support recovery by repairing damage to the energy field itself. Good examples of such stones are chlorite, covellite, danburite, fluorite, labradorite, emerald, and moonstone (especially rainbow moonstone). These gems can be worn, used in layouts, or distilled in an elixir that is sprayed in the aura to repair any damage incurred from psychic attack.

Other minerals such as aegirine, black tourmaline, cassiterite, clinoptilolite (klinoptilolith), hanksite, hübnerite, jet, pinolith, psilomelane, shungite, and sodalite help to release and draw out intrusive energies left over from psychic attack. Cleansing stones like these can be worn for continuous care or used in grids, meditations, or elixirs to clear away accumulated energy when returning home. Alternatively, several green gems help us tap into the restorative and cleansing properties of the natural world and can be used to purge unwanted and harmful energies when used with intention. These include aventurine, chlorite, emerald, jade, malachite, and green varieties of sodalite. They flood the body with the verdant power of nature to restore the natural cleansing and clearing processes to the body, mind, and spirit.

Fortifying gems like those rich in iron are good choices, too. These are generally regarded as good for overall protection, and they make for excellent companions when you're feeling depleted after psychic attack or other forms of harm. Consider partnering with bloodstone, carnelian, hematite, magnetite and others to restore your strength and bolster your defenses. Aragonite specifically speeds up recovery from psychic attack, while purpurite restores your vitality while scrubbing the energy field. Additional strengthening gems include diamond, epidote, hypersthene, jasper, mohawkite, onyx, Preseli bluestone, ruby, serpentine, and tantalite.

After experiencing psychic attack or other kinds of metaphysical harm it is also helpful to work with crystals that offset the emotional symptoms that accompany these experiences. Uplifting and comforting gems like agate, amber, citrine, calcite, jade, lepidolite, opal, rhodonite, sodalite, sunstone, tugtupite, and unakite soothe frayed nerves, support better rest and relaxation, and set the stage for complete recovery following attack.

Remember that combatting psychic attack requires proper aftercare; it isn't enough to simply sever the connection and enhance your wards. Be sure to add a few crystals to your tool kit that support a healthy recovery after psychic attack, as they will help you be more resilient, thereby minimizing future sources of psychic harm.

GRIDS AND LAYOUTS FOR COMBATTING PSYCHIC ATTACK

While there are many rituals and spells that one can use to combat psychic attack, I prefer using crystal grids and layouts. Grids can be left in place around the clock to neutralize attacks and provide a boost to your environmental wards and protections, while layouts inspire protection and healing at a deep and visceral level thanks to the stones' contact with the body. The grids described below will provide support for many instances of psychic harm as well as offer opportunities for recovery after neutralizing harm.

◆ *Neutralizing Psychic Attack Layout*

Crystals: eight flints or obsidians, one fire agate or bronzite, one tantalite or epidote, and one labradorite

When faced with psychic vampirism, malefic magick, ill-wishing, or any other kind of psychic attack, you'll need a potent and easy technique to break contact and immediately defend and repair the aura. This layout uses a handful of crystals that work together to neutralize the effects of psychic attack at their source while simultaneously removing the effects from the target's aura and psyche.

Gather your crystals, cleanse them, and begin the layout by placing the outer stones. Using either flint or obsidian, as both help sever the connection and bolster your defenses, create two overlapping squares around the body. This pattern will seal the outer layers and provide a safe space in which to recover. Place bronzite or fire agate at the solar plexus chakra to turn back the harmful and intrusive energies and strengthen your willpower. Tantalite or epidote is placed at the heart; either stone will neutralize psychic attack and promote a sense of well-being to ease recovery. Labradorite is placed on the brow to seal the psyche against further intrusion.

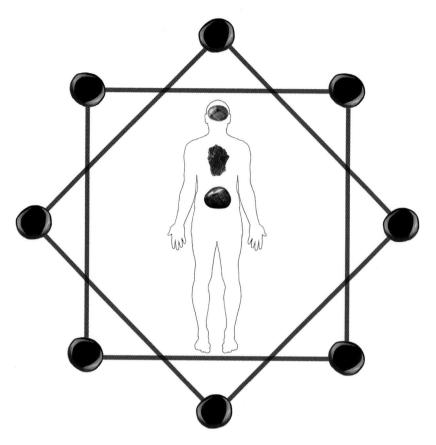

This combination of crystals makes a potent grid that
neutralizes all forms of psychic attack.

Leave the crystals in place for up to a half hour, allowing them to infuse
your body, mind, and spirit with their protective and healing energies. I find
it helpful to burn some cleansing incense or a white candle while engaging
with this layout, as it will help neutralize the energies removed from the
aura via the action of these crystals.

◈ Evil Eye Mandala

Crystals: twelve lapis lazulis, six pieces of turquoise, six quartz pieces, and
one obsidian or black tourmaline

The evil eye is a widespread belief in the ability to send psychic harm via the
gaze. Small charms or beads usually featuring blue eye–shaped patterns that

The evil eye mandala is designed around
traditional imagery to avert harmful energies.

serve as protective amulets against this phenomenon have been popular
around the world. They are known as *nazar boncuğu* in Turkey, with *nazar*
meaning "vision" or "attention" and *boncuğu* coming from the root that
means "bead." Such amulets are popular in many cultures today as jewelry,
art, and ornaments for the home. We can create a grid or mandala inspired
by this powerful motif with a handful of crystals in the appropriate colors.

Begin by collecting enough tumbled gemstones to create the evil eye
mandala, and then selecting a location where you will build and display
it. The quantities of stones listed above are enough to create a more
formal grid as depicted, or you can work with any number of stones
to build a mosaic-inspired mandala with a more free-form construction.
Cleanse all the stones thoroughly and program them to protect you.

Begin with one black obsidian or tourmaline for the center, which will
act as the anchoring point for the mandala, cutting through and discharging
harmful or intrusive energies. Next you'll surround the center stone with a

ring of turquoise; this gem thwarts psychic attack, the evil eye, and other kinds of harm. The next layer is a ring of quartz, although another protective or cleansing white stone like selenite, chalk, or marble can be used instead. Finally, create a ring of lapis lazuli around the rest of the mandala. Lapis lazuli's ultramarine color is the likely source of the evil eye amulets; the celestial hue draws power from the Divine to drive away evil and restore balance.

When the mandala is finished, hold your hands over it and draw forth your willpower and intention to power the grid. Pray or intend that this assortment of gems will conquer any harmful energies sent your way. Leave the mandala to work its magick, being sure to cleanse and empower it again as often as needed.

◆ Recovery Layout

Crystals: one aragonite, one malachite, one tugtupite, one sunstone, four aventurines, two carnelians, and two single-terminated quartz crystals

After severing ties with the source of psychic attack you can employ crystals to ameliorate the harm and hasten the recovery period. This layout incorporates many restorative and soothing stones to ensure a speedy and safe return to balance after any kind of psychic attack or other kinds of psychic harm. Be sure to couple it by thoroughly cleansing yourself and using ample protection to prevent recurrence.

Collect the stones you'll use in this layout and cleanse them thoroughly before use. Begin by placing the aragonite at the earth star chakra below the feet to draw from the regenerative power of the earth. Next, place malachite at the solar plexus, as its harmonizing qualities will soothe imbalances while lifting out any hidden vestiges of intrusive energy. A piece of tugtupite over the thymus encourages repair and recovery of the entire energy field while also soothing the mind and emotions. (If you're having difficulty finding tugtupite, try a piece of eudialyte, ruby, or rhodonite instead.) Add a sunstone to the soul star chakra above the head to draw forth light, hope, and strength. Place four aventurines in a rectangular pattern as seen in the figure above, roughly level with the neck and knees; this placement nurtures and fortifies the entire being. Two carnelians are placed approximately level with the navel, creating a horizontal axis of energy that balances the vertical one created by the aragonite and sunstone.

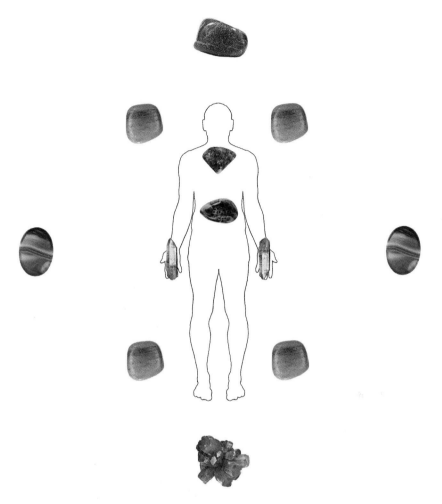

This crystal layout reverses the effects of psychic attack.

Finally, a quartz crystal is placed in each hand: one with the termination facing inward in the nondominant hand, and the other facing outward in the dominant hand.*

Remain in the layout for up to thirty minutes and repeat as often as you like as you return to full-strength after psychic attack.

---

*If you are using this layout on yourself you'll need to build it in a slightly different order. Start with the aragonite and sunstone, followed by the aventurine and carnelian. Lay the malachite and tugtupite on the body last, then place the quartz crystals in your hands.

◆ *Releasing Fear Layout*

Crystals: three rhodonites, two black tourmalines, one obsidian, one fluorite, and six smoky quartz pieces

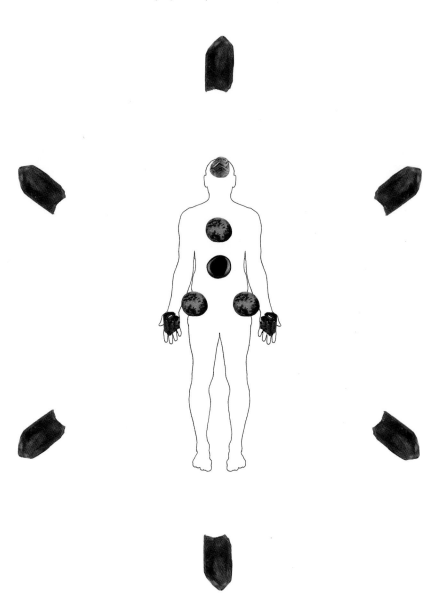

This layout addresses fear and emotional depletion,
which often accompany psychic attack.

Even when the source of psychic harm is neutralized and the intrusive energies are eliminated, many people still feel a vestige of fear. It's natural after an uncomfortable or frightening experience to feel unsafe, as if waiting for the other shoe to drop. If fear, anxiety, and emotional depletion don't dissipate after successfully clearing away psychic harm, try this layout, which is designed to release fears and anxieties while nourishing and protecting the emotional body.

Once your crystals are gathered and cleansed, begin by placing six smoky quartz crystals in a hexagonal formation around the body, as shown above. Then lay two rhodonites on the hips, an obsidian on the solar plexus chakra, another rhodonite on the heart, and a piece of fluorite on the third eye chakra. Finally, place one piece of black tourmaline in each hand. The trio of rhodonite stabilizes the heart and root chakras, soothing emotions that challenge a sense of safety and peace. Obsidian cuts through fears that inhibit personal development and willpower, and the fluorite on the brow dissolves patterns of fear and mental unrest. Holding black tourmaline in each hand helps to draw out and transmute fears and other disharmonious patterns from the psyche and aura. Finally, the ring of single-terminated smoky quartz crystals pointed outward will ground, purify, stabilize, and protect the energy field as well as contain and disperse any fears or other patterns released from the other crystals.

Lie in the grid for fifteen to thirty minutes or until a sense of peace supplants rumblings of anxiety, fear, or dread. I've found it helpful to repeat this once or twice a week as needed until you feel safe and secure and trust that the source of psychic harm has been neutralized. The added benefit of working with this grid regularly is its additional energetic protection, as it fortifies the emotional body, making it more resilient when subjected to intrusive or harmful energies.

OTHER TECHNIQUES

In addition to crystal grids and layouts, there are several rituals and recipes that can be helpful for combatting psychic attack. In the exercises below you'll discover more techniques to help you repair the aura, cut cords, and cleanse the energy field with the help of crystals.

◆ Aura Repair Elixir

Crystals: bloodstone, chevron amethyst, fluorite, danburite, labradorite, topaz, tourmalinated quartz, and unakite

Gem elixirs produce profound results across a wide range of applications. This blend of eight gemstones provides a synergistic effect that purifies, nourishes, seals, and strengthens the aura. Although designed for aftercare to regenerate the aura after psychic attack, it can also be used preventively for general maintenance of the energy field. I recommend using tumbled and polished gems in this elixir; because of the inclusion of the relatively soft fluorite, this elixir is best used for external applications.

Gather and cleanse each of the crystals listed above; give them a good rinse under running water to physically clean them. Place the stones in a glass container and fill with fresh water. Cover tightly and place somewhere that receives ambient light where it will remain undisturbed. After one week, carefully decant and strain the elixir. Mix it in a one-to-one ratio with a preservative such as vodka, brandy, or apple cider vinegar.

To use this elixir, I like to add about a dozen drops to the bathtub for a regenerative soak; feel free to add your favorite essential oils or bath salts, too. This blend also makes a versatile spray that can be spritzed through the aura daily to repair and fortify the energy field. Use it after other healing techniques such as grids, layouts, and meditations to help integrate the positive changes and seal out unwanted energies that might disrupt your progress. Sprayed around the home, this elixir purifies the environment and dissolves intrusive energies to maintain the integrity of your sacred space.

◆ Cord-Cutting

Cord-cutting is a means of ritually severing ties with someone or something. This technique has gained in interest among practitioners in metaphysical and magickal communities, and there are probably as many ways to perform a cord-cutting as there are practitioners. This method can be used to break the psychic connection driving a psychic attack. Note that while rituals of cord-cutting can provide relief from psychic attack, they almost always require additional support for lasting and permanent changes. If the underlying cause of a cord or attachment is not ameliorated, psychic cords will form again and again, no matter how many times you sever them.

First, you'll need to select a stone for use in cord-cutting. Good choices include naturally sharp or bladelike crystals such as axinite, barite, danburite, epidote, and kyanite. Flint, obsidian, and novaculite are powerful choices for cord-cutting, and they may be used in their natural state (especially when broken or fractured to reveal a sharp edge), or as flint-knapped or polished knives, arrowheads, or spear points. Selenite can be used when cut and polished into a knife or wand or as a naturally terminated crystal, and both natural and polished quartz wands are excellent choices. Cleanse and program the stone to prepare for your cord-cutting, and activate it as described in chapter 1.

Assume a stance that feels powerful, with your feet approximately shoulder-width apart if standing or with a comfortably erect spine if seated. Hold the crystal in your dominant hand and invite its consciousness to help you locate cords or attachments in the aura. You can gently move the stone through your energy field to palpate any inconsistencies in the feeling of the aura, or you can simply will the attachment to appear before you. Raise your cord-cutting tool upward, invoking the power of the heavens to help you sever the tie. Take a deep breath in and then cut through the cord in one fluid stroke, releasing the breath afterward. Repeat this several times until the cord has been completely released.

Use the crystal to direct the cord to return to its origin and immediately deactivate and cleanse the crystal. Follow your cord-cutting with a personal cleansing (such as the uncrossing bath described later in this chapter) and fortify the aura with a fresh psychic shield to prevent recurrence of the cord.

◆ Stone Limpia against the Evil Eye

Precious gemstones and finer minerals aren't necessary for combatting psychic attack. On the contrary, palm-sized pebbles of common white quartz make powerful tools for cleansing the aura and counteracting the effects of psychic attack and the evil eye. Such humble stones have a long tradition of being used for healing and protection. In folklore and living folk practices we find common stones like flint, chalk, and holey stones being used in a similar manner to clear away malevolent forces.

This technique is inspired by practices found across the world, from the use of white quartz pebbles in Great Britain, to the egg cleansings (called *limpias*) common throughout parts of Latin America, and the use of stones in the folk healing practices of the Pennsylvania Dutch. In addition to common stones there are a handful of crystals that work well for this cleansing technique, including smoky quartz, selenite, shungite, obsidian, and tektite, and they can be used in the following exercise in place of common pebbles.

Select a smooth stone that fits comfortably in the palm of the hand. I recommend using this technique with a stone you already know well, as you'll be relying on the consciousness of that stone to assist in removing the baleful energies. Cleanse it using your favorite method, such as discharging it under running water or passing it through the smoke of a cleansing herb. Gently hold the stone between the palms of your hands and connect to the indwelling spirit, the consciousness of the stone; request its help in cleansing the body, mind, and spirit of any and all harmful influences. When you feel the stone's consent, you can proceed with the cleansing rite.

Hold the stone in your dominant hand and begin to sweep it across the body, either by lightly rubbing on the body or by sweeping it through the closest layer of the aura, just a couple inches above the skin. Take care to reach each part of the body with the stone—especially the head, heart, and extremities—taking care to roll or sweep any areas that feel particularly painful, unpleasant, or energetically sticky. As you do so, imagine that the stone acts like a sponge or vacuum and draws out all the energy that doesn't belong. I often notice that the stone begins to feel heavier, sometimes even slightly sticky or prickly to the touch once it has become saturated with the harmful energy.

Once you have finished, the stone will need to be thoroughly cleansed and cleared; you may need to bury it in the earth or place it in a dish or bowl and cover it with salt overnight, or cleanse it with representations of the four elements of earth, air, fire, and water. Take care if using a softer stone like chalk or selenite so as not to damage it with your choice of cleansing method.

◈ Staurolite Uncrossing Bath

Baths present an opportunity for deep cleansing and healing when undertaken with a ritual mindset. All over the world you will find rituals of ablution that remove unwanted energies and entities, reverse magickal or psychic attack, and provide healing and comfort. Uncrossing baths are found in magickal systems influenced by African traditional religion; they have worked their way into North American folk magick and have spread far and wide with the globalization of magick and the occult. Typically, an uncrossing bath will remove negative energies, break psychic contact resulting in attack, and reverse your luck for the better. This uncrossing bath requires only two ingredients added to your bathwater: a handful of salt and a staurolite crystal. I like to use coarse-grained sea salt for this, but any salt will do. For the staurolite, try to find one that is twinned at an oblique angle (like the one depicted on page 303 in chapter 9) rather than one that forms a perfect cross with right angles, as this will symbolize the breaking of the crossed conditions.

Draw yourself a warm bath,* and when the tub is full, cleanse and bless the water to be an agent of purification and healing. Next, bless your salt to scrub away and neutralize harmful and intrusive energies. Take a freshly cleansed staurolite crystal and place it atop the salt. Hold your hands over the crystal and charge it with the task of breaking the crossed conditions; invite its spirit to remove obstacles and restore you to a state of balance. Place the staurolite in the middle of the tub and sprinkle the salt across the surface of the water. If you'd like to add any herbs, oils, or other cleansing agents, do so now. Herbs frequently associated with uncrossing include angelica, dill, cinquefoil, hyssop, peppermint, rue, and vervain; you can add a couple drops of an essential oil to the bath as well. Pray or visualize that the mixture becomes a sacred elixir that will cleanse away evil, misfortune, and all sources of disharmony. Remove the staurolite and soak in the tub, ensuring that the water touches every part of you.

---

*If you do not have a bathtub, prepare the water in a pitcher, bucket, or bowl, adapting the instructions for the salt and staurolite accordingly. You can then ritually bathe by pouring the saltwater over yourself in the shower—just be sure to remove the staurolite first so as not to damage it or lose it down the drain!

After you have soaked awhile, remove the stopper from the drain and remain in the tub as the water leaves. Visualize your crossed conditions flowing down the drain with the water. Once the bathtub has drained, take a conventional shower or bath—or at least rinse yourself off to physically cleanse away any remnants of the old conditions and give you a fresh start.

7

Banishing, Binding, and Reversal Magick

When ordinary cleansing, protection, and warding fails, I know it's time to use more heavy-hitting tools and techniques to mitigate the harm. Countermagick in the form of banishing, binding, and reversal spells can be used to counteract more concerted forms of physical, psychological, and social harm, as well as spiritual harm in the forms of magickal attacks like hexes and curses.

- **Banishing** removes an unwanted influence, either external or internal. Banishing spells empower the magician (or the person on whose behalf they are working) to eliminate the harm caused by external threats, whether mundane or magickal in nature. You can also banish your own inner demons and self-generated sources of harm like bad habits, debt, illness, fear, shame, jealousy, and so forth; think of it as turning away such influences from your life.
- **Binding** neutralizes or reduces someone's ability to implement harmful actions against you. Binding magick usually stops the target from doing something specifically harmful, as it binds someone's power or agency to prevent or cease attack or other kinds of harm.
- **Reversals** act as a kind of magickal mirror, reflecting harmful energies, entities, and circumstances such that they return to their source. Reversal magick is much more assertive, as it causes the

target to fall into a trap of their own making, but the danger of reversal is that you run the risk of causing more harm than good in certain circumstances.

Historically, practitioners of the magickal arts used a variety of techniques as countermagick. Witches, cunning folk, and magicians could be hired by laypeople for magickal services, including counterma-gick. Healers, shamans, priests, and other spiritual intercessors might fight fire with fire, sending off curses to the originator of the harm. In some cases, gods, spirits, and ancestors might be invoked to stand up to or even smite an oppressor, while some methods draw power from bane-ful herbs and even toxic minerals and metals to bind, banish, or attack the source of harm.

In today's world, magickal practitioners and spiritual folk of all persuasions often find banishing, binding, and reversal magick to be divisive topics. In some traditions, practitioners are encouraged to pro-tect themselves at all costs, while in others the mentality of turning the other cheek is deeply ingrained. For me, harm reduction is one of the key themes to reflect on when performing banishing, binding, and reversal magick aimed at another person. I have to ask myself, *Will this magickal act reduce the overall amount of harm being done, or will it magnify it?* If I feel that I'll only contribute to more harm than good, I shelve the idea and seek another way forward. However, I respect that the ethical guidelines in other people's practices may disagree with my own.

The mechanics of countermagick tend to work as a battle of wills. Without outside assistance such as from spirits, guides, or patron dei-ties, the offensive and defensive magicks ultimately play out according to whichever magician has honed the strength of their will better than the other. This means that you may stand to lose such a battle if you enter into it unprepared. Most of the time our efforts are better suited to seeking peace rather than fanning the flames of conflict. For this reason, my teacher Christopher Penczak recommends an alternative course: align your will with divine will in the form of your higher self, holy guardian angel, or a deity with whom you have a deep relationship, and operate from this higher, more expanded willpower.[1] Doing so will afford you a chance to direct your focus not to a fight, but to a meaningful solution.

Another helpful reminder is to stay centered in a place of inner peace and unconditional love whenever possible in your banishing, binding, and reversal magick. Align with divine will and perform this work from a place of clarity with the intent to seek safety. Justified or righteous anger can fuel countermagick quite effectively, but you should avoid working from a place of spite or revenge. Take time to get grounded, centered, and aligned before undertaking countermagick to ensure you don't get caught up in the drama of the situation and end up fanning the flames.

There is one more consideration before undertaking countermagick like banishing, binding, and reversal: take time to assess the situation clearly and consult a divination tool of your choice (or a practitioner who uses divination) to be certain that you are taking the best steps for remediation. Although you can banish, bind, or reverse abstract situations that aren't necessarily caused by a single culprit, you should be absolutely certain you have the right target if you are naming someone as the source of the harm you're trying to mitigate. When an attacker or source of harm is unknown, it may be better to banish the energy or situation rather than try to bind the person who may or may not be responsible for said circumstances.

It's also worth reminding you that magick complements practical action, and that no countermagick is a substitute for law enforcement or other emergency services. Always tend to your physical safety before attending to your magickal and spiritual safety.

CRYSTALS FOR BANISHING, BINDING, AND REVERSAL

Crystals can be potent catalysts for banishing, binding, and reversal spells. Crystals of a generally protective nature should be worn, carried, or placed in your environment as part of your countermagickal rituals, but certain stones lend themselves particularly well to these pursuits.

Here is a list of some of the more effective rocks and minerals for banishing, binding, and reversal spells:

Amethyst	Hematite	Pyrolusite
Barite	Hanksite	Rose quartz
Black tourmaline	Ilvaite	Selenite
Bloodstone	Jasper	Siderite
Bronzite	Jet	Smoky quartz
Cassiterite	Moonstone (especially	Staurolite
Chalcedony	the black variety)	Stibnite
Charoite	Obsidian	Sulfur (and sulfur quartz)
Chiastolite	Opal	Ruby
Ferberite	Orpiment	Tantalite
Fire agate	Pigeon's blood agate	Tektite
Fluorite	Psilomelane	Tiger eye
Galena	Purpurite	Tiger iron
Halite	Pyrite	

Historically, we find gems like amethyst, chalcedony, hematite, jasper, jet, moonstone, and even selenite used in banishing, binding, and other countermagick. Salt (halite), sulfur, and lead minerals like galena are also important materials for such work, and evidence of their use can be found around the world in virtually every age. Modern-day crystal practitioners may turn to more recently discovered gems for assistance in banishing and binding work. Some examples of these newer gems include black tourmaline, ilvaite, smoky quartz, and obsidian, which are fortifying stones that can reverse and banish harmful patterns. Others like charoite, hanksite, pigeon's blood agate, purpurite, and pyrolusite ensure that countermagickal pursuits lead to healing; they help mitigate extraneous harm while securing protection and safety. Some of my personal favorites for banishing and reversal magick among newer gems include barite, bronzite, and fire agate.

Reflective stones also have a special place in countermagick, as their optical properties highlight their magickal powers, especially in reversal magick. Consider hematite, obsidian, psilomelane, pyrite, pyrolusite, tektite, and ferberite as examples of this. Even gems with chatoyant, opalescent, and other beautiful optical effects such as bronzite, charoite, moonstone, purpurite, opal, and tiger's eye can be helpful in counterspells.

Salts, which are chemically defined as substances created when acids and bases join to create a neutral compound, have a neutralizing effect on psychic and magickal harm. For this reason, halite—the same substance as ordinary table salt—and hanksite are powerful allies for scrubbing harmful energies away in banishing spells. Selenite, fluorite, calcite, aragonite, and siderite also belong to the category of salts and may be employed in banishing and binding spells.

Saturnian rocks and minerals are essential in countermagick, as Saturn is the ruler of this type of work. Saturn is sometimes referred to as the "greater malefic" and the "lord of karma" in some systems of astrology, which implies a relationship with magickal harm (cursing, hexes, and so forth) as well as countermagick, as it helps you reap what you sow. Saturnian stones include those rich in lead and calcium (both being metals being under the rulership of Saturn), as well as all toxic or poisonous stones. Galena, schalenblende, and amazonite contain lead (as do many other minerals like cerussite, crocoite, pyromorphite, vanadinite, and wulfenite); calcium-bearing stones include aragonite, calcite, chalk, marble, fluorite, and countless more. Orpiment (and therefore bumblebee jasper) is another good example of a toxic mineral with the kind of Saturnian qualities that are essential for countermagick. Indigo and black gems may also bear the influence of Saturn and can also be added to your workings.

BANISHING MAGICK

Banishing is my first line of defense beyond the foundational practice of good spiritual hygiene and personal and environmental protection. Certain practices, like the act of making sacred space or performing basic rituals like the Banishing Ritual of the Precious Stones (see chapter 2) may involve the banishing of erratic, disharmonious, or otherwise unwanted energies. But in some cases targeted banishing magick will be necessary to drive out or turn back more intrusive forms of harm.

Depending on the ethos that guides your practice, banishing can be used as a stopgap in serious situations. Because the nature of such activities is forceful and assertive—sometimes downright aggressive—many practitioners prefer to work toward healing or sweetening a relationship while practicing good psychic hygiene and shielding techniques to mitigate harm as the healing unfolds.

Like other tactics, banishing works best when pursued as part of a holistic approach to healing the situation in question. Though I prefer banishing to binding (which I'll explain a bit later), it is often more effective in more extreme cases to bind someone or something before banishing, as this makes it harder for them to resist the banishing magick.

Banishing spells can be used with equal effectiveness whether they are focused on unwanted energies and situations or on harmful people. You can target an abusive partner, a gossiping coworker, a stalker, or anyone else causing harm. You might also try banishing illness, debt, unhappiness, or habits like biting your fingernails or procrastinating. The principles are the same, but you'll need to keep your focus on the *what* being banished, not necessarily the *who* that's behind it, even if you are directing the banishment to another person. That's largely because in both cases you are probably the common denominator, and you can't effectively banish yourself.

◆ Banishing by Stone

The simplest banishing spell needs only a common and humble stone and the strength of your willpower and emotions. The stone can come from anywhere you like, local or otherwise. Cleanse the stone under running water or incense smoke or with some other method you like, then take it someplace away from your home and work environment; a natural space with a body of water is preferable, but anywhere will do in a pinch. Hold the stone in your dominant hand (or in both hands if this feels more comfortable) and visualize the situation or person you want to banish. Let your emotions run freely by giving yourself permission to feel whatever fear, worry, anxiety, distrust, or anger the circumstances evoke. Pour that emotion into the stone as you hold it—squeeze it, if you like, to wring out every last bit of those feelings.

As the emotions drain from you and into the stone, you'll begin to feel some clarity emerge. At this point, hold the stone to your heart and authoritatively say aloud, "I banish _____ [name] from my life," three times. Take a deep breath and hurl the stone as far away from you as possible, ideally into a large body of water. Take several cleansing breaths and thank the stone for its service, knowing that the forces of nature will cleanse the stone of your emotions. As the stone is moved and shaped by the elements, so too will your situation. You will soon be free of whatever power has held you back.

◈ Banishing Grid

Crystals: one galena, four emeralds, and six jets

Saturn is the planetary ruler of banishing magick, and many of the gems traditionally used in work of this nature have Saturnian qualities. Coupling some of Saturn's gems with its astrological seal generates a powerful force that can be used for banishing unwanted influences from your life. This grid

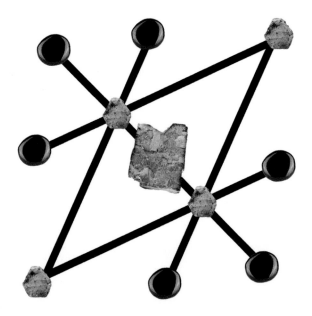

A Saturnian grid
for banishing

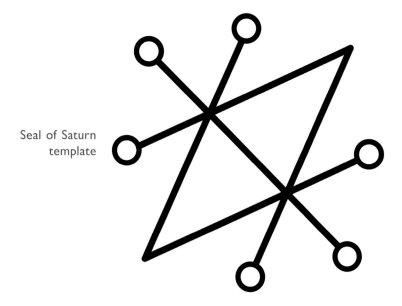

Seal of Saturn
template

employs a piece of galena, four small emeralds, and six pieces of jet. You can trace, draw, or copy the seal of Saturn depicted below to use as the template for your grid. You'll also need something to represent the target of this spell; it is usually easiest to simply write their name on a piece of paper or use a photograph. Ideally, create this grid on a Saturday, which is named for the planet Saturn, to lend additional power to your work.

Locate a place where your seal of Saturn will not be disturbed and cleanse all the crystals. Place the photo of the target or his or her name written on a piece paper underneath the seal of Saturn template so it is out of sight. The first crystal you'll place is the galena, in the center of the grid as shown in the figure above. Focus on its heft and the baneful nature of its lead content; ask that the toxicity of galena* drive out the person or situation you seek to banish. Next, place the four emeralds as shown above; hold each one and ask that as it casts out evil and harm, it replaces those influences with unconditional love. Finally, lay the six pieces of jet on the seal, petitioning each stone to shield you from harm as you exorcise and banish the source of harm from your life.

---

*Galena is safe to hold and display, though it is a good idea to wash your hands after handling it.

Activate the grid as detailed in chapter 1, then hold your hands above it and chant three times:

> By Saturn's might I drive away
> All harm and evil, you cannot stay.
> I cast you out by seal and stone.
> Begone forever, leave me alone.

Leave the grid in place until the target's influence has been removed from your life. Afterward, thank each stone and cleanse them thoroughly. Burn the seal of Saturn and the taglock and dispose of it somewhere away from your home.

BINDING MAGICK

Binding magick is a means of neutralizing harm by metaphorically tying the offender's hands. It's a practice with an ancient pedigree—inscriptions from ancient Greece, Rome, and Egypt attest to its use in antiquity. Thousands of examples of binding tablets and ligature spells unearthed by archaeologists suggest that the practice was widespread in parts of the ancient world.

Binding spells are best used in circumstances where we are otherwise unable to exorcize someone's influence from our lives. For example, you might focus your efforts on a bullying coworker, a gossiping member of your social group, or an abusive family member to keep them from doing more harm to you or a loved one. Binding also provides a chance to layer your mitigations; you might bind a particularly virulent situation before banishing it to better improve the chances of the banishing ritual taking effect.

Symbolically, many of the best binding spells involve one of the simplest tools of folk magick: cord, string, or yarn. A photograph, poppet (a doll or effigy representing the target), or the target's name written on a piece of paper can be wrapped in the length of yarn or string (black or red tends to work best) as you focus on your intent. Reciting something as simple as, "I bind you from doing harm," repeatedly as you envelop the image with the yarn produces a potent binding spell. Other bindings and binding-adjacent workings are enacted by bottling or jarring a person's name or likeness, thereby symbolically containing their agency to prevent harm; protective herbs, stones, and other *materia magica* can be added to the bottle to boost the efficacy. Another common practice today is to put someone in your freezer—symbolically, of course! Writing down the target's name (or their social media handle) on a piece of paper and putting it in the freezer helps the situation to metaphorically cool down; some practitioners put the name in a container of water (plastic freezer bags work well) before freezing for maximum effect. Let's not forget that ice is a crystal, too, so this is a good example of binding magick powered by crystal energy.

Binding spells are rarely permanent solutions; usually it is best to build a timeline into the magick itself. This might be a finite period, such as requesting that the target be bound from doing harm while you spend time together or for the time it will take for mundane protections (emergency services, legal action, and so forth) to take effect. Another route to take is to bind someone from harm until they learn their lesson or until they are rendered harmless by another means. Just be careful not to exact revenge or work from spite—always prioritize safety above all else.

Personally, I try to be very mindful about when I apply bindings. There is a teaching that what you touch also touches you; in the case of binding magick, this means your spellcraft links you and the target in some way. However minor that may be, I prefer to avoid being tethered to the person, situation, or institution being bound, and therefore only turn to binding when I am unable to extricate myself from the target's influence by any other means. If you are constantly binding others, freezing or burying their names, or using other forms of binding magick, you may spread yourself too thin to adequately protect and balance yourself. Remember that this form of countermagick is best used only when other avenues have proven ineffective.

◆ Binding Spell

The first binding spell I learned in my teenage years required only a common stone and some black yarn. Any piece of rock or stone works well for

My favorite binding spell makes use of black yarn
and a common stone.

this. Unlike other binding spells that might use an image or photo of the
target or perhaps a poppet representing the target, the stone serves as an
aniconic representation of the target of your binding spell. This means that
you could easily bind situations, institutions, or other sources of harm that
can't be visualized as a single person. It also means that it can be better
used when the source of harm cannot be identified.

Begin by choosing a stone to use in this spell. If the target is known—
and if it is safe to do so—you could choose a rock from a place near their
home, work, or any other place they frequent. Otherwise, any old rock will
do. Alternatively, you can use a piece of galena for this spell, as the lead it
contains has a long history of use in binding magick. Cleanse the stone by
any method of your choice and collect some black yarn or cord; ensure
that you've got enough to wrap around the stone and cover every bit of
its surface.

Begin your work by preparing the space according to your tradition; this
might include casting a circle or invoking divine assistance. When you are
ready to start the operative magick, hold the stone in your nondominant

hand and focus on the target of the binding spell. Create a link between the stone and the target by addressing it thus: "I name you _____ [name]; you are _____ [name]." With your dominant hand make the sign of the cross over the stone to seal this connection.

Pick up the black yarn and begin to wrap it around the stone, knotting it as needed to hold the initial wrap in place. Continue to wind the yarn around the stone and repeat, "I bind you _____ [name] from doing harm," over and over as you envelop the stone in black yarn. Proceed until every bit of the stone is obscured by the yarn, then tie it off securely so that it cannot unravel. Address the wrapped stone as the target of the spell, saying "You are bound from contributing any more harm to this situation."

Conclude your ritual and take the stone someplace away from your home where it will not be disturbed, and bury it or hurl it into a lake or pond. Once the stone is hidden from sight, turn away and don't look back.

◈ Tanglefoot Grid

Crystals: eight obsidians, four bronzites, and one hematite

In some folk magick traditions you'll find variations of a spell known as a tanglefoot. This is usually performed by knotting a piece of cord, though I've seen alternative methods that involve winding thread or cord around nails or needles. However it's enacted, the goal is to trap or entangle someone energetically so they can no longer cause harm; think of it as a bit like tying their shoelaces together, hence the name tanglefoot. This crystal grid combines the idea of a tanglefoot charm with a grid called "tangling web," from D. J. Conway's *Crystal Enchantments.*[2] I've chosen the crystals in this layout to create a potent and immediate effect.

To create this grid you'll need eight pieces of obsidian, four pieces of bronzite, and a piece of hematite. Trace the figure (at right) on a piece of paper and cleanse your stones. If you have a specific target in mind, write their name on a small piece of paper or use a photo and place that in the center of the grid; otherwise, without a specific target in mind you can use this to generally trap or entangle harmful psychic energy in your environment. Next arrange the stones as depicted above, with each bronzite flanked by two obsidians in each of the four directions, and the hematite resting atop the name or photo.

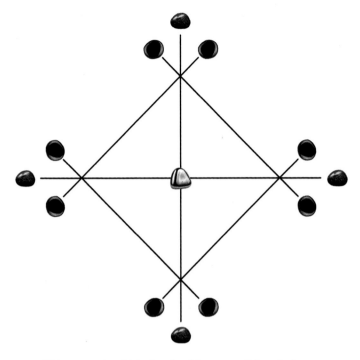

This crystal grid is inspired by a traditional charm
known as a tanglefoot.

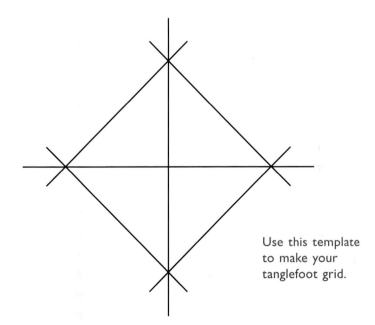

Use this template
to make your
tanglefoot grid.

Obsidian's sharp, incisive energy grabs hold of errant, intrusive, or outright harmful energies, while bronzite binds said energies from causing harm. Finally, the hematite acts to weigh down the will and psyche of the source of the harm, making it rather difficult for the target to continue causing harm. Alternatively, if you create this grid without a specific target in mind, it can entangle and collect harmful and misplaced energy in your home to prevent it from causing harm. I've had success with this grid for myself and loved ones; it can stave off psychic attack, ill-wishing, and harmful magick. Be sure to cleanse all the crystals and refresh the grid at least once per lunar cycle.

Selenite Defixio

Crystals: one flat piece of selenite

There is a unique category of countermagickal artifacts stemming from the Greco-Roman world and beyond known as *defixiones* (singular *defixio*, meaning "to bind" or "to fasten down"). These magickal tools were typically made from lead or a lead alloy, though they could also be made of pottery, ceramic, limestone, gems, papyrus, or wax. The British Museum houses dozens of examples of defixiones inscribed on natural slabs of selenite from the island of Cyprus. These spells are reminiscent of modern-day petitions, as they draw from the power of the written (and probably spoken) word to achieve a magickal effect. Many such curse tablets are more accurately considered to be binding tablets, as they were used to bind enemies, rivals, and abusers from perpetuating harm. Other tablets cursed the target outright as a means of achieving justice, with eye-for-an-eye morality steering the way for the magick to work.

Defixiones usually work by invocation of supernatural forces; historically this meant appealing to gods, angels, tutelary spirits, and the spirits of the dead. This typically manifested in three primary ways in which the tablets work: a performative utterance ("I bind _____"), a prayer invoking supernatural forces for a result ("May the power of the gods bind _____"), and persuasive analogies that link the outcome with characteristics of something used in the spell ("May _____ be

An updated version of an ancient
binding spell using selenite

as cold and dull as this lead.") Note that one, two, or all three mechanisms
may be evident from the inscriptions or from the rituals used to empower
the tablets.[3]

With just a few simple ingredients you can create a modern version of a
binding spell that is inspired by the Cyprian defixiones in the British Museum;
this version uses selenite. My preference is for a natural transparent slab of
cleavage, though polished plates, discs, and other shapes made from fibrous
satin spar selenite will work beautifully. You'll also need an iron or steel
nail to carve or etch the words of power on the selenite. To complete the
ritual, you'll need a bit of salt, two candles—one black and one white—and
any protective incense or other ritual implements of your choosing. If you
like, cast a circle or prepare your ritual space according to the customs of
your tradition, calling forth any gods or spirits connected to your craft. Light
the candles and cleanse the selenite by sprinkling salt on both sides of the
slab while saying, "By the power of salt, may this selenite be exorcized of
all evil and rendered a clear slate for this spell."

Next, hold the selenite between your hands and quiet your mind until you feel its inner light pouring forth. Ask the selenite to lend its power to you so that its light can transform the harmful situation you seek to bind. Now take the nail in your hands and repeat the process of connecting to its strength, inviting it to direct your will to seek protection and justice.

Carve your intention into the selenite with the nail, naming the person, situation, or institution that you wish to bind. You can create a simple inscription, such as "I bind _____ [name]," or a longer one that describes the effects you seek in greater detail. When the inscription is complete, take the defixio in your hands and ask the Divine to help you seek justice. Recite the following charm nine times:

> _____, whose name is on this selenite,
> Do no harm; you are bound by light.

As you chant, envision the target being flooded by prismatic white light so dazzling that it dissolves any trace of harmful or evil intent. Imagine the target being immobilized by the light, such that going forward all their actions must be aligned with the light of the Divine otherwise their actions will fail them.

Thank the selenite and any deities or spirits you've invoked for assistance. Snuff out the candles, conclude your ritual, and place the selenite tablet in a location where it cannot be disturbed. You might choose to bury it or tuck it away in an attic or cupboard. Historically, defixiones were sometimes placed in springs, or they might be broken (or bent and pierced when made of lead), with the broken bits left somewhere liminal, like a hole in the ground or a crossroads.

REVERSAL MAGICK

When someone opposes you with harmful magick, reversal is often a useful method of countermagick. Because reversal magick directs hexes, psychic attacks, or other malefic powers back to their source, it can sometimes succeed where ordinary measures of cleansing and protection have failed.

Part of the power of reversal magick lies in its ability to offer a lesson to the source of the magickal or psychic harm. Reversals of this nature only work when harm is actively sent your way—in other words, as the harm is directed your way, the person directing this harm will experience their efforts being returned to them. In theory at least, when presented with mishaps of their own making, the person will be faced with the opportunity to change course and choose not to harm others.

Considering the Crossfire

Unlike most countermagick and apotropaic workings, reversal magick can potentially bring more harm than good in some circumstances. As the harmful energies and magick reflect off your shields and spells, they travel back to their source. Along the way they could cross paths with many an innocent bystander if your magick does not have certain safeguards built into it.

The terms *blowback* and *crossfire* describe the harm caused by energies, intentions, spirits, and spells that are deflected by your magick. Blowback is often thought of as the harm that comes to the people around you, as they may be left undefended when maleficia bounce back. Take note that when you perform any protective magick or build any shields there is a small chance that harmful energies can spill over to those around you unless you create effective shields that cover your household or community. Asking that your shields and spells harm none offers a layer of protection built into your work that mitigates the risk of blowback.

Another way that such energies can cause more harm than good is when a less skilled or less diligent practitioner aims harmful magick your way. At worst you might experience such a jinx or hex as a minor inconvenience thanks to your regimen of daily spiritual hygiene, personal protection, and adequate wards. At best, no harm will come to you at all. If you focus on reversal magick in these instances, the full effect of the harm will make its way back to its source. Chances are good that this practitioner won't have all the protections and spiritual hygiene in place, thus your reversal will hit them hard. In these cases, minor protections and cleansings are almost always sufficient.

It's important to consider all the factors when practicing any magick, especially reversal magick. If it is still the best course of action, consider working with crystals that help mitigate the effects of blowback to prevent the people you love as well as innocent strangers from being caught in a deluge of energy they didn't ask for. Barite, bronzite, shungite, amber, and jet are wonderful stones to prevent accidental harm, and amethyst, charoite, and sugilite can transmute harmful energies rather than reflect them back to their source. Crystal author and expert Judy Hall recommends a wide array of additional crystals for preventing blowback, including black tourmaline, fire agate, pinolith, rose quartz, shungite, smoky quartz, tourmalinated quartz, and elestial crystals.[4]

Apart from reversing the effects of curses, hexes, and psychic attacks, reversal magick is sometimes used to reverse your own fortune. In this case the reversal magick can be adapted not to send harm back to its source (especially since I wholeheartedly believe that we mostly make our own luck), but instead to reverse the trend of events for the better. The Smoky Quartz Reversal Spell on page 189 can easily be adapted to this use.

◈ Hematite Mirror Cage Grid

Crystals: thirteen pieces of hematite (optional: an additional four pieces of shungite or black tourmaline)

Mirrors are the traditional staples of reversal magick; there are countless spells using reflective surfaces to symbolically return baneful magick and malefic forces back to their source. Practitioners might burn candles or place ritual objects atop a mirror for reversal magick, or they might line a small wooden box with mirrors and place the target's name or image inside. This grid draws inspiration from similar techniques and uses hematite's reflective qualities to reverse the flow of harmful energy.

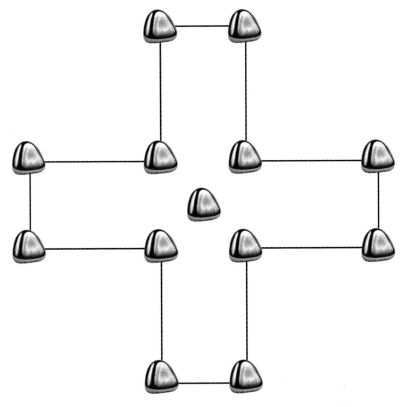

Harness the mirrorlike power of hematite to reflect harm back to
its source with this crystal grid.

Collect thirteen pieces of hematite for this grid; if you would like to
neutralize the harmful energy without it rebounding back on you (or causing
fallout that harms anyone else, for that matter), you'll also want four pieces
of shungite or black tourmaline. Cleanse the stones and arrange twelve of
the hematite crystals in the pattern above, which is shaped like a crossroads
or an equal-armed cross. Place something to represent the target in the
center of the grid: their name written on a piece of paper, a photo, or
something belonging to them. If the attacker is unknown, simply write
"attacker" or "source of harm" on a piece of paper and place that in the
middle of the grid. Lay the final piece of hematite atop the symbol of the
spell's target. At this point you may also place the four pieces of shungite or
hematite just beyond the four arms of the hematite crossroads to contain

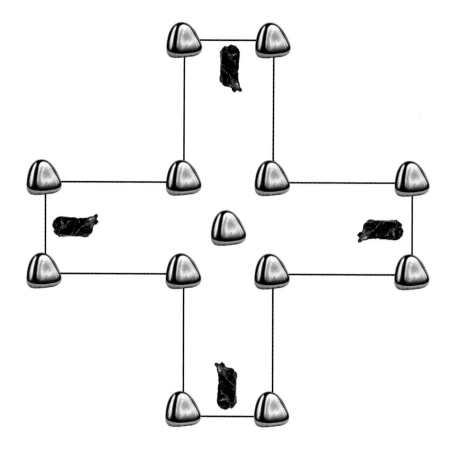

Adding shungite (pictured) or black tourmaline to
this grid helps to neutralize all harmful energy and
reduce the chances of blowback.

and neutralize the harm, essentially transforming this into more of a binding
than a reversal.

Activate or empower the grid to return the harmful energy to its
source and remove any trace of its influence from your life. Leave the grid
in place for as long as needed for urgent situations, but probably not more
than one lunar cycle. If the situation persists after the grid has run its course
it may be necessary to focus on banishing the influence rather than simply
repelling it.

◈ Smoky Quartz Reversal Spell

Crystals: one single-terminated smoky quartz (or a piece of black tourmaline, ilvaite, or aegirine with a termination at one end), four tumbled black stones (obsidian, onyx, or black tourmaline), and four tumbled white stones (selenite, magnesite, or quartzite)

Some of the most common reversal spells involve burning candles. Popular versions use specialty reversal candles, which can be burned upside down to symbolize their reversal of fortunes and overturning magick that's been cast against you. To perform a crystal version of this reversal, you'll need a bowl or cauldron (or any other receptacle) full of sand or salt, an elongated, single-terminated smoky quartz crystal (natural or polished), four tumbled black stones, and four tumbled white stones. In place of the smoky quartz, you could use a piece of black tourmaline, ilvaite, or aegirine, as long as it has a termination at one end.

Inverting a piece of single-terminated smoky quartz
is the central action in this simple ritual to
reverse harmful magick or bad luck.

Begin by setting up your work space with the sand- or salt-filled cauldron or bowl on your altar or other flat surface and place all the crystals nearby. Cleanse all your tools—with smoke, for example—and prepare yourself for the ritual according to your tradition. When ready, begin the working by holding the smoky quartz crystal in your dominant hand with the point facing upward. Focus on the situation you seek to reverse, whether it is a harmful spell that has been cast on you, or a wave of misfortune you seek to turn the tide on. Flood the crystal with your intention to reverse the scenario or return the harm to its source.

Now invert the crystal and gently thrust it point-downward into the vessel filled with sand or salt. Place the rest of the stones in a circle around the smoky quartz, alternating the black stones with the white ones to signify reversal and balance. Hold your hands over the arrangement of stones and recite the following charm three times:

> *Harm, abuse, attack, and hate*
> *No longer shall I tolerate.*
> *I send your curses back to thee,*
> *And reverse all harm that's sent to me.*

Charge the stones with your willpower as you chant, feeling their influence expanding to reach all parts of your life and turning back any harm that has been sent your way. Allow this mental image to fade and relax your hands. Close the ritual and leave the stones in place for three days before taking them down and cleansing each one thoroughly. Discard the salt or sand somewhere safe—such as a crossroads, body of water, natural space, or a dumpster—with the intention that any vestiges of magickal harm leave with it.

OFFENSIVE MAGICK

I won't sugarcoat the truth: sometimes people do inexcusable and unforgivable things to us or our loved ones. From physical and emotional abuse to violent crimes, the human race has its fair share of problems. Spiritual practitioners are exempt neither from experiencing nor perpetuating harm, and there may come a time when the harmful actions, mundane or magickal, that you face cannot be solved by ordinary countermagickal measures. This is traditionally when one might consider using offensive magick, such as a hex or curse.

There is a fine line between defensive and offensive magick, and historically the delineation has not always been very clear. Folk healers, cunning folk, and other magickal practitioners have long employed curses for a net positive result. Even today it is frequently said that a witch who cannot hex cannot heal, or one must be able to curse in order to cure. This doesn't mean that you need to perform malefic magick—merely that understanding the mechanics of it and being able to raise the caliber of willpower required for cursing will serve you well in the beneficent arts, from healing to attracting abundance or love. You can curse the agents of disease and hex systems of oppression to bring justice.

I don't take offensive magick lightly, and I suggest you don't either. To enact a curse or hex is to incur the karmic weight of your actions. Every stone cast causes ripples in the pond, and not every ripple is a pleasant one. In my decades of magickal practice there are precious few situations that have ever necessitated it. Admittedly, I've been more apt to consider using such work against transpersonal forces—oppressive systems like white supremacy, racism, misogyny, and transphobia—than to wield them against individuals.

If you do take the route of offensive magick or maleficia, the most ethical route is to add a lock to the curse, such that it will only affect the target if they should cause more harm.[5] Set your intention (perhaps by writing it down or stating it out loud) that the curse you are about to enact will only activate if and when the abuser or target perpetuates harm again. This places them in an active role.

How do you know when it's right to curse? My sincere hope is that you'll never have to consider it. However, the world hits hard, and sometimes we have to know how to hit back to protect ourselves and our loved ones. I urge you to consider divination to confirm whether or not this is the best action. There are basically three yes-or-no questions worth asking:

- Will a curse be effective in stopping (or minimizing) the harm coming from the target?
- Will a curse result in less harm overall?
- Will this put myself or my loved ones or client in more danger than we are already in?

Ideally, the answers you are looking for are, respectively, *yes*, *yes*, and *no*. Any other responses should raise a red flag and invite you to rethink your course of action. Instead, turn your attention to other forms of countermagick: binding harm, banishing your attacker, and reversing the harm sent your way.

It is also important to remember that offensive magick—like all magick—is never a substitute for sensible mundane actions to remove yourself or your loved ones from harm. That said, I leave you with a single example for performing this type of work.

◆ Crystal Curse

Crystals: clear quartz, fluorite, amethyst, or obsidian

I hesitated to include this technique in this book, but there are times when simply focusing on protective and preventive measures are not sufficient. Cursing, hexing, and jinxing are not to be taken lightly, but they are historically part and parcel of the *ars magicae*. Thus, I thought it might be helpful to provide an example of how baneful magick can be adapted to a modern-day approach that uses crystals. Consider this crystal curse to be a last resort when you have exhausted all other approaches. Curses and malefic workings are often used by practitioners to invoke justice when other means of remediating a situation have failed repeatedly. You might choose this working when you are in imminent danger with an impending threat of spiritual or physical harm—just be certain that you are ready to take on the karmic repercussions of this extreme action. No matter when or why you lean into the act of cursing, bear in mind that like all magickal acts it should never replace practical actions to preserve your health and safety.

The ritual itself is very simple and needs few tools—little more than a black candle and an appropriate crystal. I suggest clear quartz, either tumbled or a natural point, but you may also choose from fluorite, amethyst, or obsidian. In a pinch just about any crystal or gemstone will do. You'll also need a small piece of black cloth or a black pouch to wrap the stone in, a hammer or something comparable to break the stone, and a dish in which to place the broken bits. If you like you can also use commercially available or handmade oils such as crossing oil, black arts oil, confusion oil, or justice oil to name a few commonly available. If you are inclined to make your own, you can find recipes online and in books.

Place the items before you and prepare for the ritual according to the tradition that you follow, perhaps by cleansing the room or casting a circle. Invoke any assistance from the Divine by calling the gods, ancestors, or other spirits of your craft. State your intention to levy a curse at your attacker that will activate only if and when they enact further harm. Ask that this work be divinely guided so that it will reduce harm and not augment it.

Carve the name or initials of your attacker or other target into the candle. Before you light it, focus on your present circumstances. Allow all the raw emotions to bubble up to the surface without losing control; these

When all else fails, use this ritual to petition for
justice to overcome your attacker.

feelings are the fuel for your magickal act. Light the candle, summoning the burning of your willpower as you do so.

Wrap the crystal in the black cloth, pick up the hammer, and channel your inner flame of righteous anger into it. When ready, break the crystal. Put the pieces in the dish. Lift the lit candle and hold it over the shards of crystal so the wax drips over them. Imagine that the power of your curse immobilizes your attacker just as the wax immobilizes the crystal fragments. Snuff the candle and wrap the candle end and the wax-encrusted shards in the black cloth. Bury it far from where you live, or dispose of it at a crossroads to complete the spell. Know that your work will help you achieve justice and safety.

8

Dealing with Spirits

Historically there have been periods and places in which spirit activity has had greater relevance to humankind than it does in the modern Western world today. In times past, various afflictions were attributed to displaced, mischievous, or even malevolent spirits, and a host of methods for banishing and exorcising these entities can be found in cultures around the world. Lapidary texts from the medieval period and even earlier describe gems that have an affinity for casting out unwanted spirits, a tradition continued by modern crystal practitioners today.

It's unlikely that you'll have a pressing need for the techniques in this chapter. Hauntings and other paranormal phenomena aren't exactly uncommon, but it is rare for malicious entities to be their sole cause. Rather, they are usually caused by lesser orders of spirits, conscious energy patterns, or thought forms generated by people or events that attach to your home. Many times paranormal phenomena result from memories or imprints stored in a home, not unlike the way crystals store energy and information when we program them. In most instances, diligent cleansing and warding is often enough to mitigate the unusual phenomena. But if spirits and other entities are involved, you'll need to turn to more advanced procedures.

Similarly, true possession is quite rare. Most spirits aren't capable of possession, and most are also quite ambivalent about humankind. You are far more likely to encounter other kinds of attachments, like psychic debris, negative thought forms or emotions projected from other people or from traumatic experiences, or displaced lower-order astral entities that linger because of the light and warmth offered by the human energy field. Again, diligent cleansing and shielding will often take care of such situations, but stubborn attachments may require more focused techniques.

Though rare, it may be that you encounter something that requires spirit release or exorcism. Please note that the symptoms of possession often overlap with those of mental illness. This being so, it will be necessary to consult a qualified mental-health provider when these signs manifest before proceeding with any magickal remedies. Just as with psychic attack, use divination or another diagnostic tool of your choice to determine the nature of the psychic harm and whether further action is necessary. If you feel out of your depth, reach out to someone with experience in spirit release or exorcism to assist or guide you or to take the reins in the situation.

Throughout this chapter you'll find a variety of techniques to turn to when you feel there is indeed a spirit or some other entity taking up residence where it shouldn't. Some of the methods are fairly simple and passive, while others include more in-depth workings. Remember to practice good spiritual hygiene and keep yourself shielded whenever taking on cases requiring spirit release—it's a good idea to add more layers of protection than you might ordinarily use in your everyday life. And always call on a higher power of your choosing to help release, banish, or exorcise unwanted spirits, particularly harmful ones.

ASSESSING THE SITUATION

Learning to correctly identify hauntings, attachments, and possessions requires patience, clarity, and experience. As already mentioned, spirit possession is quite rare. Instead, you are more likely to encounter spirit attachments that have resulted in hauntings or obsessions rather than full-blown possession. Possession displaces or battles with the host's personality and/or consciousness; obsession, on the other hand, more subtly infiltrates a person or place to leave a general sense of unease or harm. Generally speaking, there are a number of signs common in cases of spirit attachment, haunting, obsession, and possession. These include:

- Subtle shifts in the energy of a space
- Unexplained sounds and disembodied voices
- Unusual and unpleasant aromas, like sulfur, decay, and filth
- Disturbing visitations in dreams and meditations
- Household items being inexplicably moved or lost
- Interference with electronics and appliances
- Sudden change in animal and human behavior
- Shadows or movement seen in one's peripheral vision
- Sense of being watched or followed
- Being touched by unseen hands, which may or may not be accompanied by marks and bruises without apparent cause
- Strong emotions without identifiable cause, typically fear, paranoia, or disgust
- Uncharacteristic compulsions, affinities, or aversions
- Sudden precipitation of slime, mold, and other substances

As with the symptoms of psychic attack, many of the aforementioned signs overlap with the signs of mental imbalance, which would require the help of a licensed health care provider. Always be sure that someone seeking magickal assistance has first consulted their health care practitioner.

It may sometimes be difficult to discern the difference between an ordinary psychic attack and paranormal phenomena like hauntings and attachments, especially as magickal and psychic harm can be enacted via spirits deployed by the magick-maker. As with other cases of psychic and magickal harm, do due diligence via careful observation coupled with divination to rule out other possibilities.

UNDERSTANDING EXORCISM

Spirit release and exorcism comprise a broad category of spiritual practices that aim to remove a spirit or other presence from a person, place, or object. Although definitions will differ based on tradition and practice, I consider spirit release to be more passive work that virtually anyone can perform. This might be achieved through prayer, meditation, crystal grids and layouts, or with other spiritual tools. Exorcism, on the other hand, is a much more active approach.

The word *exorcism* derives from two Greek roots: *ex,* meaning "out," and *horkizein,* meaning "to swear an oath." The idea is that the exorcist uses their spiritual authority—perhaps derived from swearing an oath to a higher power—to cast out or otherwise command spirits. Spiritual authority is the key here. The exorcist is merely a link in a chain to the higher power being invoked, and that higher power is who's doing the real work. Author and magician Jason Miller describes exorcism as a battle of wills and advises that "in order to win, your will must be linked with something beyond your own personal wants and desires. Your will must be identical to the will of the Gods."[1] Thus the exorcist must also strive to maintain a clear connection to divinity and keep their vessel free from contaminants, thereby enabling divine will to manifest through the ritual.

If you are faced with the need to perform any kind of spirit release, exorcism, or similar work, be extra diligent about your spiritual hygiene. Spend time in quiet meditation or prayer and surround yourself with whatever nourishes your spirit. Connect to your team of guides, guardians, angels, ancestors, saints, and deities to build yourself up spiritually. Shield yourself and strengthen the wards in your space; consider coupling these techniques with a ritual like the Banishing Ritual of the Precious Stones found in chapter 2. Avoid alcohol and other activities that may make you more vulnerable to the influence of harmful forces during your preparation.

Truthfully, if you are new to the world of exorcism and spirit release, mindlessly laying down some crystals in a pattern will not be very effective. There are other, more advanced techniques that require experience and a strong platform of personal practice (really, it can be any kind of spiritual practice as long as it is done regularly enough that it forges a strong connection to the higher power of your choosing). Spirit release for lower entities and psychic debris can be accomplished by most anyone, but genuine exorcism for hauntings, possessions, and similar intrusions should only be attempted by someone with expertise. Moreover, such rituals must, once begun, be carried out to completion.

A few other words of caution are worth mentioning here. If someone reaches out to you requesting exorcism because they believe they are possessed, first refer them to the appropriate professionals in both the occult and mental health spheres. If you are experienced enough to attempt exorcism or spirit release for a house or a person, it is helpful to have an experienced assistant in case things go awry; that way a second person can step in if your abilities waver, and an extra pair of eyes and hands is always welcome in unusual circumstances. Also, bear in mind that the person performing spirit release and exorcism must have complete faith in the outcome of the actions. For more advice, consider reading *Protection and Reversal Magick* by Jason Miller and *The Exorcist's Handbook* by Josephine McCarthy.

GENERAL GUIDELINES FOR SPIRIT RELEASE

Before practicing any of the techniques outlined in this chapter it will be helpful to familiarize yourself with these general guidelines for spirit release. Ensure that you understand each of the steps and pay special attention to your personal preparation before attempting to remove unwanted, intrusive, or harmful spirits. In lieu of formal ritual instructions for releasing and exorcising spirits, I'll lay out some general guidelines that experienced practitioners use to craft their own rituals. If you aren't comfortable doing so, it's best to seek the expertise of someone with adequate experience in these kinds of workings.

The first step in readying yourself for any kind of spirit release is self-preparation. This consists mainly in cleansing and shielding. It's best to add some additional steps or select more intensive options than you might use in your ordinary, everyday life, just to ensure that you don't bring any of your own baggage into the ritual and to prevent any kind of foreign energy or entity from following you home. You can refer to chapters 2 and 3 for inspiration on your spiritual hygiene and personal protection needs. Also spend time engaging in your spiritual practice to connect to a higher power. Meditation, prayer, and ritual can be meaningful ways to do this, as can readings from scripture and other sacred texts. Surround yourself with uplifting music, symbols, and other fonts of spiritual inspiration. Avoid places, people, and media that drag you down into fear, worry, frustration, or doubt as you prepare for the spiritual work ahead of you. Be absolutely certain that you are plugged into a power higher than yourself, and that the ritual actions you undertake come from that authority. Any assistants or observers should be encouraged to follow suit by preparing themselves ahead of the ritual itself.

Finally, you'll need to prepare your space. Cordon off the object, room, or person that will be the focus of your work. In some traditions a consecrated cord or stole is draped over the person who is the focus of your work; you could also surround them with a ring salt or a circle of insulative gems such as amethyst, obsidian, or amber. This helps contain the presence that will be removed as you prepare the rest of the space. Select your working area, remove unnecessary clutter, and follow that with a thorough space cleansing. Lay out any tools you've selected to work with and enter into a prayerful state to reaffirm your connection to your higher power.

When the time comes to perform the ritual of spirit release, bring the person or object into your working space. Invite your higher power to come into the space to oversee the ritual. Then address the harmful presence with authority. Don't mince words by trying to avoid uncomfortable terms like *evil* or *harmful*; command that these hostile forces be banished through the higher power that you've invoked. Call to the higher power to uproot the evil from its hold over the person, place, or object being exorcized—I like to visualize a horde of fierce and luminous angels carrying it away. You might choose to abjure the malicious presence via the elements, using symbols such as smoke, holy water, salt, and flame to command the spirit to leave. Continue doing so until the ritual is successful.

When the ritual is successful, an experienced practitioner will feel a shift in the atmosphere—in fact, even less sensitive practitioners may note a feeling of relief or a lightness that alights in the ritual space. It's imperative to thank the higher powers—whatever team of gods, saints, angels, ancestors, or other beings of light that supported you—and immediately cleanse the subject of your ritual with any of the personal hygiene methods described in chapter 2. As well, cleanse the space with a final ritual such as the Banishing Ritual of the Precious Stones, found in chapter 2, and then set up whatever wards or protective amulets are desired to prevent any further incursions by malefic forces.

CRYSTALS FOR SPIRIT RELEASE

Traditional lore describes an array of gemstones that banish, repel, cast out, or otherwise neutralize harmful spirits. Medieval and classical lapidary texts list gems whose primary curative virtues include exorcising all manner of ghosts, devils, and unclean spirits that were believed to cause maladies. Many of these gems are the very same allies we can turn to today for support in times of spiritual crisis. Here is a short list of rocks, minerals, and other gemstones with either traditional or modern associations with spirit release and exorcism:

Aegirine	Emerald	Opal
Amethyst	Galena	Orpiment
Ametrine	Hypersthene	Peridot
Aquamarine	Ilvaite	Phantom quartz
Astrophyllite	Jasper	Pinolith
Black moonstone	Jet	Ruby
Botswana agate	Lapis lazuli	Selenite
Chalcedony	Marble	Sphalerite
Chiastolite	Muscovite	Stibnite
Chlorite	Nuummite	Sulfur (and sulfur quartz)
Diamond	Obsidian	Tektite

Most crystals that can be used for rites of spirit release and exorcism fall into two categories: those with strong ties to the divine or angelic realm, and those that reach deep into the dark, uncomfortable parts of the psyche. For example, diamond, for its long associations with divinity and invincibility, is a powerful ally in spirit release work, and emerald, for its associations with paradise and angels, also has a long tradition of being used to cast out spirits. Other stones like ilvaite, jet, obsidian, and stibnite belong to the second class of gems—those that release and purge attachments from the deepest parts of the self.

Other trends emerge when considering the above-named crystals. Several of the stones listed here may be toxic if mishandled, and their apparent baneful nature drives out unwanted spiritual influences. These minerals include galena, orpiment, stibnite, and sulfur. Others on the list form under metamorphic conditions, and the extreme pressures they've endured help us face crisis and danger with greater ease. Such stones include aegirine, astrophyllite, chiastolite, emerald, hypersthene, lapis lazuli, marble, nuummite, and tektite.* Some stones, when properly programmed, act as spirit traps, particularly obsidian and phantom quartz. No matter which stones you work with, be sure to thoroughly cleanse and program them to ensure a safe and effective outcome.

When astral parasites and semiconscious thought forms attach to a person's energy field, it can feel like a spirit attachment. These attachments can be extracted or released with sulfur, stibnite, muscovite, opal, Botswana agate, laser wand quartz, and phantom quartz. Oftentimes such entities can be removed with simple techniques like the Cord-Cutting ritual found in chapter 6, but you might occasionally need more formal rituals such as those described here to draw them out of their host.

GRIDS AND RITUALS

The remainder of this chapter describes a handful of grids and other techniques that can be used to support your work to remove spirits and dispossess an object, person, or place of harmful spirits. Bear in mind that sites with intense paranormal activity will require more than a mere grid, thus you are invited to consider these to be starting points for fleshing out your own rituals. However you employ these crystal grids and rituals, always be sure to thoroughly cleanse your stones before *and* after you use any of the exercises that follow.

---

*Though it is not a metamorphic rock, tektite undergoes rapid transformation due to meteoritic activity.

◈ *Ring of Amethyst*

Crystals: nine single-terminated amethysts

If you are sensitive to spiritual forces and the occult, you may encounter an object that seems to exude a dark or oppressive influence. These may be finds from second-hand, vintage, or antique stores, or they may be found or inherited items ranging from everyday objects to jewelry or furniture. While the source of the discordant energy may vary from one situation to another, the owner will invariably believe it to be haunted or cursed. One of the first techniques I'll try before attempting longer curse-breaking or spirit-release rituals is a deceptively simple procedure that requires only nine single-terminated amethyst crystals, some salt, and (if the item is small enough) a bowl or dish for the object in question.

Thoroughly cleanse the amethysts and the space where you'll perform this easy rite. I suggest doing this in a space where it won't be disturbed,

A ring of amethysts placed around an object can
eliminate the influence of spirits and baneful magick.

like a spare room or a less-trafficked part of a common space. If you are cleansing a small item such as a piece of jewelry, fill a dish or bowl with salt—preferably sea salt, rock salt, or kosher salt—and cleanse and bless the salt to be an agent of exorcism that neutralizes all harm. Place the item in the dish, and then build the ring of amethysts around the object by surrounding it with the crystals, placing them one-by-one, moving counterclockwise, with the points facing outward. If you are cleansing a larger object such as a piece of furniture, skip the dish of salt and instead sprinkle a little blessed salt around the object before encircling it with the crystals.

Once the amethysts are in place, call on the higher power of your choice to cleanse, purify, and transmute the object within the amethyst ring. Ask the consciousness of amethyst to help you remove any and all baneful influences. Leave the object within the ring of amethysts for at least a week, but note that it may take up to a full month to completely clear and discharge the harmful energy or entity attached to it.

◈ Spirit Trap Spiral

Crystals: obsidian or phantom quartz, and as many single-terminated quartz crystals as you can gather

This crystal grid is a simple continuous spiral with either an obsidian or a phantom quartz in the center. It is inspired by an ancient Middle Eastern prophylactic device called an *incantation bowl* or *demon bowl*, which archaeologists date back to 400–800 CE. These terra cotta bowls were commonly inscribed with incantations written in a spiral starting from the rim and moving toward the center. Protective seals or magickal figures were sometimes drawn in the center, and the finished bowl was placed upside down at the threshold or in the central part of the home or courtyard as a means of capturing spirits, demons, or other malefic entities. Wayward spirits, harmful entities, and even the influence of the evil eye were thought to get caught up in the flowing spiral of the inscribed incantation and rendered inert under the bowl.

To create this grid, make a spiral out of as many single-terminated quartz crystals as possible, preferably in a pattern like that depicted above. Place the crystals as close together as possible, ensuring that they are gently touching. In the center of the spiral you can place either a piece of obsidian

This spiral grid inspired by an ancient protective amulet
neutralizes harmful energies and entities in your environment.

or a phantom quartz crystal (chlorite phantom is ideal), as both can be
effective at containing or neutralizing spirits and other entities. Leave the
grid in place in the central part of your home or workspace, preferably in
an area where spectral phenomena occur. Over time, the grid will draw
the influence of a harmful or displaced spirit, entity, or other sources of
psychic harm into the central stone, where it can be safely contained until it
is effectively cleansed and neutralized.

Take care to program or charge the central stone with the intent to
securely hold any entity or energy directed into it via the grid until that
energy can be safely removed. Once it feels as though the center stone
is saturated or has otherwise performed its duty, I will dismantle the grid
and place the central stone in a dish of salt for several days to a month;
sometimes I also place it inside the spirit release grid depicted in the next

exercise. You can also cleanse it with the smoke from an exorcising and sanctifying blend of herbs such as rue, rosemary, or frankincense. Always cleanse the central stone and all the crystals in the spiral after they have performed their duty, and it is helpful to allow the crystals to rest once they've finished their work.

◈ Spirit Release Grid

Crystals: selenite, chlorite, carnelian, and ruby

Early in my crystal journey I began exploring other fields of paranormal, psychic, and spiritual experience. This included a brief window of ghost-hunting in my second year of college. The local cemetery near the university housed a number of old, historic graves, and the entire place was brimming with spirit activity at night. One of the most effective combinations of crystals I worked with for helping those spirits move on consisted of chlorite, carnelian, and ruby, as described in Melody's book *Love Is in the Earth*.[2]

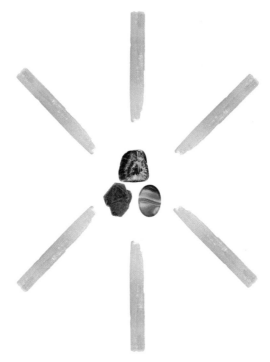

Try this hexagonal grid to release earthbound spirits.

Originally I experimented with this stone combination by merely placing them roughly in the shape of an equilateral triangle around the affected area in which spirit activity occurs; over time I developed the hexagonal grid with selenite added, as depicted.

This spirit release grid is most effective when built around a site with noticeable paranormal activity or strong spirit energies. If you use fairly large stones they can effectively cover a large radius and can neutralize some hauntings, spirit attachments, and similar unwelcome astral guests within a few hours or days. There are two approaches to erecting this crystal grid. The first is to place the stones close together, as shown in the facing image, wherever the paranormal activity is centered, such as in the room or other space with the most activity. A second approach will require larger stones (preferably selenites longer than seven inches and palm-size examples of chlorite, carnelian, and ruby); the selenites are placed equidistant around the exterior of the building or other space, with the chlorite, carnelian, and ruby placed in the room or area with the greatest concentration of spirit activity.

Minor attachments to a person's aura can also be released after lying in a modified form of this grid and visualizing its light dissolving and transmuting any hitchhikers in your energy field. This is similar to using the second approach to assembling this grid around a building, only on a smaller scale. Place the selenite around the body in a roughly hexagonal shape, and place the trio of chlorite, carnelian, and ruby over the heart or solar plexus. Leave the stones in place for fifteen to thirty minutes, then cleanse the stones, yourself, and the space thoroughly.

One-Way Crystal Portal

Crystals: chlorite-included quartz, stibnite wand, and a selenite bar; optional nine or twelve flints or small pieces of quartz

Judy Hall describes this one-way portal in the fifth volume of her *Crystal Prescriptions* series.[3] Gently lay down a chlorite-included quartz, a stibnite wand, and a piece of selenite in the configuration pictured on the following page, and activate this simple grid to create an energetic doorway through which entities can be released; it will be a one-way opening, thus

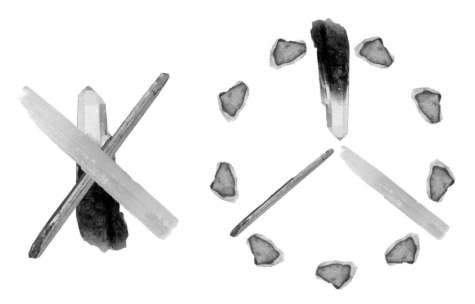

This simple configuration permits you to banish and
release unwelcome spirits, ensuring they do not return.
Judy Hall's version is on the left, and an updated
version is depicted on the right.

preventing the entities from returning. In lieu of stacking the crystals as
shown on the left, you can create a triangular grid out of them with small
pieces of quartz or flint to connect the stones to one another, as pictured
above on the right.

This crystal configuration draws in negative or harmful energy, including
spirits, psychic debris, and unwelcome thought forms, and projects them out
beyond the earth plane and into the light of the cosmos, where they can be
effectively neutralized or returned to their point of origin. I do not find it
helpful to leave this grid up for long periods of time; rather, it works best
when erected for dedicated healing or spirit release sessions, after which it
should be disassembled and cleansed thoroughly. Although it functions well
as a standalone practice, the one-way portal is a great addition to formal
rituals of spirit release, exorcism, and banishing, as it offers a safe outlet for
removing spirits or other entities.

◆ Sulfur and Salt Exorcism

Crystals: one natural sulfur crystal

Both sulfur and salt are minerals with ancient associations with driving out evil, and when partnered together they pack a potent punch against many kinds of entities. This simple rite combines the powers of these minerals with candlelight to exorcise malevolent forces. You'll need a small dish or bowl, one piece of natural sulfur (alternatively use a piece of sulfur quartz), an ample amount of salt (use rock, sea, or kosher salt), and four white candles. Use this rite as a standalone spell to clear away harmful forces, or use it as the central focus of a formal ritual of spirit release or exorcism in more urgent scenarios.

Placing a sulfur crystal on a dish of salt in the center
of a fourfold ring of candles becomes a
powerful focal point for a ritual of exorcism.

Gather your supplies and arrange them as shown in the image above with the sulfur in the center of the dish of salt, surrounded by the four white candles. Take care to select a location where the dish of salt and candles can sit undisturbed without causing a fire hazard. When you are ready to begin, cleanse your space, light a protective or cleansing incense if you desire, and face the items you've arranged for the spell. Hold your hands over the center of the dish, and invoke the spirits of salt and sulfur as follows:

> I call to the spirit of sulfur, the blue flame of
> brimstone, to cast out evil and harm.
> I call to the spirit of salt to bless and purify this
> space, sealing it so that nothing harmful
> returns.

Visualize a blinding blue-white light emanating from the dish of sulfur and salt. Light the candles in a clockwise fashion and intend that the flames of the candles carry the energy of the minerals to the far reaches of the building or space you are exorcising. Recite the following:

> By the power of sulfur and salt
> By the flames of the four directions
> Deliver this place and all who reside here from
> harm.
> Cast out evil and leave only love in its wake.

Leave the candles to burn undisturbed until they are spent. Afterward, dispose of the wax and scatter the salt around the property or along the thresholds of the space. A word of caution: keep the sulfur away from the lit candles; if it accidentally kindles, it will produce noxious fumes that are dangerous to inhale.

Directory of Protection Crystals

This chapter is an A-to-Z guide to crystals that can be used for psychic self-defense. Many of the stones you'll find here are outright protective, bolstering your body, mind, and spirit against external (and internal) forces. Some of the crystals cleanse and purify, while others turn back harmful energy and malicious forces. You'll meet a wide variety of minerals for breaking spells and reversing psychic attacks. Other stones are shining examples of allies for aftercare, as they help nurture and restore vitality when we are depleted, whether as a result of mundane or mystical causes. I've endeavored to include many old favorites—some known since antiquity—in addition to many new and exciting crystals that have only recently entered the crystal healer's toolbox. Use this chapter as a reference to help you select the crystals that will best support your own psychic self-defense as you navigate an ever-changing and sometimes challenging world.

The rocks, minerals, and gems found in this directory are organized alphabetically. Whenever varieties or special formations of a given stone are included, they will be listed after their "parent" or "base" stone: for example, black tourmaline will be found under the *tourmaline* section, and red jasper is listed below *jasper*. Further, there are a handful of stones mentioned in preceding chapters that do not appear in this directory.* Truthfully, there is such an abundance of gems available to us, that they could not all be squeezed into a single book. Thus, you'll likely discover many more crystals that offer protection and otherwise strengthen your skills of psychic self-defense than just the ones found in this book.

---

*The stones mentioned elsewhere that do not appear in the directory include amblygonite, cerussite, chrysoprase, coquina, coral, crocoite, eudialyte, fossil echinoids, goethite, goshenite, iolite, kunzite, marcasite, natrolite, petalite, pyromorphite, quartzite, realgar, stilbite, thomsonite, vanadinite, and wulfenite.

Aegirine

Prismatic aegirine from Malawi

Aegirine is a member of the pyroxene group of minerals. It is commonly greenish black, but fibrous specimens may be a lighter shade of green. It is mined in several locations around the world, including Canada, Greenland, Kenya, Malawi, Norway, Russia, Scotland, and the United States. Its iron content makes it stabilizing, grounding, and generally protective. Aegirine is celebrated as a stone that invites positivity and concentration, lending itself well to warding against harmful influences in your environment, including others' emotions, electromagnetic pollution, and other sources of psychic harm. Working with aegirine is helpful when recovering from psychic attack because it fortifies and cleanses the aura and helps overcome trauma and harmful emotional patterns as it improves one's sense of self-worth.

Aegirine is helpful in removing attached entities and thought forms from the aura, as it is very effective at coaxing earthbound spirits to move on. Try wearing or carrying this stone when performing an exorcism, or grid the affected area for a more passive approach. Aegirine helps boost your confidence so you can use your resources to be a more effective healer, magician, and exorcist. I have found that aegirine is an excellent ally for shamanic journeying too, as it facilitates spirit contact while protecting against harmful beings.

Agate

Level-banded agate from Brazil, exhibiting a thin layer of fortification banding along the exterior

Agate is a banded variety of chalcedony, a fibrous, cryptocrystalline form of quartz. Its bands vary in color and translucency, and agates, which are found in locations around the world, have many unique and distinct patterns. Agate has been regarded as an apotropaic gem since ancient times, when it was thought to ward off venomous creatures, storms, and disease. Agate was also carried for gifts of persuasion, strength, luck, and dominion over spirits. Agate is an excellent all-around healing stone, too. The bands of this gem help to fortify and nourish the aura, conferring additional resilience in the face of stress, environmental harm, and psychic attack.

There are three distinct formations of agate that are considered especially protective: eye agate, fortification agate, and level-banded agate. Eye agates crystallize in round or spherical patterns, built from the inside out. When cut or polished they reveal eye-shaped spots. Their ocular patterns have long been believed to watch over anyone who carries them. Fortification agates, on the other hand, are formed as silica crystallizes in bands from the outermost layer inward. They generally have starkly pronounced bands resembling walls and are generally quite shielding. Level-banded agates—sometimes known as water-line, water-level, and spirit-level agates—display parallel bands that may reflect changes in the water level or saturation; this variety of agate strengthens your aura's natural defenses from the ground up and seals off any leaks or tears in the aura.

Tumbled blue lace agate

Blue Lace Agate

Blue lace agate is a popular variety of agate with wispy bands of blue, white, and lavender. Most blue lace agate is found in Namibia, Malawi, and Kenya, though it also occurs in Brazil, China, Georgia, Mexico, Romania, and the United States. This gem offers an uplifting energy to the mind and environs. It sends out waves of energy that help us sift through the layers of body, mind, and spirit to find and release patterns that do not belong to us, thereby making it an ideal stone to support energetic cleansing and recovery from psychic attack. Blue lace agate boosts one's confidence, releases fear, and calms the mind. It is especially protective during sleep, offering a safe and sacred space for your dreamtime journeys. Blue lace agate is well-suited to protection for children; placing it in their room fosters restful sleep and a loving, peaceful environment for play.

Tumbled Botswana agate

Botswana Agate

Botswana agate, named for the country where it is mined (although a near-identical agate with similar properties is also mined in Iran), typically displays pronounced bands of white, gray, cream, black, and pink. This gemstone is protective and comforting; wearing it is like wrapping yourself in a favorite blanket on a cool day. It helps you feel emotionally safe and secure, all while protecting your aura from leaks and attachments. Stones that exhibit eyelike bands are ideal protection stones, as they avert harmful energies and act as sentinels to watch over you.

Botswana agate exerts a centering influence over the mind and aura. It achieves this by recalling scattered energies and inviting a state of mindful awareness. This gemstone encourages optimism and creativity, and it initiates creative problem-solving skills as well. This makes for a gemstone that can help us avoid harmful or negative situations as well as overcome such situations with ease.

A polished slice of Dulcote agate from Somerset, England, with a hidden pocket of druzy quartz

Dulcote Agate

Dulcote agates, also called *Mendip potato stones* and *Bristol diamonds*, are agate nodules found in Somerset, not far from Glastonbury, in England. Though they are predominantly cryptocrystalline quartz (chalcedony or agate), these nodules often contain inclusions of goethite, calcite, and celestite, and opening one sometimes reveals a druze of quartz, amethyst, or citrine. There is some speculation that these stones may have been used by Celtic peoples as sacred stones.

Traditional lore tells us that Dulcote agates were used for protection, especially during travel.[1] Overall, the energy of these nodules is protective, and carrying them thwarts negative magick while promoting well-being. These stones connect to the intelligence of nature and nature beings such as fair folk and devas. They help us perceive the beauty of all life and teach us to celebrate this beauty. Meditating with Dulcote agate helps you connect with the otherworldly realms to learn the wisdom and magick kept there. It empowers you to gain control over the elements and enhance your psychic gifts, thereby strengthening your innate ability to defend your energy field. Dulcote agate is soothing and comforting, and you can turn to this gentle gem whenever you feel rundown to prevent energetic intrusions, psychic vampirism, and parasitic entities from taking advantage of a weakened state.

Polished fire agate

Fire Agate

Formed when minute crystals of limonite are sandwiched between bands of chalcedony, fire agate exhibits iridescent flashes of gold, orange, red, and brown. Fire agate is found in Mexico and the southwestern United States. Of all the members of the agate family, fire agate is the most strongly protective. It embodies the dual elemental forces of water and fire, allowing it to purify and transmute harmful energies wherever it is placed. The iron content of the limonite offers a gently grounding effect as well.

When worn, fire agate shields and protects the aura. It deflects psychic attack, harmful magick, and other negative energies and returns them to the sender. It is a stone of inspiration and personal power, helping you to claim sovereignty and loosen the hold of others over your life. Fire agate severs unhealthy cords and attachments, and it helps both parties involved understand how and why those energy cords have formed.

Tumbled pigeon's blood agate from Utah

Pigeon's Blood Agate

Pigeon's blood agate is found in the desert of southeastern Utah. It ranges from white, cream, and brown, to orange and red background colors with bright red speckles, plumes, and dendrites that resemble flecks of blood. Like all members of the agate family, this gem invites healing, strength, and overall protection. The vibrant vermillion inclusions contain hematite, another protective mineral, and they send out a kind of psychic warning to deter magickal and psychic attack.

Pigeon's blood agate offers a sense of renewal and strength, making it a helpful ally for cultivating resilience and recovery after psychic attack. It is one of the premier allies for counteracting psychic, emotional, and even social harm that can result from our relationships with other people. Partner with pigeon's blood agate to banish a toxic or abusive partner or to overcome a difficult coworker. This gemstone also promotes reconciliation, friendship, and loyalty, and it can help you manifest the support you need to get through troubled times.

Polished Shiva eye agate

Shiva Eye Agate

Shiva eye agates are fancy agates* from India that are cut and polished in the shape of an eye. They are sometimes called *lucky eye agates* or simply *eye agates*. As a variety of fancy agate, they lack the pronounced bands typical of most other agates and instead form indistinct zones of color. Shiva eye agates are considered sacred to their namesake god, Shiva, one of the principal deities of Hinduism. Shiva is regarded as both creator and destroyer, and is considered to be fiercely protective, so the stone bearing his name is thus similarly protective.

---

*These stones may be called agate, jasper, or sardonyx by various collectors. They belong to the chalcedony family and bear a composition and appearance roughly between that of jasper and agate. For this reason, they can be considered *jasp-agate*, a term once more popular than it is today.

Use Shiva eye agates around your home to guard against negative energy, ill wishes, and harmful magick. The eyelike shape of these stones stimulates clairvoyance and psychic perception, thus alerting you to psychic attack or other harmful energies. They encourage you to take proactive measures to prevent harm. Shiva eye agates are also gently grounding, and they nourish you with nature's energies. They promote recovery following psychic attack and help you handle stress and transitions of all sorts with relative ease.

Amazonite with smoky quartz and black tourmaline

Amazonite

Amazonite is a variety of blue-to-green feldspar colored by trace amounts of lead and occasionally iron. It is common in many parts of the world, with some of the finest specimens hailing from Brazil, Canada, China, Madagascar, Malawi, Mozambique, Russia, and the United states. It has a long history of magickal use, as it was prized by the ancient Egyptians as a protective amulet. Amazonite represents hope and luck, and it leads us toward success in our endeavors while thwarting harmful energies that might otherwise interfere with our goals. Amazonite is popularly employed for protection against harmful electromagnetic fields as well. This gem also has a strong filtering effect that is useful against geopathic stress, mental patterns (including other people's thoughts), and stress. It is an excellent stone for empaths.

One of the key themes that amazonite embodies is that of personal truth. This gemstone clarifies your vision of truth and strengthens your personal identity, thus empowering you to live your best life. Amazonite can thus help you pursue and defend your truth and overcome obstacles. Work with this stone when you feel as though you need protection and guidance on your life's path.

Amber

Raw amber from Indonesia

Amber isn't a true crystal, as it is the solidified resin of ancient trees. Important sources of amber include Austria, Belgium, China, Colombia, Czech Republic, Dominican Republic, Germany, Indonesia, Italy, Latvia, Lithuania, Mexico, New Zealand, Poland, Russia, Spain, Ukraine, and the United States; additional discoveries have been made in several more countries across the world. This stone has been used ornamentally since prehistory (circa 45,000 years ago), and it has been regarded as sacred and protective ever since. This organic gem's golden hue evokes the energy of the sun and the earth; it is grounding, uplifting, and helps nurture success. Wearing or carrying amber is a good overall apotropaic.

When I was still relatively new to the world of crystals, I remember admiring my friend's amber necklace. She explained that amber is an exceptional psychic shield—it prevents others from tapping into your energy field and protects your aura from other unwanted energies. I've noted that amber is of particular help to those who identify as empaths and highly sensitive people, as it creates a sort of buffer and boundary against the outside world. In addition to protecting against harmful external influences, amber serves to clear internal ones, especially fear and feelings of inadequacy. Amber offers comfort, peace, and support from ancestral guides and guardians, thus making it an excellent ally for recovering from psychic harm or baneful magick.

Amethyst

Natural amethyst point from Uruguay

Amethyst occurs when traces of iron lend quartz a violet hue. A popular gemstone, amethyst is found in many places around the world, with some important deposits found in Australia, Bolivia, Brazil, Canada, China, France, Madagascar, Mexico, Namibia, the United States, Uruguay, and Zimbabwe. Amethyst is often associated with wisdom, peace, healing, psychic development, and overcoming obstacles. It has an alchemical nature that transmutes and purifies energies, thereby making it an excellent gem for psychic protection.

Traditional lore going back to ancient times ascribes a benevolent, protective influence to amethyst; it was worn in battle to prevent defeat and kept by sailors to protect against accidents at sea. Amethyst is well-suited to everyday protection, although it is also useful in more extreme circumstances. Medieval lapidaries recommended engraved amethysts for protecting against evil spells, demons, spirits, thieves, and intruders in one's home. Modern crystal mystics sometimes recommend it for psychic attack and for dispelling harmful energies in the home. Surrounding an object with a circle of nine amethyst crystals will remove negative or harmful energies from it and transmute them (see the Ring of Amethyst grid on page 203).[2] This can be especially useful for secondhand or antique objects that may hold unpleasant energies, as well as for items that may have been used in malefic magick.

Tumbled chevron amethyst from South Africa

Chevron Amethyst

Chevron amethyst, which can be found in many places around the world, exhibits pronounced bands of white or pale lavender quartz amid the dark purple color of amethyst; when polished, these bands often display a V-shaped chevron pattern. This variety of amethyst connotes a strong sense of boundaries, so it offers a more potent boost to your psychic protection than other types of amethyst. It is known to repel negative and harmful energies while simultaneously cleansing and sealing the aura. Some crystal healers use it to bolster the body's immune system; I find it similarly helpful for enhancing one's psychic and spiritual immunity, as it removes and breaks down intrusive thoughts, emotions, and energies. Try combining chevron amethyst with larvikite, obsidian, or amber for a psychic shield that doubles to help you stay invisible to psychic spies and wayward spirits.

Zones of smoky quartz and amethyst come together in this crystal from Namibia.

Smoky Amethyst

Smoky amethyst occurs when quartz crystals exhibit distinct smoky and amethystine zones of color, and it can be found in many places around the world. Some may appear as ordinary amethyst or smoky quartz until held to the light to reveal the layers of color within. Smoky amethyst offers a unique blend of the energies of both amethyst (page 218) and smoky quartz (page 300) as well as a handful of additional effects.

This bicolored gem is deeply cleansing, protective, and grounding. It ushers high spiritual energy into the physical plane in such a way that it can dislodge and transmute stubborn and stagnant sources of psychic harm. Smoky amethyst is a dynamic shield against psychic attack. Crystal healing expert Judy Hall offers that this stone repels negativity while calling in positive vibrations.[3] Consider working with this combination gemstone when you need extra support from your spiritual guides and guardians.

Ammonite

A trio of ammonites

Ammonites are the fossilized remains of the ancient ancestors of the modern-day nautilus. These fossil shells have an elegant spiral form that has been regarded as magickal and holy throughout the ages. The coiled shape evokes that of a ram's horn, and so this fossil is named for the ram-headed Egyptian god Amun (or Ammon). Ammonites were known by many names—*serpent stones, ophites* (from Greek *ophis*, meaning "snake"), and *draconites* (from the Greek *draco*, for "dragon"), all of which allude to the serpentine form of this fossil. Ammonites once lived worldwide, and their fossils are widespread, having been found virtually everywhere that oceans once existed on Earth.

Ammonite, like many fossils, has been employed as a protective amulet since antiquity. Ammonite fossils have traditionally been carried to protect against snakes and venomous creatures, to ward off disease and bad luck, and to avert malefic forces of all sorts. Ammonite invokes aid from benevolent protective spirits such as ancestors, saints, dragons, and goddesses. These stones can also rectify sources of geopathic stress and help activate latent ley lines and vortices of earth energy.

Gemmy aquamarine crystal

Aquamarine

Aquamarine is a variety of beryl whose blue-to-green color derives from traces of iron. The name is taken from *aqua marina*, Latin for "seawater," a reference to its color. Aquamarine is found in locations across the world, including Australia, Brazil, China, Mozambique, Myanmar, Namibia, Ukraine, the United States, and Vietnam. The ancient Egyptians used aquamarine as a protective gemstone, and Greek and Roman sailors would carry this stone for safe passage, which suggests its connection with safe travel up through the medieval period. Aquamarine is also an excellent all-around healing stone that invites inspiration, mental clarity, communication, and spiritual growth.

Aquamarine excels at cleansing stagnant, outdated, harmful, and foreign energies from the body, mind, and spirit. Drinking, bathing in, or spraying aquamarine elixir removes anything that no longer serves you and helps eliminate harmful, toxic, foreign energy patterns from every part of your being. It draws out the light of the soul to rise above the powers of darkness. Its traditional association with protection extends even beyond travel safety to its historical use in casting out and protecting against malefic spirits. Aquamarine can be used around the home to brighten and uplift the energies around you, and it can be hung from your car's rear-view mirror to protect you when you're on the go. Aquamarine is a versatile gem that can treat psychic attack and help eliminate internal sources of psychic harm as well.

Aragonite

A starburst-shaped cluster of aragonite from Morocco

Aragonite, a common mineral composed of calcium carbonate, is found worldwide in a broad range of colors and formations, including the popular starburst clusters called *sputniks*, pictured here. This mineral is closely attuned to the energies of the earth and helps you stay grounded and supported even when stressed or under attack. Aragonite starbursts are among the best crystal companions for contending with geopathic stress and unbalanced energies in your environment. The radiating forms of this crystal offer a sense of dynamic movement while still providing grounding and protection.

Aragonite cleanses, clears, and aligns the aura. It gently shields and balances the entire energy field. I find it especially helpful for empaths and other people who find themselves easily affected by others' emotions. This mineral is also useful for communication with nature spirits and the angelic realm, helping you find and befriend spirit allies that can join you in building defenses against disruptive energies. Aragonite starbursts or sputniks also alleviate blocked or stagnant chakras and facilitate soul retrieval, thereby making them good choices for hastening recovery from psychic attack and other forms of harm.

Arfvedsonite

Polished arfvedsonite from Russia

Arfvedsonite, a member of the amphibole group, is found worldwide in metamorphic environments and frequently occurs as iridescent, swirling fibers in a quartz-rich matrix and as opaque blue and green prismatic crystals that appear nearly black in color. It is often mistakenly sold as astrophyllite. This underappreciated mineral teaches us about the nature and value of fear as an expression of the ego's defenses; it invites us to replace fear with curiosity and wonder, thereby negating much of our need for traditional protection. It helps transform internal sources of psychic harm and allows our inner light to shine. Arfvedsonite is an ideal stone for the proverbial "dark night of the soul," as it stands with us through difficult periods as a trusted friend and guardian. This stone allows us to embrace our shadow self and undertake our spiritual journey fearlessly. It facilitates trancework, astral travel, and other forms of journeying, enabling us to bypass the ego—with its inherent fear—to work from a place of unity and love. Wearing or carrying arfvedsonite invites you to claim your personal power and stand your ground when you are challenged by life's uncomfortable moments.

Astrophyllite

Iridescent astrophyllite crystals in a white quartz matrix

Astrophyllite is a rare and complex silicate mineral with a brownish, often metallic color. It is usually found as small, bladelike crystals in a quartz- and feldspar-rich matrix, and it sometimes forms radial aggregates resembling starbursts. First found in Norway, astrophyllite may now be found in several places around the globe; most commercially available astrophyllite is mined in Russia. Many crystal therapists turn to astrophyllite for catalyzing out-of-body experiences such as astral travel and access to the Akashic records. Its iron content and crystal form make it excellent for breaking up and warding off stagnant and negative energies, and it bolsters the aura's natural boundaries.

Astrophyllite is a light-bringing stone that clears darkness from the soul, mind, and environment. This stone is an excellent ally for transforming defensive emotions into effective psychic shields by redirecting the energy and effort it takes to push everyone away so we can focus on creating healthy emotional and spiritual boundaries instead. Crystal expert Samaya K. Aster (formerly known as Naisha Ahsian) suggests working with astrophyllite to assist in exorcism and entity removal.[4] Since astrophyllite also promotes discernment and mental clarity, it can be used in meditation to determine whether or not you are experiencing genuine psychic attack or have encountered a real entity. This gemstone also wards against electromagnetic pollution, geopathic stress, and other sources of energetic harm.

Aventurine

Tumbled green aventurine

Aventurine is a form of quartz that is composed of minute grains of quartz crystals with inclusions of trace minerals that provide both its distinct color and a twinkling optical effect called *aventurescence*. Aventurine is common around the world, and some of the most valuable sources of this gem include Austria, Brazil, Canada, India, Russia, Tanzania, and the United States. While aventurine comes in many colors, green remains the most popular (and abundant) on the market; its color comes from fuchsite, a chrome-bearing mica, and it often contains some pyrite. Green aventurine is usually praised for offering a soothing, healing energy overall, and it is also enjoyed for attracting love, luck, and prosperity.

As a protective stone, aventurine nurtures our inner resiliency and invites a sense of emotional safety. By releasing fear and tension, this gem works preventively to reduce the likelihood of psychic harm coming from a variety of sources. Aventurine also reinforces emotional and psychic boundaries to prevent loss of energy due to psychic vampires and geopathic or electromagnetic sources. Placed over the spleen, this gem can help prevent, remove, or recover from psychic cords and hooks.[5] It's also a useful balm for recovering from psychic attack; try holding it in meditation, spraying its elixir in your aura, or placing the gemstone over your heart, solar plexus, or spleen to help regenerate psychic boundaries and replenish lost energy.

Axinite

Axinite crystal from Afghanistan

Axinite refers to a closely related group of minerals that typically crystallize in blade-shaped structures resembling an ax. This mineral ranges in color from brown to purplish brown, and is found in some kinds of igneous and metamorphic rocks in many locations worldwide. Axinite's energy can be directed in two areas: honing the mind, and grounding the entire self. This mineral protects the mind against deception by imparting a sense of discernment. It is skilled at removing and preventing conditioning acquired from religion and politics, and it helps one think critically in all areas of life.

Axinite is a powerful ally for maintaining continuous grounding, thereby allowing one to release unhealthy energies and draw nourishment from the earth. This prevents outside sources from depleting your energy, especially in cases of psychic attack. Axinite invites you to step into your power while maintaining a sense of diplomacy. It can help you resolve potentially dangerous situations by using creative thinking, while simultaneously helping you cut any energetic ties to the parties involved. Axinite's sharp, bladelike crystal forms make for a potent tool for cord-cutting ceremonies as well as for warding off harmful thoughts from others.

Barite

Barite from Linwood Mine in Buffalo, Iowa

Barite is an extraordinarily heavy stone owing to its barium content. This dense sulfate mineral is found in an array of colors and crystal forms. It can be colorless, white, gray, brown, gold, blue, red, or green, and its habits often include bladed crystals and rosettes. Some important sources of barite are Australia, China, Morocco, Poland, the United Kingdom (particularly England and Scotland), and the United States. Barite is a valuable industrial material because of its high specific gravity and subsequent weight. It is used to insulate against radiation, reduce corrosion, and prevent blowouts when drilling for oil and gas. These mundane uses hint at its value in psychic self-defense.

Barite's relative heaviness makes it inordinately grounding. At the same time it draws down light and energy to expand your consciousness. Barite can seal the aura to prevent psychic attack, and it also lessens the chance of blowback from bindings, reversals, and other forms of countermagick. This stone is excellent for when you feel you are spread too thin, as it increases your focus and diminishes your vulnerability to outside influences. Barite strengthens boundaries and encourages independence and assertiveness. It is valuable when you feel as though you are easily swayed by others, whether magickal influence is involved or not. It is a stone of transformation and freedom that cuts through harmful psychic cords and reveals your inner light.

Basalt

Rough basalt
from Brazil

Basalt is the name given to extrusive igneous rocks with a mafic composition, meaning they are rich in silicates of iron and magnesium. Before it erupts as molten lava, basalt originates deep in Earth's mantle—in fact it is the most abundant form of volcanic lava on the planet, and thus occurs in many parts of the world. Fine-grained and usually very dark gray or black in color, basalt has been an important carving medium throughout human history. In ancient Egypt this stone was associated with the underworld and with the powers of regeneration and eternal life.

Basalt is associated with courage, strength, and resilience. Its mineral content is both grounding and regenerative, initiating cycles of renewal after periods of change, depletion, or illness. Crystal expert Judy Hall notes that basaltic eruptions often form shield volcanoes, symbolizing the protective nature of this common rock.[6] Basalt imparts creativity, inspiration, and clarity; use it to maintain a sense of healthy detachment when faced with uncomfortable truths or potential harm. This volcanic rock can transmute fiery emotions like anger, resentment, and jealousy, which means it can overcome psychic harm caused by the evil eye. Try gridding the home with basalt when the energy is heavy, stagnant, or unbalanced to bring a sense of safety and healing to your space.

Bloodstone

Polished and tumbled bloodstone

Bloodstone is a jasper with a green background color speckled with iron-bearing flecks of red. This gemstone, which is found worldwide, fortifies the body, mind, and spirit, conferring protection and courage no matter the circumstances. Because its physical appearance evokes the image of blood, it has traditionally been used to thwart physical injury and is today used to boost the body's ability to repair and heal itself. Bloodstone strengthens the immune system, the body's built-in defense against pathogens, in much the same way it prevents harm via psychic attack and negative energy.

In addition to being generally protective, bloodstone is helpful in banishing magick and conferring victory. Talismans of bloodstone were believed to render their wearer invisible, and so wearing this stone can be useful when you want to remain unnoticed. This green and red gem is sometimes used to promote success and granting justice, making it an ideal ally for protecting those who feel disempowered, victimized, or oppressed. This makes bloodstone effective for protection and support when you are the target of bullying, as recommended by crystal healer and author Adam Barralet.[7] This gentle and grounding gem ensures protection, strength, and victory in all situations.

Boji stones are often used in pairs; the male stone is on the left and the female on the right.

Boji Stones

Boji stones are unusual concretions rich in pyrite that are only found in Kansas, in the United States. Also known as *Kansas pop rocks*, boji stones are usually worked with in pairs: one with a smooth surface (the "female" stone) and one with large crystals of pyrite and/or other sulfides extruding from the surface (the "male" stone). Viable geological information about the source and composition of boji stones is scarce, but it is likely that these concretions formed in the far distant past and contain traces of palladium, a rare and precious metal. Thanks to their iron content, boji stones are helpful for general protection.

Boji stones have a dynamic energy that aligns, balances, and strengthens the disparate elements of the human energy field. Holding one in each hand creates an almost instantaneous sensation of buzzing as they work their magick to harmonize the aura and chakras. By aligning and fortifying all parts of your energy field, these rocks can seal the aura against harmful and intrusive energies. Boji stones have a deep connection to the energies of the planet and can be used to heal out-of-balance ley lines and vortices. Masters of grounding, boji stones quickly discharge harmful energies and dissolve cords and attachments in the aura. These strange stones also repair holes and tears in the aura, lending them to restorative work after experiencing psychic attack or malefic magick. Holding boji stones alleviates pain and helps you feel more connected to and nurtured by the planet.

Bronzite

Tumbled and polished bronzite

Bronzite (often erroneously identified as axinite in the market) is an iron-bearing member of the pyroxene group of minerals, found in many locations, such as Antarctica, Australia, Austria, Brazil, Czech Republic, Madagascar, Norway, Spain, Tanzania, and the United States. As an orthorhombic mineral (i.e., characterized by three unequal axes at right angles to one another), bronzite is extremely balancing and can focus the mind to improve decision-making skills and prompt us to take decisive action. It teaches discernment and fosters a state of awareness about the overall safety of your environs, both physical and spiritual. Its iron content strengthens your sense of personal power, making it an ideal ally for times when you feel powerless because of the actions of others. Bronzite also helps enforce healthy boundaries, and it therefore provides relief and support to empaths.

Bronzite is hailed as one of the best gemstones for counteracting curses and negative magick. Crystal authority Judy Hall offers that this stone returns negative magick and harmful intentions to their source and magnifies these energies along the way.[8] Bronzite helps us counteract jealousy and malice with confidence, and assists us in maintaining our composure when faced with challenging situations. It is one of my favorite all-purpose protection stones, as it invites strength, power, and a feeling of safety in troubling times.

Brucite

Yellow brucite from Balochistan, Pakistan

Brucite is an uncommon magnesium hydroxide mineral found in several locations worldwide, including Australia, Austria, Canada, Germany, Italy, Russia, South Africa, Sweden, and the United States. It typically crystallizes in fibrous masses and botryoidal (i.e., having the form of a bunch of grapes) habits. Yellow specimens of brucite from Balochistan, Pakistan have become popular on the market in recent years. It is used industrially as a buffering agent in cement and in the production of flame retardants—two uses that echo its protective qualities.

Brucite is an excellent protective stone because it creates a neutral buffer between its wearer and any potential sources of harm. Rather than constructing an impenetrable wall to keep out any and all energy, brucite permits you to consciously accept the energies you want to receive from the world at large while guarding against external sources of harm. It can also be used to dampen or smother harmful or disruptive energies in your environment. Yellow brucite, the most commonly available specimen right now, boosts confidence and is especially capable of neutralizing emotional energies from people around you, particularly heavy emotions such as depression. This makes it an excellent ally for empaths. Brucite can help you decide when it is best to remove yourself from a situation that doesn't serve you, whether it's a stale career or a space teeming with disharmonious energies or entities. It tends to absorb negative or disharmonious energies, resulting in a pure and clear environment—just be sure to cleanse your brucite often!

Golden calcite mined near Rochester, New York

Calcite

Calcite is an abundant calcium carbonate mineral found worldwide. It comes in a massive range of colors and crystal forms—perhaps in more forms than any other mineral species. Calcite is relatively soft and exhibits perfect cleavage in several directions. Transparent pieces demonstrate birefringence, or double refraction, which is to say it creates a double image when something is viewed through it. Very little ancient lore about calcite exists, though it has been used as a carving material and occasionally for magickal and medicinal purposes. A popular healing stone today, calcite is a tool that enables adaptation, clarity, and expanded consciousness.

In the context of protection and psychic hygiene, calcite is proficient at dissolving blockages from the energy field and overcoming states of fear, confusion, and disempowerment. Not strongly protective of its own accord, it is nevertheless helpful for detaching from harmful situations and finding stability. Calcite has been used in Chinese medicine for removing parasites, and I find that it works similarly to remove astral parasites and other energetic attachments, making it ideal as part of a regular spiritual hygiene practice. Black and red calcite confers strength and is the most protective of the family, though golden calcite lends the necessary willpower to overcome obstacles when you're the target of a psychic attack. Calcite's double refringence also lends us its ability to see a scenario from more than one perspective. Meditate with it before engaging in offensive magick to better understand how it will impact others, so you can practice harm reduction with compassion, yet with strong boundaries.

Carnelian

A polished cabochon of banded carnelian

Carnelian is a member of the chalcedony group, usually ranging in color from red to orange (though occasionally it can be yellowish or pinkish). Its color range is due to its iron oxide (hematite) content. It is found worldwide and has been revered as a sacred stone and protective amulet since antiquity. Carnelian seals, amulets, and talismans are found across the ancient world, having been used for safe childbirth, protection from storms, averting evil magick, and inviting vigor and health.

As an iron-bearing gem, carnelian carries the blessings of Mars. It is therefore a warrior's stone that confers strength and protection in all kinds of battles. This gemstone was considered sacred to the goddess Isis, whose magick restores wholeness and is especially protective of women and children. Carnelian has also been prized for neutralizing anger since ancient Egyptian times; it defuses and disarms our own anger as well as anger directed at us by others. Islamic tradition maintains that carnelian rings invite protection from difficulty and worry, bring luck, and avert the evil eye. Carnelian is regarded by crystal healers today as an invigorating, fiery stone that purifies the body, mind, and spirit; it burns away negative energy and harmful magick while helping you claim your personal power. Carnelian is an excellent choice for general protection and for recovery after psychic attack.

Cassiterite

A dipyramidal example of cassiterite from China

Cassiterite, tin oxide, is the chief ore of tin. It often forms lustrous, metallic dipyramidal (consisting of two pyramids base-to-base) crystals and is very heavy. The most important sources of cassiterite today include Bolivia, Malaysia, Russia, Rwanda, Thailand, and the Democratic Republic of the Congo;

historically it was mined in China, England, the Czech Republic, France, Germany, Italy, Portugal, and Spain. Tin and its ores are attributed to Jupiter, the planet known as "the greater benefic" for the joy and positivity it radiates. Cassiterite is often linked to fairy lore in England, having been used to call on the aid of benevolent fairies and to dispel mischievous and malevolent ones.

Cassiterite exerts a powerful protective influence. Its constituent metal, tin, prevents other metals from oxidizing; in a similar fashion it protects the outermost layer of the aura from being penetrated by harmful energies. Cassiterite invokes the jovial nature of its ruling planet to invite optimism, equanimity, motivation, and pleasure while simultaneously banishing fear, rigidity, and self-destructive habits. It is strengthening and regenerative, making it helpful for drawing out negative forces and recovering after psychic attack. This mineral also attracts good fortune and can be used for uncrossing rituals. Cassiterite sparks feelings of stewardship of planet Earth and helps us live more balanced lives that in turn reduces harm to ourselves, our loved ones, and the very planet on which we live.

A polished example of catlinite

Catlinite

Catlinite, also known as pipestone, is a reddish variety of argillite found in Minnesota, Utah, and Wyoming in the United States, and in Ontario, Canada. Formed when mudstone is transformed into metamorphic rock, catlinite is relatively soft and easy to carve. Its main constituents include pyrophyllite, muscovite, diaspore, and small amounts of hematite, the latter of which provides the characteristic red color of pipestone. It takes its common name, *pipestone*, for its traditional use by Native Americans, who use it in carving ceremonial pipe bowls. Very little authentic pipestone is available on the market today, as its extraction is protected to prevent overmining.

Catlinite has been used by indigenous peoples for thousands of years; in light of this, care and respect should be taken when purchasing and working with this stone. In addition to ceremonial pipes, catlinite effigies and other carvings have been found in archaeological sites throughout the United States. Many healers today find the energy of this sacred stone to be protective. Since catlinite forms in platelike layers, it has the ability to insulate and shield the energy field. Its porous makeup absorbs harmful energy, transmuting it into positive, uplifting vibrations. Grounding and nurturing, catlinite helps protect against and breaks down harmful social patterns like racism, classism, sexism, and xenophobia by highlighting the commonalities of the human experience and promoting feelings of fellowship, compassion, and unity.

Cat's Eye

Tumbled cat's eye

The name of this gemstone suggests its characteristic optical phenomenon, called *chatoyancy*, wherein a polished stone reveals a band of light resembling the reflection in the eyes of cats. Cat's eye stones are the result of a fibrous structure or inclusions of fibrous minerals within the gemstone. The variety pictured here is the common cat's eye, which is quartz with inclusions of riebeckite or crocidolite. Other cat's eye gems include apatite, beryl, chrysoberyl, nephrite, scapolite, sillimanite, tiger's eye, tourmaline, and many other mineral species. Cat's eye gems can be found in many places, including Brazil, China, India, Madagascar, Pakistan, Russia, Sri Lanka, Tanzania, and Zimbabwe. While this entry focuses on quartz cat's eye, similar effects can be achieved with any other strongly chatoyant gemstone.

Ancient lore ascribes great spiritual power to gems with lively optical phenomena such as cat's eye, moonstone, and star sapphire. These gems were sometimes thought to be the dwelling places of powerful spirits that could be commanded to do the bidding of their owner. Cat's eye gems are frequently worn for protection. They reveal hidden dangers, as though the gem's ocular symbolism keeps watch over you. They can be worn to repel the ill effects of the evil eye and wayward negative emotions. Cat's eye can also help you enforce boundaries, strengthen your etheric body to make it more resistant to disruptive energies, and thwart both psychic spying and psychic attack. Hanging a cat's eye gemstone near the front door turns away negativity from the entire household, and placing one above or near the bed ensures restful sleep free from the influence of disruptive energies and bad dreams.

Celestite

Blue celestite from Madagascar

Celestite (also called *celestine*) is a strontium sulfate mineral that usually forms in tabular, bladelike, or needlelike crystals, as well as in compact and fibrous masses. Named for its characteristic soft, celestial shade of sky blue, celestite may also be colorless, gray, golden, orange, red, brown, or green. Found in many places worldwide, including Canada, Italy, Libya, Madagascar, Poland, Spain, the United Kingdom, and the United States, celestite is beloved among healers today for its connection to the angelic realm and its ability to soothe the mind and spirit.

Celestite's energy is clear and sweet. Hold this stone when petitioning the angels or other celestial beings for help and guidance; it will strengthen the protection conferred by your spirits and guides. Crystal healing pioneer Katrina Raphaell discovered that celestite imparts inner strength and helps us maintain a sense of personal security as we grow and evolve.[9] This gemstone invokes trust, openness, and compassion as manifestations of strength; we can thus use it to completely step outside of harmful patterns and negative energies rather than trying to block or reflect them. This gentle gem cools hot tempers and clarifies turbid minds, surrounding its wearer in a bubble of love and trust. For this reason it is sometimes carried to protect against bullying.[10]

Chalcedony

Tumbled chalcedony

Chalcedony is a variety of cryptocrystalline quartz; in other words, its component crystals are too small to be seen with the naked eye. This gem's name is derived from the ancient town of Chalcedon, in what is now modern-day Turkey, though this stone is found worldwide. Chalcedony is most often translucent and can be found in virtually any color; when it has pronounced bands it is called *agate*, and when it is opaque it is known as *jasper*. Other varieties of chalcedony include bloodstone, carnelian, chrysoprase, onyx, and sardonyx.

Chalcedony has a soothing, nurturing energy that counteracts fear, worry, and stress. Amulets carved from this gentle gem have been worn for protection since antiquity, especially those fashioned into seals and signets. White and blue chalcedony are thought to be especially powerful for protecting mother and child, and all varieties were worn to grant victory over enemies and obstacles alike. Other traditional uses for chalcedony include banishing spirits, averting the evil eye, preventing nightmares, and protecting against storms and accidents. Modern-day crystal healers sometimes use chalcedony to confer additional safety and protection during times of political unrest.[11]

Red chalk from Norfolk, England, and white chalk from Wiltshire, England

Chalk

Chalk is a soft, porous form of limestone found worldwide; notable sources include Australia, Denmark, Egypt, England, France, Germany, Sweden, and many parts of the United States. It is a sedimentary rock made chiefly of calcite, and it often contains deposits of flint and fossils. Chalk has a long history of use by humankind as a carving medium, building material, and pigment. Outcroppings of chalk are often considered sacred, and this common stone helps us forge a link to the spirits of the land.

Chalk defends the aura against disruptive, harmful energies. Thanks to its porous nature it acts as an energetic sponge that siphons off harmful energies from the aura or the space around you. It is quite effective when used to grid rooms or buildings with especially toxic auras. Be sure to cleanse your chalk often—it responds best to being cleansed in bright sunshine. Chalk also conveys a sense of inner security, as its calcite content nourishes the inner child and promotes mental and emotional balance. Rough chalk can be used to draw protective sigils and signs on whatever you are using to boost your magickal defenses.

Charoite

Polished charoite

Charoite is a violet gemstone with chatoyance, formed by metamorphic processes and found only in Russia. It was discovered in 1949, and the name *charoite* is said to derive from either its discovery near the Chara River, in Eastern Siberia, or from the word *charovat*, meaning "to charm," referring to its enchanting appearance. Because it was only confirmed as a mineral species in the 1970s, there are no traditional myths or lore connected to this gem. Modern-day crystal writers often attribute to it powers of psychic development, transmutation, and deep healing on all levels of one's being.

As a protective gemstone, charoite serves to reveal sources of psychic harm, often helping by reconciling and integrating your inner sources of negativity. This gem offers an alchemical means of transmuting negative, disharmonious, harmful energies in the aura and environs to help purify yourself and your space. Thanks to its ability to transmute heavy and harmful vibes, charoite can be a powerful aid when performing reversal magic or for recovering from psychic attack. This enchanting gem also strengthens and maintains wards placed around your home by reducing harmful and stagnant energies that can wear your protective measures thin.

Chiastolite

Polished chiastolite with its namesake crosslike appearance

Chiastolite is the name given to a twinned variety of the silicate mineral andalusite, whose name is taken from the Greek *khiasmós*, meaning "marked with an X." It exhibits a cross or X-shaped pattern due to carbonaceous inclusions in its twinned lattice. Some of the best known sources of chiastolite include Australia, China, England, France, Myanmar, Portugal, Spain, and the United States. This unusual gem was known in the seventeenth century, when it was referred to as *lapis crucifer*, or "cross stone." Chiastolite was once believed to have fallen from the heavens, and it was traditionally favored for drawing luck and conferring protection, making it a popular gem among pilgrims and travelers.

Traditional lore tells us that chiastolite was employed for protection in a variety of circumstances. It was believed to be potent against the evil eye, and gemologist G. F. Kunz reports that its protection was so powerful it would drive away evil spirits from the neighborhood of its wearer.[12] Chiastolite is beloved by healers today for its powerful ability to ground and center, as well as for concentrating one's spiritual and magickal powers. Chiastolite is celebrated for its ability to repair damage to the aura, sealing it against harm while also removing attachments, cords, and foreign energies. Working with this gem supports success on many levels, enhances perception and discernment, and promotes positive changes, thereby making chiastolite a welcome ally for many endeavors.

Chlorite

Chlorite is commonly available as inclusions in quartz (left, from Japan) and as the gem variety of clinochlore, better known as *seraphinite* (right, from Russia).

Chlorite refers to a group of related minerals that share a similar composition and structure rather than a reference to a single mineral species. Chlorite minerals are most often found as constituents in igneous and metamorphic rocks, but fine specimens are available to crystal healers in the form of chlorite-included quartz and seraphinite, a gem-quality variety of the mineral clinochlore. Chlorite is a common rock-forming mineral, and thus is available worldwide. Fine examples of chlorite-included quartz are known from Brazil, Japan, Nepal, Pakistan, Russia, Switzerland, and the United States, and gem-quality, chatoyant seraphinite is known only from eastern Siberia, Russia.

Chlorite-group minerals are considered powerful healing stones that detoxify and strengthen the energy field of any person or place. They can remove cords, attachments, intrusive energies, and stale or disharmonious energies from the entire being. Chlorite is often combined with carnelian and ruby to release earthbound spirits as well as for prevention and treatment of psychic attack.[13] I've found this combination of minerals to be highly effective in dealing with hauntings and aggressive spirits. Chlorite is deeply restorative and regenerative, and on its own it can be effective for recovery after psychic attack.

Citrine

Polished natural citrine from Zambia

Citrine is a yellow or golden variety of quartz, whose color is derived from traces of aluminum, lithium, and/or iron. Most citrine on the market is actually heat-treated amethyst, although natural citrine is increasingly available. Though rarer than other varieties of quartz, natural citrine is found in many countries, including Australia, Brazil, Democratic Republic of the Congo, Madagascar, Namibia, Russia, the United States, and Zambia. This gem is considered among the best stones for supporting manifestation, abundance, and success. It strengthens the ability to let go of what doesn't serve you to embrace a bigger, brighter future.

In your psychic self-defense practice citrine is adept at promoting good spiritual hygiene as it facilitates the release of energies that impede your well-being. This golden gemstone cleanses, aligns, and revitalizes the body, mind, and spirit to support health and balance on all levels. Citrine works to help you digest and break down unhealthy, outdated, and harmful patterns, while encouraging optimism and confidence. It eliminates blockages and stagnancies in the aura and chakras, too. As a member of the quartz family, citrine strengthens the entire energy field to provide greater resiliency and balance.

Clinoptilolite

Tumbled clinoptilolite

Clinoptilolite (sometimes spelled *klinopti-lolith*) is a member of the zeolite group, a family of tectosilicate minerals with exchangeable cations, mined primarily in Russia, with other sources in locations such as Austria, Canada, Chile, Germany, India, Italy, Namibia, New Zealand, the Philippines, Spain, Madagascar, and the United States. It is a relatively soft and porous mineral with a high water content. Its unique chemical properties make clinoptilolite invaluable as an industrial material, where it is added to building materials, used as a desiccant, and employed in the remediation of nuclear radiation. It is sometimes used internally in veterinary medicine as a detoxifier, although the therapeutic value for humans is still being studied.

Energetically speaking, clinoptilolite is a powerful absorber of harmful, misplaced, stagnant vibrations. This stone acts like a sponge that neutralizes disruptive energies, including electromagnetic pollution, geopathic stress, and the energies of other people and spirits. It cleanses and detoxifies the entire energy field; you can sweep it through your aura to remove psychic debris following ritual or meditation, or when simply venturing out into the world, when you can carry it with you for round-the-clock clearing. It may be one of the most potent stones for combatting geopathic stress, and it can draw intrusive energies from the aura such as those that result from psychic attack. Be sure to cleanse this stone frequently, as its porous nature holds onto energies readily.

Covellite

Polished covellite

Covellite is an uncommon mineral composed of copper sulfide and typically found alongside other copper-bearing minerals, in locations all over the world where copper is mined. It is an iridescent blue, bearing the metallic luster that is common to most sulfide minerals. Covellite is used by modern-day crystal healers for reducing stress, anxiety, and sleeplessness. This gemstone is also strongly stimulating to the psychic senses. It is deeply regenerative, and because it prompts introspection, working with it can reveal emotional wounds and psychic blind spots that enable intrusive energy to find a way into your energy field.

Covellite is helpful whenever you feel unprotected and vulnerable. It works to reduce sensitivity to other people's energies and helps you define and enforce healthy boundaries. It works equally as well on psychic and emotional energy as it does on geopathic stress. Whether you wear, carry, or even spray its essence into your aura, covellite strengthens and defines the energy body and teaches it to filter out unwelcome energy while permitting loving, nourishing energy to feed the aura. Covellite can be a welcome ally when engaged in any type of astral travel, lucid dreaming, channeling, or other work with spirits, for it shields against malevolent beings and ensures that only helpful and truthful messages come through. Covellite can also be worn to prevent or recuperate from psychic attack.

Danburite from Aurora Mine in Charcas, Mexico

Danburite

Danburite is an orthorhombic mineral that often forms four-sided crystals with chisel-shaped terminations. Typically it is white or colorless and occasionally pink; other localities may produce blue, gray, brown, or golden specimens. Most danburite on the market today is sourced from Mexico, but it is also found in Bolivia, Japan, Madagascar, Russia, the United States, and other places worldwide. Danburite has the ability to remove negative patterns from the energy field, psyche, or life of a person. It ushers such a strong field of light into the body, mind, and spirit that there is little room left for negative patterns. Danburite is also helpful in cases where cords, thought forms, and entities are attached to the aura.

Danburite offers a clearer line of communication to the spirit ecology all around us. This gemstone comes as a blessing when we seek guidance from angels, nature spirits, guides, or ancestors, thereby making it a wonderful ally in building relationships with our helpers-in-spirit. By promoting a healthy, thriving, balanced spiritual ecosystem (and fostering a positive relationship with said spiritual beings), danburite bolsters the natural defenses of your home or other spaces. Wearing this gem can create a bubble of light around your aura that keeps most unhelpful (and often harmful) spirits away and helps you build a solid connection with the rest of the spirit world. The brilliant light this gem emits on the astral plane provides protection and guidance while dissipating harmful energies, emotions, and entities in your immediate environment.

Diamond

Rough diamond from South Africa

Diamonds, among the rarest, most brilliant, and most durable gemstones, are composed of crystalline carbon. Some of the most prolific diamond mines are found in Angola, Australia, Brazil, Canada, Ghana, India, Ivory Coast, Liberia, Myanmar, Namibia, Russia, Sierra Leone, South Africa, Venezuela, and Zimbabwe. The name *diamond* derives from the Greek *a damas*, meaning "unconquered," a testament to the hardness of this radiant gem. Traditionally, diamonds have been used for all manner of healing and magickal defense, as they were believed to eradicate illness, drive out the forces of evil, and overcome oppression. Diamond lore tells us that these gems are also effective at cutting through fear and illusion.

Diamond confers a special kind of invincibility through its unconquerable radiance and hardness. This special gem teaches the power of unconditional love—the only truly unconquerable force in the cosmos. Partnering with diamond reminds you that surrendering to unconditional love evokes a protection that cannot be overcome by outside forces. The innate hardness of diamond strengthens the body, mind, and spirit by infusing every aspect of your being with light, thereby making you less permeable by harmful influences. Diamonds, though expensive, are potent allies that cut through blockages, dissolve evil through the power of love, and restore our inner light to its original perfect state.

Dolomite

Pearly crystals of dolomite from the United States

Dolomite is calcium magnesium carbonate, and it usually forms as tabular and columnar crystals in compact masses, and as stalactites and stalagmites. Dolomite in its pure form is colorless, but it is more often found in shades of white, gray, beige, brown, yellow, and pearly pink; traces of other minerals yield green, blue, magenta, or reddish hues. Dolomite is a common mineral and is found across the globe. Folkloric references to dolomite are few, but the Dolomites, a mountain range in the northern Italian Alps rich in their eponymous mineral, has been frequently connected to otherworldly creatures and guardian spirits.

Dolomite is calming, soothing, and detoxifying. Combed through the aura, a cluster of dolomite can sweep away attachments and intrusions. One of its greatest gifts is seeing the spiritual amid the everyday. Judy Hall suggests that dolomite "protects by activating the realization that spirituality is a matter of pragmatic interaction with the everyday world, rather than something experienced in another dimension."[14] Thus dolomite helps you live a more grounded, embodied, and conscientious life, one less likely to attract harmful energies. Dolomite's association with spirits and other guardians makes it an excellent choice for building a relationship with the spirits of a place and the nature spirits that inhabit your home environs; dolomite invites their protection, favor, and assistance and helps you maintain a happy, healthy, and safe household.

Emerald

This Ethiopian emerald has a pronounced hexagonal cross-section.

Emerald is a chromium-bearing variety of beryl and thus is a sister stone to aquamarine, heliodor, and morganite. This gemstone usually forms in metamorphic environments in a variety of places around the world, including Brazil, China, Colombia, Ethiopia, India, the United States, Zambia, and Zimbabwe. It has long been regarded as sacred, and it has been employed as an apotropaic since prehistory. Emerald is also employed in rites of healing, love, prosperity, and alchemy.

Folklore reveals that emerald was believed to cast out unclean spirits and ward off venomous serpents. This verdant gem was also used for breaking enchantments and revealing deception. A heart-centered stone, emerald invokes the power of unconditional love to protect, transform, uplift, and heal all scenarios. It is known for transmuting disharmony and for renewing vitality when we feel depleted, and that makes it helpful after psychic attack or other forms of magickal harm. Emerald's loving energy can be used in workings aimed at diffusing and healing jealousy, misunderstanding, resentment, and spite—all of which may be fuel for unconscious psychic attacks or for malefic magic to be sent your way. This sacred gem also invokes the power of the angels to intervene on your behalf when you feel too vulnerable to take action yourself.

Epidote

Fan-shaped cluster of epidote from Pakistan

Epidote is a silicate mineral common in metamorphic rocks that ranges in color from yellowish green to greenish brown. It forms as grainy masses and prismatic, bladed crystals, and is often seen as inclusions in prehnite. Epidote is found worldwide, as it is an abundant rock-forming mineral. Epidote is a balancing stone that magnifies the patterns within the psyche, intensifying both positive and negative thoughts, feelings, and behaviors. By bringing latent negativity to the surface, this mineral invites us to make lasting changes that will improve our overall well-being, thereby eliminating internal sources of psychic harm.

Epidote is regenerative and protective of the life force. It restores depleted vital energy and blocks others from siphoning energy from us, and its bladelike crystal formations are excellent tools for severing cords and excising foreign energies from your aura. Epidote reveals the unhealthy coping mechanisms that have created a false sense of self, and encourages us to release these patterns and behaviors, replacing them with joy and a healthy sense of self. Epidote reveals the positivity in every situation and encourages us to embrace change. This mineral is particularly protective of our animal companions—one of my dear friends considers it to be among the best for keeping her horses safe.

Ferberite

Ferberite crystal in matrix from Saxony, Germany

Ferberite is an iron tungstate mineral closely related to hübnerite (page 254). It generally forms as blade-shaped crystals and as compact masses; ferberite's color is black to brown, with a metallic luster. It was discovered in Spain in 1863, and it is mined in dozens of other countries including Algeria, Argentina, Bolivia, China, Finland, Kazakhstan, Peru, Portugal, and Thailand. It is an important ore of tungsten, with many industrial and technological applications.

Because ferberite is a dense, iron-bearing mineral, it offers immediate and effortless support for grounding and centering. It safely and instantly discharges intrusive and harmful energies that accumulate in the aura and chakras. Ferberite strengthens the energy field, making it impervious to needy, vampiric personalities. This mineral assuages anxiety, worry, and fear, offering protection and calm during tumultuous experiences. Ferberite promotes innovation, adaptability, and surrender, making it excellent for overcoming limitations and obstacles; it is particularly helpful when you are isolating and releasing internal sources of psychic harm. Try adding ferberite to rites of uncrossing, banishing, and binding to boost their efficacy.

Flint

Raw flake of flint from Glastonbury, England

Flint is a sedimentary rock composed of minute grains of quartz that replace calcium minerals in chalk and limestone. Flint is a common stone found worldwide that has been revered since antiquity for its apotropaic qualities. This rock is grounding and strengthening, helping you stand your ground when faced with the unexpected. Flint can alleviate geopathic stress and guard against harmful environmental energies, too. It can be worn for a powerful sense of general protection or used in ritual to release attached entities.

Flint has been carried since antiquity for protection against harmful energies and malevolent entities, which explains why the deceased were frequently buried with flint carvings and tools to protect them on their journey to the afterlife. Similarly, this stone can be used in meditation to promote safety during astral travel and other spiritual journeys. Carrying, meditating with, or placing flint on your altar invites the protection and blessings of your ancestral line. The incisive nature of flint makes it an ideal stone for cutting cords and excising foreign energies from the aura.

Fluorite

Purple fluorite from Morocco

Fluorite, a calcium fluoride mineral, is an ever-popular stone for healing, as it crystallizes in a wide range of colors and is found around the world in many different crystal forms. This gem is celebrated for lending stability and mental clarity, improving concentration and focus, and facilitating meditation and psychic development. Fluorite clears psychic debris from the energy field, and rainbow fluorite in particular repairs leaks and tears in the aura. When the symptoms of psychic harm bring up confusion, fear, or a sense of overwhelm, fluorite comes to the rescue. Despite being relatively soft, fluorite's density and cubic crystal structure give stability and coax order to emerge out of chaos. Coupled with its ability to cleanse and repair the aura, this makes fluorite a powerful choice for psychic self-defense.

Tumbled galaxyite displaying its characteristic flashes of color

Galaxyite

Galaxyite is the trade name given to rocks containing small grains of labradorite in an andesine matrix. To date, galaxyite is mined only in Quebec, Canada. This formation is also known as *starstone* thanks to its brilliant flecks of labradorescence resembling stars against its dark background color. This sidereal symbolism links this gemstone to themes of hope, faith, guidance, and divine assistance. Galaxyite shares some of the properties of labradorite (page 261), and is therefore a potent tool for protection.

Galaxyite draws down the power of starlight to confer protection, inspiration, and hope. Crystal healing pioneer Katrina Raphaell describes this stone as the polar complement to the light of the sun, writing that it "will transmute the deepest despair into the faith and knowing that everything is truly in divine right order."[15] Galaxyite is far more grounding than labradorite, anchoring the body, mind, and spirit in any situation, simultaneously invoking compassion, clarity, and a higher perspective. This mineral combination surrounds you in a cloak of protection to support and enhance your spiritual work, including meditation, ritual, healing, shamanic journeying, and psychic practices. Galaxyite shields against harmful energies and deters engaging in draining, hostile, or antipathetic situations. It can be worn, carried, or meditated with to magnify magickal and metaphysical pursuits of all kinds.

Cubic crystal of galena from the United States

Galena

Galena is the principal ore of lead; it's a soft, heavy mineral with a metallic luster that forms cubic crystals. It has been mined since antiquity as a source of both lead and silver and is found all over the world. Despite its toxicity, galena was once ground to a fine powder and applied to the eyes as a cosmetic and used as a pigment in ceramics. Exercise some care when handling galena; wash your hands to remove any residue, and *never* make an elixir from it via the direct method; use only the indirect method, as described in chapter 1.

As an ally in psychic self-defense, galena creates a near-impenetrable shield to keep out unwanted psychic spies, wandering spirits, and baneful magick. Its lead content correlates with the planet Saturn, making galena helpful in banishing and binding magick. Lead minerals like galena have historically been used for malefic purposes, including curses and other harmful magick, based on the homeopathic principle of *similia similibus curentur*, or "like heals like." Accordingly, in crystal healing today, galena is usually touted for neutralizing toxicity, infection, melancholy, and immaturity. A simple and effective binding spell requires only a specimen of galena, a length of string or yarn, and the name of someone causing the harm written on a piece of paper. Tie the paper to the galena with the name facing the stone and knot it tight while repeating your intention to neutralize that person's harmful intentions or actions.

Garnet

Reddish crystal of almandine garnet

Garnets reflect a group of closely related silicate minerals belonging to the cubic crystal system. They are typically dense, lustrous, and often brightly colored. Although red may be the classic shade of this gem, garnets are found in all colors of the rainbow. This family of minerals is common worldwide, as they are common ingredients in a wide range of rock types. Garnets have been praised for millennia for their curative and spiritual properties. Today, garnet is considered the gemstone par excellence for promoting overall health, abundance, attractiveness, and success. It brings a stabilizing influence that clears away confusion, chaos, disharmony, and disruption. Wear or carry garnet to invigorate body, mind, and spirit, especially after experiencing psychic attack.

In premodern times, garnet was employed for protection against sickness, injury, poisoning, drowning, nightmares, demons, and general danger. The Greeks favored garnet for protection in travel, and other cultures harnessed the warriorlike nature of this gem of Mars for battlefield protection and to stanch the flow of blood. Similarly, in modern-day crystal healing garnet is employed to stop the aura from hemorrhaging as a result of psychic attack and to extract negative energy from the chakras. Traditionally, when a garnet's owner was imperiled it was believed the gem offered a warning through a sudden change in its luster or color. Wear it to stay levelheaded, grounded, and aware of your surroundings so as to be alert to any potential harm, psychic or otherwise. Garnets were used in days of yore as projectiles to inflict lethal damage to enemies, and today their potent energy can be used for both defensive and offensive magick to neutralize an opponent's magick if necessary.

Granite

Tumbled granite
from Brazil

Granite is a common stone found worldwide. It is classified as an intrusive igneous rock, meaning it forms when molten rock intrudes into cavities in preexisting rock in Earth's crust. This allows it to cool slowly, such that relatively large crystals (called *phenocrysts*) of feldspar, quartz, mica, and other minerals appear in its makeup. Granite is a humble stone that has a long history of protective uses, from mundane protection offered by granite walls, to spiritual protection rendered by amulets, talismans, and sacred statues.

Granite is a stone whose vibration is both earthy and expansive on account of its general composition. It has garnered a reputation for supporting psychic and spiritual endeavors for its ability to provide a firm foundation for long-term growth and personal development. It can be worn to safely close down psychic connections following meditation, psychic readings, rituals, or other metaphysical endeavors, thus ensuring that no extraneous energies or entities tag along. Granite stabilizes the energy of one's environment, too, providing a sense of sanctuary in the home. Wearing it strengthens the aura, making it much less permeable to external thoughts, emotions, and energies. Granite is a dynamic stone of protection that imparts discernment and pragmatism, thereby counteracting fear and allaying paranoia. This makes it an excellent choice for neutralizing the effects of psychic attack. As well, gridding with granite alleviates geopathic stress and deflects harmful electromagnetic frequencies.

Graphic Granite

Graphic granite contains a striking combination of smoky quartz and feldspar.

Graphic granite is an igneous rock chiefly composed of feldspar and smoky quartz inclusions that are intergrown in such a manner as to resemble runic, cuneiform, or other written characters—hence the term *graphic*. This unusual and visually arresting rock typically forms as portions of granitic pegmatites (i.e., igneous rocks), and there is often a noticeable lack of other minerals.

Graphic granite also goes by the names *graphic feldspar, runic feldspar, script stone, Hebrew stone,* and *zebradorite*; it is found in Canada, Germany, Madagascar, Norway, Poland, Portugal, Russia, and the United States. In addition to the general properties of granite (page 248) and smoky quartz (page 300), this unusual rock is believed to cleanse the chakras, remove blockages from the energy field, and facilitate divination.

Graphic granite offers a strongly balancing energy as represented by the contrasting colors of the microcline feldspar and smoky quartz in its makeup. It is simultaneously grounding and expansive, helping you stay present no matter the situation. This rock is strongly protective and is said to grant stealth and invisibility when traveling through the shamanic realms.[16] Graphic granite strengthens bonds with guardian angels, familiar spirits, and other protective allies who can accompany you in this world and in dreams, meditations, and shamanic journeys.

Halite

Pink halite from Searles Lake in San Bernardino County, California

Halite is the proper geological name for the mineral more commonly known as salt, which is found almost everywhere on the planet. It has been considered a sacred and magickal tool since recorded history. Halite's uses as a purifying and preserving agent have been celebrated for millennia, and this carries over to its spiritual qualities. Salt can effectively be used to cleanse the energy of ourselves, our homes, and anything imaginable. Sprinkling salt around your home or at the entrances, such as doors and windows, creates a protective barrier to keep out unwanted influences. This mineral has a long tradition of being used in banishing and curse-breaking, too.

Natural specimens of halite help clear energies wherever they are placed. You can harness this power with a fine specimen, a lump of rock salt, a salt lamp, or even a simple dish of salt. The deeply purifying power of halite scrubs the human energy field and the energy of your environs to purge cords, attachments, wayward spirits, and other entities. Crystalline specimens of halite draw light into the aura and chakras to seal the energy field from intrusive patterns. Halite also has the ability to neutralize harmful beliefs and behaviors, thereby eliminating internal sources of psychic harm just as efficiently as it neutralizes external ones. Salt has traditionally played an integral role in spells and rituals of protection, unhexing, curse-breaking, and healing.

Hanksite

Hanksite crystals from California (left) and Turkey (right)

Hanksite is a curious mineral with an unusual composition, containing both sulfate and carbonate in its makeup. This mineral can be found in mostly arid regions, including parts of Argentina, Canada, China, Sweden, Uganda, and the United States. It usually crystallizes as double-terminated hexagonal crystals that may be colorless, gray, brown, or green; its colors are usually owed to inclusions of clay and other minerals. Soft and highly soluble, take care with this evaporite mineral, as it cannot be cleansed in water and must be kept in a dry environment.

Hanksite is one of the best crystals for scrubbing your energy field of unwanted energies. It is extremely detoxifying to the body, mind, and spirit, as it purifies your entire being and clears the energy of the space where it is stored or displayed. Hanksite stimulates the solar plexus chakra to spark creativity, willpower, and a healthy sense of self. This mineral helps you reclaim your personal power and channel it for the good of all rather than for selfish gain.[17] It dispels illusion and overcomes deception and cleanses the psyche of fear, anger, resentment, envy, vengeance, and aggression, making it a good adjunct to binding, banishing, or reversal spells as it ensures that the work is truly undertaken for the benefit of all rather than out of personal revenge. Hanksite draws out and transmutes the remnants of psychic attack, malefic magick, and the evil eye. As a result of its absorptive action, hanksite requires frequent cleansing, which can best be performed by placing it on some uncooked brown rice, dried flower petals, or on a bed of salt.

A natural mixture of pyrite and magnetite creates the dramatic contrast in healer's gold.

Healer's Gold

Healer's gold is the trade name given to rocks composed predominantly of magnetite and pyrite and found in the desert of Arizona. This dynamic combination reveals a dramatic black-and-gold appearance when polished, and it has earned its name due to its popularity among healers. As a mixture of iron minerals, healer's gold is grounding, strengthening, and beneficial for overall healing and balance. Both magnetite (page 267) and pyrite (page 283) are effective protection stones in their own right, and healer's gold synthesizes them into something even more potent.

Many healers, empaths, and highly sensitive people are drawn to healer's gold because it prevents one's energy from being drained or otherwise influenced by others. Initially, the effect of healer's gold is grounding and balancing; it realigns the aura and chakras and clears out stagnant patterns. From there it works to strengthen the boundaries of the aura, discharging and transmuting harmful energies that you encounter by directing them into the earth. It's excellent for promoting protection without curbing personal magnetism; you can shield yourself from unwanted situations while still attracting what you desire.

Hematite

Raw crystalline mass
of hematite
from Morocco

Hematite is an abundant iron oxide mineral displaying a shiny, silvery-gray color that becomes reddish when powdered. It is found worldwide and has a long history of use, spanning several millennia and many cultures. In ancient Egypt, hematite was fashioned into amulets worn by the living and interred with the deceased. The Babylonians carved seals from hematite that were employed to destroy the bearer's enemies, while in the Classical Era it served as a battlefield charm meant to stop the flow of blood and ensure victory.

Modern-day healers and magicians celebrate hematite as one of the most potent allies for grounding and mental clarity. Melody writes that this humble stone dissolves negative energy and transmutes it into light and unconditional love.[18] Ethan Lazzerini, author of *Psychic Protection Crystals*, calls this gem "the gladiator of the mineral kingdom" and notes that the reflective nature of hematite acts like a psychic mirror to deflect and disintegrate harmful energy; hematite reflects this back to the source of psychic harm, helping the attacker understand that the ripples are being caused by their own actions.[19] Hematite consolidates willpower, improves strength, activates survival instincts, and even cloaks the aura when directed to do so. It is a powerful ally for neutralizing harmful energy and overcoming baneful magick.

Herkimer Diamond

Gemmy Herkimer diamond quartz

Herkimer diamonds aren't diamonds at all— they are brilliant, double-terminated crystals from upstate New York that because of their exceptional luster and clarity are called diamonds. Some crystals contain black anthraxolite inclusions, while others are tinged golden or brown as a result of clay or iron oxide content. Though they display all the general properties of quartz (page 285), Herkimer diamonds are especially known for being consciousness-raising crystals that expand, enhance, amplify, and uplift the energies of other stones and the human energy field alike. Herkimer diamonds induce mental clarity and expedite the healing of body, mind, and soul.

Herkimer diamond's energetic qualities of activating and expanding the energy field are helpful in protective magick. These gemmy crystals strengthen the body and energy field's natural defenses and can be useful for transmuting dense, stagnant, or unhealthy energy in your aura and environment. Small Herkimer diamonds can be added to witch bottles and spell pouches or buried at the perimeter of your home alongside other protective stones to augment their apotropaic function. You can also use Herkimer diamonds to cleanse and clear yourself and your environment; sweep one through your aura to eliminate dense or harmful energies plaguing you, or spray an elixir of Herkimer diamond around your home to clear and uplift its energy.

Holey Stone

Holey stone from a Florida beach

Holey stones, also called *hag stones* and *Odin stones*, have long been considered powerful apotropaics. Found everywhere in nature, stones that are naturally pierced with holes stand out as unusual, and they are thus ascribed preternatural influences. They act as guardians when hung over doorways or over the bed, preventing disturbances from harmful energies, nightmares, and negative magick; they are traditionally hung from a red cord or ribbon for this purpose.

Holey stones' shape has been likened to the birth canal, and this symbolic connection to the life-giving power of the Divine counteracts deleterious energies. The holes that pierce these rocks also act as energetic filters, trapping harmful energies that attempt to enter your space. They can be empowered as protective amulets for both personal and home use; water-worn holey stones are discreet-looking objects that can be imbued with great power.

Peruvian hübnerite
accented by quartz

Hübnerite

Hübnerite (sometimes written as *huebnerite*) is manganese tungstate that forms in high-temperature environments as reddish-brown to black crystals with a nearly metallic luster. It is an extremely dense mineral due to both the manganese and tungsten in its makeup. A relatively rare species, hübnerite is found in relatively small amounts in dozens of locations around the world.

As a healing stone, hübnerite is best known for its grounding properties. It instantly anchors high-consciousness energies into the material plane and discharges excessive, harmful, or foreign energies into the earth to be transmuted. This rare mineral seals the aura in a bubble of safety, helping you feel secure, safe, and grounded when facing uncertainty or danger. It is effective when the fight-or-flight response is activated, as it increases vigor, stamina, and mental clarity. Hübnerite also helps you trust your choices and find answers.[20] This mineral is a powerful energetic detoxifier that unravels karmic patterns playing out and readies you for new, more peaceful cycles after periods of stress or unrest. Meditating with hübnerite brings your conscious mind into alignment with your true will to enhance your magickal prowess and empower your practice.

Hypersthene

Polished hypersthene

Hypersthene is a pyroxene mineral found in igneous and metamorphic rocks. Nearly all commercially available hypersthene is from Canada, but it has also been found in locations such as Germany, Italy, Japan, New Zealand, Tunisia, and Oregon in the United States. Its name is derived from the Greek *hyper* and *sthenos*, meaning "beyond strength," referring to its hardness being greater than hornblende, a mineral with which it is sometimes confused.

Energetically, hypersthene draws forth one's inner strength and helps catalyze deep, soul-level healing. It confers protection by fortifying the energy field, and it promotes critical thinking and problem-solving skills. An excellent stone for empaths and highly sensitive people, this gem helps you maintain healthy boundaries and filter out others' emotions. In times of trauma, confusion, or attack, hypersthene quickens recovery and regeneration.

Ilvaite

A natural crystal of ilvaite

Ilvaite is a silicate of iron and calcium, frequently containing traces of manganese and magnesium in its makeup. A monoclinic mineral that results from contact metamorphism that forms black prismatic crystals, it is most frequently found in Australia, China, Greece, Greenland, India, Italy, Mexico, Russia, and the United States. Ilvaite calms the temper, promotes patience, and encourages a pragmatic approach to spirituality. It has a Saturnian energy that is generally helpful for protection, banishing, and exorcism.

Ilvaite may be the most effective grounding stone I've ever encountered. By keeping the psyche and the emotional body grounded, it makes us less susceptible to outside influences of all sorts. Ilvaite thus prevents psychic vampirism and removes cords. This mineral helps empaths and those who are psychically sensitive to not take on others' energy, and instead it offers a safe route from which to observe said energy and release it via grounding.

Isua Stone

A tumbled piece of Isua stone, among the oldest rock formations on the planet

Isua stone formed as part of the Isua Greenstone Belt, a geologic formation in southwestern Greenland. It is a metamorphic rock derived from both igneous and sedimentary rocks that have transformed over a span of more than three and a half billion years. Isua stone has a highly variable composition that includes amphiboles, pyroxenes, serpentine, peridot, quartzite, and iron-bearing minerals like hematite. Often banded, Isua stone is colored reddish, brown, green, black, and silvery gray.

Isua stone is considered to be a stone of ancient wisdom and spiritual evolution. Many of its constituents are protective and grounding, and so this ancient rock deflects harm, removes blockages, and roots the soul back into the body.[21] The strata of Isua stone represent its ability to realign the subtle bodies of the aura, restoring balance and harmony after psychic attack, stress, or other disequilibrating experiences. As well, Isua stone can provide much-needed levity when life feels heavy, especially when we are in the midst of negativity, change, or psychic attack.

Jade

Tumbled nephrite jade

Jade is the name given to two different gems: jadeite and nephrite. Both are metamorphic rocks made of silicate minerals that have been treasured as gemstones for millennia. Although green jade may be the most popular today, this gemstone is also found in shades across the spectrum and is mined in many places worldwide. Jade's healing qualities and peaceful character have been revered throughout time, and it is still regarded as the tool par excellence for attracting wealth, health, and inner peace.

In Chinese medicine, jade is said to fortify chi, the life force, thereby preventing putrefaction and decay. It is closely associated with the kidneys, our body's filters, in folklore worldwide; similarly, this gentle gemstone strengthens the natural ability of body and spirit to filter out harm and eliminate what no longer serves, thus we find that jade's blissful energy is a potent medicine for the effects of psychic attack. In magickal lore the protective nature of jade is said to guard against accidents; Scott Cunningham recommends wearing jade or placing it on the altar amid purple candles to support defensive magick.[22] However you choose to use it, jade supports your well-being and wards off harm of all kinds.

Jasper

Tumbled jasper from Ireland

Jasper is a variety of chalcedony, a type of cryptocrystalline quartz. It is typically opaque, and its appearance varies in color and pattern depending on its origin. Jasper is a durable stone found worldwide that can be carved with relative ease, and thus it has garnered much attention and lore since ancient times. Take heed, though: many materials called "jasper" that are on the market are not true jasper and thus will have different compositions and vastly different energies; some of these include bumblebee jasper, kambaba jasper, leopardskin jasper, shell jasper, and countless others.

Jasper remains an accessible and able helpmeet in magick and healing. Its lore, which spans millennia, indicates that jasper offers protection against all manner of harm, such as accidents, injury, poisoning, sickness, evil spirits, and insanity. Modern healers prescribe it for alleviating burnout, thwarting psychic attack, and preventing harmful EMFs from affecting one's health and well-being. Jasper is extremely grounding; it nourishes soul and body alike by replenishing vital energy. This makes it a useful gem for any period of stress or transition. Because it offers a supportive, grounding energy, jasper is useful for achieving gentle, prolonged change. It can also be used in rituals to banish gossip.[23]

Polished slab of bumblebee jasper from Indonesia

Bumblebee "Jasper"

Despite its common name, bumblebee jasper is not a true jasper—it is a rock composed primarily of calcite, realgar, and pyrite. A form of travertine, this gemstone is found in volcanic fumaroles at Mount Papandayan, in West Java, Indonesia. Realgar is a toxic sulfide of arsenic, and while it typically requires caution to handle, it is relatively safe when mixed in small amounts in the calcite matrix of bumblebee jasper. The potent mix of minerals in this stone helps protect the energy field and invites positive change in a number of ways.

Bumblebee jasper combines the earthy, protective nature of iron pyrite with the fiery qualities of sulfur and arsenic to initiate and stabilize alchemical processes. This gemstone burns away the dross of everyday life, including psychic debris, unwelcome entities, and other disharmonious energies. Bumblebee jasper is also noted for overcoming weakness and replenishing vital energy after strenuous periods or draining interactions with others. Crystal expert Judy Hall writes that this gemstone encourages triumph over the unfeasible, just like the bumblebee who seemingly defies physics to achieve flight.[24] This makes bumblebee jasper a helpful ally when malefic energy, geopathic stress, or mundane social situations seem to prevent you from thriving. Place a piece of this stone on the solar plexus and another over your crown to restore healthy movement to your energy field and recharge your batteries.

Tumbled Judy's jasper, or eye of the storm jasper

Judy's Jasper

Named for internationally regarded crystal expert Judy Hall, who died in 2021, Judy's jasper is found in Rio Grande do Sul, in the southernmost part of Brazil. This stone ranges in color considerably, from red and pink to green, blue, white, gray, and brown, and it occasionally exhibits zones of pinkish amethyst. Judy was reportedly very fond of this gemstone, and she wrote that it "helps you to stay grounded and centered within the turbulence of the bigger picture. Showing you where you have hyped-up problems, it offers a wider view."[25]

Judy's jasper is also known as *eye of the storm jasper*, a name that suggests its ability to combat fear, panic, and hopelessness—feelings common among those experiencing psychic attack. It instills a sense of self-worth and helps you find your personal power amid turmoil. Like all jaspers, it is protective, but the energy of this variety brings a sense of immediacy and power; work with it when you feel a sense of loss or victimhood, as it transforms powerlessness into strength and anchors you during times of change.

Tumbled red jasper

Red Jasper

Red jasper derives its color from hematite, an abundant iron oxide mineral. It is common worldwide, with notable deposits in Australia, Brazil, India, Indonesia, Madagascar, Namibia, Russia, South Africa, and the United States. Its use as an ornament and amulet goes back to the Stone Age. Notable uses in the ancient world include cylinder seals made by the Etruscans and Romans, which were often carried for their protective qualities. Red jasper was known to the Egyptians, too, and figures of Isis carved from this gem have even been found in Roman sites in England. Folklore attributes red jasper with the power to drive away harmful spirits, ward off curses, and attract luck. It has also been used to invoke passion, love, creativity, and drive.

Red jasper is a reliable, friendly gem that confers a sense of safety and accelerates all-around healing. Witches and magicians often use this earthy gem in defensive magick, especially for protection, banishing, and reversals. Red jasper is emotionally supportive, too, a helpful catalyst when taking a stand against bullying, abuse, and violence. In Germanic lore, red jasper was inlaid in the sword of Sigurd (Siegfried), the dragon-slayer, to grant him the courage necessary to face his beastly foes.[26] Red jasper is excellent for forging relationships with land and nature spirits, and it may win their favor when you need such allies to fortify the energy of your home or office.

Jet

Polished jet from
Whitby, England

Jet is the name given to wood that has transformed into lignite coal; it is light-weight and black in color. Jet is some-times known as *witch's amber*, and it can be found washed ashore in England, France, Germany, Poland, the United States, and other places worldwide. This organic gemstone has been known and used since great antiquity—Paleolithic burials have revealed pendants, beads, and statues carved from jet, confirming that this stone has been used as a talisman against evil since the Stone Age.

Wearing or carrying jet averts dangers both physical and metaphysi-cal. When ground and burned on a charcoal, jet can be used for rites of exorcism, too. Medieval lore says it has been used to make devils, ser-pents, and sickness flee. Jet has been worn in many cultures to avert the evil eye, protect mothers and children, and insure safe travel. It makes a powerful apotropaic amulet, and it easily absorbs unwanted to unhelpful energies. Jet should be cleansed often as it is so energetically porous—cleansing by smoke is the easiest method. I tend to work with jet when situations are dire; it is a useful rescue stone when toxic or malefic forces are at hand. Sit within a circle of jet or wear a piece in jewelry to purify and bolster the aura.

Blue and black kyanite
from Brazil

Kyanite

Kyanite is a silicate of aluminum that often forms in metamorphic rocks. Though commonly blue in color, kyanite can also be black, green, and orange. It can be found as bladelike crystals or schistose masses, often accompanied by biotite mica. Kyanite's name is taken from the Greek word *kyanos*, the same root as the word *cyan*, meaning "dark blue." It is found worldwide, and some important sources include Australia, Brazil, Switzerland, Tanzania, and the United States.

When held, kyanite begins to align and balance the chakras, meridians, and subtle bodies. It clears energy pathways in the body and overall energy field and helps detox the entire being. The tabular, blade-shaped crystals of kyanite make excellent tools for directing energy, cutting cords, extracting foreign energies from the aura, and sealing the energy field against invaders. All varieties of kyanite reduce the aura's permeability to harmful low-vibration energies, thereby enhancing our natural defenses. Black kyanite is particularly helpful for promoting spiritual hygiene. The fanlike formation of this crystal makes it a first-rate tool for combing out unwanted and unhealthy energies from the aura and chakras. Black kyanite can then transmute and transform the negative energy so that it won't be picked up again.

The iridescent sheen of labradorite hints at its protective virtues.

Labradorite

Labradorite is a member of the feldspar group, a family of aluminosilicate minerals comprising about 60 percent of Earth's crust. Labradorite rarely forms euhedral crystals and is instead found in masses of brown or gray stone (though white or clear varieties are known as *rainbow moonstone*). Labradorite's brilliant iridescence, known as *labradorescence*, is owed to two closely related feldspar minerals in its composition, albite and anorthite, which form submicroscopic layers that diffract light moving through it. Labradorite is commonly mined in Canada, China, Finland, Madagascar, Norway, and the United States.

If you walk into any crystal shop and ask for a stone for psychic protection, labradorite is sure to be one of the first stones you'll be shown. The resplendent play of colors in this gem symbolizes its ability to brighten and strengthen the aura, making it less permeable to harmful, stagnant, foreign energies. Labradorite repairs damage to the aura and chakras, including that which is caused by psychic attack and harmful magick. This luminous gem also helps you set more effective boundaries as it filters out others' emotions and unwanted or unhelpful psychic information, thereby making it one of the best stones for empaths and other sensitive people. Labradorite enhances magickal prowess and manifestation skills overall, making it one of the best stones to accompany any magus.

Large crystals of bytownite contrast the fine-grained basalt in this tumbled lakelandite specimen.

Lakelandite

Lakelandite is a type of igneous rock also known as a *basalt porphyry*; it contains large phenocrysts of bytownite feldspar against a fine-grained background of basalt. Lakelandite takes its name from the Lake District of England, where eons ago its sole source was exposed from beneath a large layer of sedimentary rock thanks to the erosive power of glaciers. Porphyritic rocks—those with textures like lakelandite—have traditionally been held in high regard in cultures like those of ancient Egypt, Rome, and Greece, as they symbolized power, authority, and divinity. For this reason, similar stones have long been used for sacred sites and burials, as they confer divine protection that lasts into the afterlife.

Lakelandite has reached the crystal market only in relatively recent years. Crystal healers often note that it opens the heart to alleviate pain, grief, and fear. This stone provides endurance, as evidenced by its resistance to glacial erosion, and it strengthens the outer layer of the aura to prevent it from becoming frayed or torn. An excellent stone for alleviating harm resulting from geopathic stress, lakelandite also helps to break generational curses and heal the ancestral line. Last year my closest friend (who is also a noted crystal expert and author) Ashley Leavy shared with me that lakelandite is a powerful stone of protection that draws on the power of the generations that have gone before you to evoke the wisdom and guidance of the ancestors as they surround you with a protective barrier. Work with this stone to combat feelings of powerlessness, isolation, and disconnection, and it will help you claim your personal power and find success.

Lapis Lace Onyx

Polished lapis lace onyx from Turkey

Lapis lace onyx is a layered mixture of calcite and dolomite, with traces of iron that produce this rock's characteristic bright blue patterns resembling lace. It is only mined in Turkey. Initially, this material was incorrectly identified as containing scheelite, a calcium tungsten mineral, due to its similar fluorescence under short-wave ultraviolet light, and the market still prefers the misnomer *blue scheelite*. It is mostly celebrated for being a stone of peace and serenity, as it calms the emotions and improves one's outlook. Lapis lace onyx sparks creativity and draws inspiration while improving communication.

Curiously, this sedimentary rock has a hardness of 5 on the Mohs scale despite both calcite and dolomite typically ranking a 3. Because it is more resistant to abrasion, it helps fortify our own energy field. The layers in this stone symbolize the way it sorts through the subtle bodies to center and realign them, while encapsulating the energy field in a protective barrier that allows light, joy, and peace to flow freely as harmful or disruptive energies are filtered out. Lapis lace onyx is excellent for removing obstacles, and it can be used in uncrossing spells with good success. Because it is so peaceful, this gem counteracts feelings of powerlessness, frustration, and fear that may accompany psychic attack. An angelic stone, lapis lace onyx invokes help from the spiritual planes to make you feel safe and secure wherever you are.

Lapis Lazuli

Polished lapis lazuli

Lapis lazuli is a metamorphic rock composed mainly of blue lazurite, white calcite, and metallic pyrite; it may contain dozens of accessory minerals that are usually too small to be seen with the naked eye. This richly colored gemstone is found in only a few locations worldwide, including Afghanistan, Angola, Canada, Chile, Myanmar, Pakistan, Russia, and a couple locations in the United States. Its name translates from the Latin as "blue stone," its celestial connotation referring to its appearing like the night sky. This gem has been employed for protection for thousands of years, as it was believed to ward against illness, injury, evil spirits, and harmful magick. It may also be the original material used for the construction of amulets against the evil eye.

Nowadays this azure gem is prized for its ability to protect against envy, harmful spirits, baneful magick, and even electromagnetic pollution. Wearing lapis lazuli thwarts many kinds of psychic harm, and meditating with a piece on the brow or third-eye chakra helps you perceive the sources of psychic harm in your life. Lapis is a restorative gem that fosters your spiritual growth, helps you recover from psychic attack, and reminds you of your inner divinity. Meditate on lapis to reclaim your sovereignty and make yourself less permeable to all kinds of psychic harm.

Larvikite

Polished Norwegian larvikite

Larvikite is an igneous rock rich in various feldspars, notably plagioclase. It is sometimes known as *blue pearl granite*, *black labradorite*, *blue pearl moonstone*, and *elven moonstone*. Its primary source is

Norway, though it is also mined in Canada, Mexico, and Russia. Larvikite is an apotropaic stone much like other members of the feldspar group. This gemstone prevents psychic attack and neutralizes harmful magick directed at you. My first experience holding this stone was akin to donning a cloak of invisibility, a trait corroborated by my friend and fellow crystal author Ethan Lazzerini. Carrying larvikite often renders you undetectable to people and forces that may not have your best interests in mind. It shields against invasive psychic endeavors such as remote viewing or psychic stalking.[27]

Larvikite supports people who find themselves in the role of guardianship. It encourages us to be protective of others and is thus an ideal stone for parents and other stewards.[28] This stone nurtures a sense of responsibility and stewardship for the land, initiating protection of us as we protect the earth. Larvikite initiates contact with otherworldly guardians such as angels, ancestors, and the spirits of the land, helping you build relationships with those allies who can, in turn, help protect and watch over you when you most need it.

Rough lepidolite from San Diego County, California

Lepidolite

Lepidolite is a lithium-bearing variety of mica. It is found around the world in scaly masses and platelike or sheetlike formations much like other micas, and it is most often found in a shade of lavender, purple, or violet, while more rarely it may be golden, yellow, greenish, gray, or bluish. Lepidolite is celebrated by modern-day crystal healers for its calming, nourishing properties; it is often used for pacifying anxious thoughts and dispelling stress. The lithium content of this mineral prevents energetic stagnation and is effective against electromagnetic pollution.

Lepidolite is a mildly protective stone. It offers flexible boundaries and dissipates negative or erratic energies from one's environs. It has a bit of a filtering effect as well, thereby keeping out foreign vibes that can affect mood and perception. This gemstone is adept at granting a sense of buoyancy and emotional ease, making it one of my favorites to turn to when recovering from psychic attack. Lepidolite's warm, friendly nature soothes the internal disquiet that accompanies psychic attack and deepens your connection to your own spiritual nature. Grid your bedroom with it if you are troubled by nightmares or other nocturnal disturbances, and this gem will enable restful and regenerative sleep.

Polished luxullianite from Cornwall, England

Luxullianite

Luxullianite is a granite unique to England, specifically the Cornish town of Luxulyan, after which it is named. This igneous rock is composed of pink feldspar, whitish quartz, biotite mica, and black tourmaline, and occasionally has traces of cassiterite. This special igneous rock combines the properties of granite and tourmaline, thereby packing a strongly protective energy. It clears stagnant, harmful, stale energies from the aura and assists in dynamic grounding.

Work with luxullianite when your emotions prevent you from addressing situations rationally, as this stone enables you to see the big picture. It is most useful when you are under psychic attack or suffering from other sources of psychic harm, as it helps you stay grounded and see things as they really are. Luxulliante delivers a much-needed dose of realism to those who are unwilling or unable to see the truth. The revelatory nature of this rock is excellent for identifying the inner sources of psychic harm, allowing us to integrate and heal the traumas we carry. It forms when boron-rich fluids initiate a gradual replacement of feldspar by tourmaline, which hints at its ability to leverage available resources to clean and transmute harmful or intrusive energies. Luxulliante can also provide environmental protection; try gridding with this stone to eliminate harmful earth energies.

Magnetite

Polished magnetite

Magnetite is an iron oxide mineral that demonstrates a strong magnetic charge, hence its name. It belongs to the cubic crystal system and is common in rocks of igneous, sedimentary, and metamorphic origin. Also known as *lodestone* when it exhibits strong ferrimagnetism, this mineral has a long history of shielding its wearer against harm. It has been found in tens of thousands of locations; some important sources include Australia, Canada, France, Italy, Norway, Portugal, Scotland, and several parts of the United States. Modern crystal healers use it to harmonize the electromagnetic field of the body and for balancing the aura, chakras, and meridians. Magnetite also has a reputation for alleviating pain and attracting positive outcomes. I love using magnetite to promote self-discovery and to help navigate life's ups and downs.

Magnetite protects the aura from all kinds of psychic attacks, harmful energy, and misfortune. The dual nature of magnets is thought to draw positive influences and repel negative ones. Holding a pair of natural lodestones in your hands can extract deeply embedded cords and spirit attachments, and due to the stone's iron content it fortifies your entire being to prevent future attachments. Magnetite is strongly grounding, connecting your energy to the earth to stabilize, nourish, and strengthen you from the ground up.

Malachite

Polished malachite from the Democratic Republic of the Congo

Malachite is a carbonate of copper that is typically found in beautiful masses colored by swirling shades of green. It is sourced in arid regions, in the oxidation zones of copper deposits, often alongside other copper-bearing minerals like azurite and chrysocolla, in places such as Democratic Republic of the Congo, Mexico, Morocco,

Namibia, Russia, and the southwestern United States, among many others worldwide. Malachite has long been used as a decorative material and talismanic gemstone since the days of ancient Egypt. Medieval lapidary texts assert that malachite is indicated for averting the baleful influence of accidents, storms, night terrors, and malefic magick, and that it is especially protective of children.[29] It is a versatile stone for overall protection and well-being whose popularity has persisted to the present, perhaps owed to the eye-like patterns revealed when many specimens are polished.

Crystal healers often note that malachite is well-attuned to drawing out latent, repressed emotions. In so doing it alleviates the inner obstacles to claiming your power, thereby endowing this mineral ally with the ability to boost manifestation skills and foster a general sense of well-being. This gemstone can purge the vestiges of foreign energies after experiences of negative magick, psychic attack, or ill-wishing to subsequently harmonize one's inner and outer worlds. Crystal healer and witch Cassandra Eason recommends keeping malachite by the computer and other electronic devices to energetically thwart hacking attempts and for neutralizing envy directed at you via social media.[30]

Veined marble from the ancient Roman city of Sabratha, Libya

Marble

Marble is a metamorphic rock composed chiefly of calcite. Pure marble is white and often appears luminous, but traces of other minerals in its composition yield a wide array of colors, patterns, and textures in marbles coming from different sources around the world. The word *marble* is taken from the Greek word *marmaros*, meaning "shining stone." This relatively soft stone is easily carved and thus throughout history has been valued for art and architecture, as well as for magick and medicine. In ancient Rome, marble was believed to ward off evil spirits, and in India it is said that marble not only deters evil spirits, it draws helpful ones toward you.

Common marble forms when limestone has been subjected to heat and pressure, causing its components to recrystallize. Because it has undergone such an intense transformation, marble is similarly able to bring relief during tumultuous or painful periods of growth and change in your life in order to facilitate transformation. Spending time near marble invites communion with your higher self and helps you see the sacred in the everyday. Given all these qualities, marble makes for a stone that helps you rise above negative or harmful energies and cultivate greater peace.

Isla rose marble from the Hebrides, Scotland

Isla Rose Marble

Isla rose (sometimes called *isla rosa*) is a pink marble speckled with crystals of dark green diopside and blackish pyroxene. It is found only on the island of Tyree, off the west coast of Scotland. A similar pink marble was said to have adorned the great hall of Camelot, which housed King Arthur's fabled Round Table. Isla rose soothes the emotions and imparts gratitude and grace. Like other marbles it is gently protective and uplifting, and it restores vitality, boosts the immune system, and improves overall health.

This gentle pink stone dispels negative energy and prevents cords and attachments from taking root in the aura. I've found isla rose marble to be excellent for chasing away nightmares, anxiety, and a sense of impending doom; for this reason I often use it in tandem with more strongly protective stones to diminish the effects of psychic attack. When negative energy, psychic harm, or burnout produce long-term effects, isla rose offers perseverance, hope, and healing to reverse the trend and bring relief. This gem also wards against cynical, skeptical, and pessimistic attitudes, and it helps empaths and other sensitive people remain receptive to positive attitudes and helpful energies while filtering out harmful vibes.

The brilliant greens of this Scottish marble result from serpentine.

Highland Marble

Highland marble, also known as *Scottish greenstone* and *Scottish green marble*, is a metamorphic rock from Scotland consisting of marble with ribbons and veins of serpentine running through it. Local tradition says it was beloved by fishermen, who carried it to protect against drowning, and many a legend asserts that this green gem is protected by the fairy folk. A popular stone for overall healing, highland marble reduces stress and balances each of the chakras. As an amulet, highland marble has a tradition of protecting against poisons and malefic magick.[31] Kept in your home or sacred space, highland marble clears away psychic debris and prevents stagnation of energy; it can therefore prevent psychic attack by uplifting the vibrations of your space. This vivid green gem also prevents harm from geopathic stress and environmental pollution, while deepening your connection to the spirit of place to promote rest, repair, and regeneration.

Mohawkite

A nugget of mohawkite

Mohawkite is the name given to a variety of copper ore found in Michigan; it is named after the Mohawk Mine, where it was first discovered in 1900. In addition to being rich in copper, mohawkite also contains algodonite and domeykite, two forms of copper arsenide, as well as traces of iron, cobalt, and nickel. Mohawkite may sometimes have patches of quartz, which lend stability and reduce the toxicity of this rock due to its arsenic content. Handle unpolished specimens with care and never prepare elixirs from mohawkite using the direct method; only use the indirect method, as described in chapter 1.

This rare ore of copper and arsenic creates a strong psychic shield in the aura. It strengthens the outermost layers of the energy field to prevent cords, entities, and negative emotions from attaching. Mohawkite also deflects psychic attack and psychic spying, and it can be used to restore and heal the aura after attack or other psychic harm. Its inherent toxicity enables it to combat toxic energy and actions through the law of similars; think of it as fighting fire with fire. This stone is effective for revealing the source of psychic harm, particularly in cases of ritual harm such as cursing and hexing. Mohawkite also offers dynamic grounding, and it nurtures and stabilizes in periods of intense change and deep healing.

Moonstone

Two specimens of moonstone displaying different colors

Moonstone is a gem variety of feldspar that displays an iridescent, shimmering effect known as *adularescence*. It exhibits a range of colors and is found worldwide, in places like Armenia, Australia, Austria, Brazil, India, Madagascar, Mexico, Myanmar, Sri Lanka, and the United States. The Romans believed moonstone to be congealed rays of moonlight and thus considered it sacred to the lunar goddess Diana, who would bestow wisdom, good fortune, and protection to any who bore her gem.

Moonstone is chief among stones for safe travel; just as the moon travels through all twelve signs in a lunar cycle and returns to its starting point, this luminous gem ensures you'll make it home safely after any voyage. Moonstone keenly enhances psychic skills while also filtering out harmful energy and warding against deception. Try meditating or using a divinatory tool (tarot, pendulum, crystal ball) in a circle of seven moonstones to better reveal the truth in a given situation or pinpoint the source of harmful energies. This lunar gem is also worn for general protection, as the moon represents the Great Goddess who watches over and protects all her children. All varieties of moonstone offer protective qualities, but two in particular pack an extra punch: black moonstone and rainbow moonstone. The former is excellent when faced with the need to move about psychically unnoticed, while the latter helps repair damage to the aura after psychic attack.

Muscovite

Rosette of hexagonal
muscovite crystals

Muscovite is the commonest variety of mica, a family of phyllosilicate minerals famous for their perfect cleavage and platy, sheetlike forms. Also known as *Muscovy glass, isinglass, glimmer,* and simply as *mica,* muscovite is found throughout the world, in white, silver, golden, pinkish, greenish, brownish, and other metallic hues. Its resistance to heat, its transparency, and its ability to split into thin sections has led to its various mundane uses—as insulators, windows, and in a variety of other applications. As a healing ally, muscovite is often praised for bringing mental clarity, supporting self-reflection, and instilling mental and emotional flexibility.

Muscovite is an excellent stone for all-around protection as it helps insulate the aura from unwanted and intrusive energies. Since it simultaneously fosters insight, intuition, and inner vision, this mineral is especially effective for psychics, empaths, and sensitive people who are prone to taking on energies from outside themselves. Muscovite and other micas prevent overwhelm from psychic stimuli, and they help seal the aura after the removal of cords, implants, and entities to prevent reattachment. Muscovite imparts objectivity and clarity, enabling you to better discern genuine psychic harm from your own projections, while helping you remain calm and collected in the face of genuine crises.

Novaculite

Polished novaculite
from Arkansas

Novaculite is a very fine-grained variety of chert or flint with a waxy luster and a white, gray, tan, or black color. Its name derives from Latin *novacula,* meaning "razor," on account of its sharp cleavage and its use as a whetstone for sharpening blades. Found in several parts in the United States as well as in Japan,

Syria, Lebanon, and Israel, this stone is more compact than ordinary flint because it has endured low-grade metamorphism. It has been used historically for producing weapons by indigenous peoples of the Americas, and colonizers in the Americas used it for sharpening blades since at least the eighteenth century. Novaculite has therefore been associated with protection through its material uses for several centuries or more.

Modern crystal mystics employ novaculite for protection, curse-breaking, cord-cutting, and removing obstacles. Novaculite refines and polishes every aspect of your being, from your energy field to your personality, and it eliminates challenges and releases sources of psychic harm along the way. Like flint (page 244), novaculite is adept at restoring environmental harmony by soothing geopathic stress. It is excellent for removing attached entities and assisting with spirit release; novaculite also helps alleviate some of the symptoms and stresses caused by spirit attachments.

Tumbled nunderite

Nunderite

Nunderite (also spelled *nundoorite*) is an aegirine-rich syenite rock. Most metaphysical books and vendors erroneously describe this material as consisting of andalusite, feldspar, and epidote, or as a mix of jadeite and feldspar, however, deeper research reveals that it is largely composed of aegirine, orthoclase feldspar, nepheline, and natrolite. Originally found in Nundora Station, New South Wales, Australia, most nunderite on the market today comes from other unconfirmed locations but nevertheless displays a makeup similar to the original. Modern crystal mystics consider nunderite a grounding gem that boosts confidence, compassion, and cooperation.

As a protective gem, nunderite has several applications. It can be worn or used in grids when you need to be undisturbed. Melody says that it protects against being discovered when engaged in underground, clandestine, or secret activities, allowing you to blend into the environment.[32] This makes it a good choice to prevent spying eyes and allay gossip. Judy Hall recommends working with it to make the outer edges of the aura impenetrable, thus making it an excellent stone when you're experiencing prolonged psychic attack.[33] Meditate with a piece of nunderite over the solar plexus or navel to remove psychic debris and harmful cords, and to seal yourself against intrusions and energy vampires.

Nuummite

Tumbled nuummite with its characteristic flash

Nuummite is an ancient metamorphic rock—one of the oldest rocks on Earth. It contains anthophyllite, gedrite, biotite, cordierite, and several other accessory minerals, which come together to form a flashy, iridescent mass. Nuummite is relatively rare, as it's found only in Greenland; note that several other materials (like arfvedsonite, anthophyllite, and coppernite) are sometimes mistakenly sold as nuummite. It is a deeply shamanic stone ally that supports astral travel, soul retrieval, psychic development, and integrating soul lessons.

Nuummite is a potent protection stone, as it shields against negativity and repels astral parasites and other low-level spirits. Wearing nuummite provides a bubble of protection when undertaking any kind of spiritual journey or astral travel. This metamorphic rock also repairs damage to the aura and chakra column, particularly when caused by spirit attachments and malefic magic. Work with nuummite to alleviate ancestral wounds, karmic baggage, and generational curses, thus helping your body, mind, and spirit become more resilient. Nuummite awakens your sense of purpose and helps you manifest your personal power to attain self-mastery and all-around magickal proficiency.

Obsidian

An obsidian spear point

Obsidian is naturally occurring volcanic glass found worldwide. While most obsidian is black, some varieties (such as rainbow obsidian, snowflake obsidian, and mahogany obsidian) exhibit additional colors and patterns. This stone is one of the most popular choices for protection. It has been used for defensive magick since prehistory, when blades and arrowheads of obsidian were worn to ward off harm on many levels. Obsidian grants the gift of perspective, enabling us to see where and why we truly need protection. It hones the mind to a fine point, helping to cut through the dross of insecurity, doubt, and aimlessness to reflect back to us our inner sources of psychic harm by calling out the parts of our psyche that require some tending to. Although frequently used to deflect harmful energies, this volcanic stone is better suited to helping us accept our circumstances and work with them, rather than against them.

Carrying obsidian can shield against psychic attack and prevent psychic intrusions of all kinds. This stone is also helpful for cutting cords and revealing our own true nature and the nature of those around us. A helpful stone for empaths, obsidian boosts confidence and guides us to exercise healthy boundaries. Although obsidian is a popular stone for general protection, it can be a bit too insulating when used as a shield, as it can be rather brittle for long-term use. Instead I suggest harnessing obsidian's gifts of reflection to help us identify sources of psychic harm and then use this insight to cut the ties that bind us to them.

Black onyx

Onyx

Onyx is a form of chalcedony, a fine-grained type of quartz, though the term *onyx* is often applied to massive banded forms of calcite and aragonite. It is found worldwide, with some important sources in Brazil, Germany, India, Madagascar, and Uruguay. True onyx is black, white, and/or gray, and it is often treated to achieve an even coloration. As a talismanic gemstone, onyx has been used for millennia for protection and courage in battle and for dispelling unwanted or harmful forces. This gem was once believed to imprison demons and ward off other frightful entities. Onyx is a strongly shielding stone and is a general ally for protection, especially during times of conflict.

The energy of onyx is grounding, thereby counteracting feeling scattered, spacey, or unfocused. It nourishes the chakras, especially the root chakra, and it fosters better connections in our chakra system as a whole. Working with onyx can help us release bad habits, thereby eliminating sources of psychic harm that we unknowingly direct at ourselves. This gemstone provides the strength, focus, and stamina needed to make healthy changes on every level. It teaches the appropriate use of willpower, and it supports us to face our fears by surrendering them with love. Onyx reminds us that the state of vulnerability may feel like a dark room, and that cultivating compassion and kindness will light our path regardless.

Opal

Opal is beloved for its play of colors.

Opal is an amorphous silica with a high water content. Precious and nonprecious varieties exist; the former are translucent, bearing iridescent flashes of color, while the latter are usually opaque. Opals demonstrate a wide color range that spans the entire spectrum, with the rarest and most valuable often having a blue-to-black background color with a brilliant play of color. Important sources of precious opal include Australia, Ethiopia, and Nevada. Opal has many magickal and therapeutic uses, as it brings light and movement to the aura and emotions.

Folkloric sources abound with tales of opal's magic. This stone is said to protect against misfortune, sickness, and ghostly apparitions, and prevents its bearer from being restrained by all kinds of bonds. Much lore contends that opals confer invisibility, and thus these gems can be worn to prevent psychic spying and to prevent unwanted spiritual attention during meditation, sleep, ritual, and astral travel. The inner light represented by opal's play of colors banishes darkness, density, and stagnant energies, and its power can be channeled into rituals that break through blockages, reverse binding spells, rend curses and hexes, and otherwise promote liberation from magickal harm. Add opal to your protective magick when you feel that you may be the target of harmful intentions, and it will help your light shine unhindered.

Orpiment

Russian orpiment demonstrating pearly luster on its cleavage planes

Orpiment is a vibrantly colored arsenic sulfide mineral. Its brilliant shades of yellow and gold are the source of its Latin name, *auripigmentum*, or "golden pigment," and indeed this mineral has traditionally been used as a beautiful—albeit toxic and unstable—pigment in art. It is found all over the world as prismatic crystals, fibrous or grainy masses, botryoidal formations, and foliated crystals with a pearly luster. Orpiment has been coveted by artists, employed by alchemists in the pursuit of the philosopher's stone, and used to make poison-tipped arrows. Handle this mineral with great care due to its toxicity: do not inhale flakes and *never* make a gem elixir via the direct method; only use the indirect method, as described in chapter 1.

Orpiment is a crystal that embodies the homeopathic principle of *similia similibus curentur,* or "like heals like"; in other words, its toxicity serves to eliminate similarly toxic energies, ideas, and people from your life. Ancient manuscripts in Tibet and Nepal were sometimes treated with orpiment to prevent damage by insects, and this crystal works energetically in a similar way to deter astral parasites, low-level spirits, and other entities from roosting in the environment where it is placed. This crystal is sometimes used for home protection, particularly for warding against invasion and burglary. Thanks to its toxic nature, this mineral is also helpful in banishing, binding, and both curse-making and curse-breaking. Orpiment's energy is transformative, heroic, and alchemical; it restores and repairs damage from psychic harm at the most fundamental levels and strengthens one's personal power.

Peridot

Gemmy peridot

Peridot is the name given to gem-quality specimens of the mineral olivine, a silicate of magnesium and iron. The principal source of peridot today is in the United States in the San Carlos Apache Indian

Reservation in Arizona. It is also mined in Arkansas, Hawaii, Nevada, and New Mexico as well as Australia, Brazil, China, Egypt, Kenya, Mexico, Myanmar, Norway, Pakistan, Saudi Arabia, South Africa, Sri Lanka, and Tanzania. Because peridot is formed in igneous rocks, it therefore has a fiery quality to its energy. It has a generous and luminous nature that symbolizes new beginnings, wealth, wisdom, and clarity. Peridot's use as a protective amulet dates back to ancient Egypt, where it was worn to protect against envy, while medieval traditions held that peridot conferred protection against nightmares, burglary, and evil spirits.

Since it is skilled at combating jealousy, resentment, and spite, peridot is a perfect companion for alleviating the effects of the evil eye and other forms of psychic harm. The warm and inviting energy of this stone stimulates processes of repair and regeneration while simultaneously shielding the aura. Working with peridot as a follow-up to your regular spiritual hygiene routine bolsters its natural defenses and keeps out unwanted or intrusive energies to maintain the health and clarity of your energy field.

Petrified Wood

A polished slab of petrified wood

The once-living tissue of ancient trees undergoes the process of fossilization to produce petrified wood. Most examples of this stone consist of silica—that is, quartz in the form of agate or chalcedony—that has replaced the organic tissue, leaving behind a colorful fossil in its place. Petrified wood can be found all over the world. In Native American communities, petrified wood is frequently viewed as a protective gem. For example, the Hopi explain that petrified wood contains guardian spirits, while the Apache people describe petrified wood's inability to burn (unlike organic wood) as protecting against harm by fire.[34]

Petrified wood is hands-down my favorite grounding stone. This ancient fossil provides a deep and immediate connection to the earth, and it invites renewal, regeneration, and repair, making it the perfect ally when your defenses are low. Petrified wood helps you leverage the resources around you to become stronger and more resilient, thereby boosting your psychic shields and deterring psychic attack and other disruptive energies. Work with this gemstone ally for general protection and to reduce the side effects of psychic harm, as it helps you overcome obstructive and destructive forces in your life.

Pietersite

Tumbled pietersite showing its multicolored chatoyance

Pietersite is a close relative of tiger's eye, a combination of riebeckite fibers in chalcedony. Pietersite is formed when the parent stone is broken down and sutured together by the earth in a process called *brecciation*, which results in a swirling mass of chatoyant reds, blues, and golds resembling stormy clouds. Originally discovered in Namibia, pietersite is also found in China and in the United States, in New Jersey. This gem is also known as *tempest stone*, a name that reflects its resemblance to stormy, swirling clouds and this stone's ability to help us weather the storms in life.

It is no secret that pietersite is my favorite gemstone. Over the years that I have worked with it, this gemstone has served to bolster my confidence and protect my energy field time after time. Like its sibling tiger's eye, this gem is a good overall protector. The chaotic chatoyance that provides pietersite's characteristic patterns breaks up stagnant energy and sparks processes of adaptation, transformation, and healing. It soothes unbalanced emotions, prevents outbursts, and provides the clarity and perspective needed to understand difficult or challenging circumstances; these qualities make it excellent for uncrossing rituals. Pietersite alleviates burnout that results from physical, emotional, and magickal overwhelm, which makes it helpful when harmful energies or entities drain your vitality. Pietersite generates enough momentum to release especially stubborn and stagnant attachments and oust unwanted energies from the body, mind, and spirit. Take care with pietersite, as it can unleash a little chaos along the way!

Pinolith

Tumbled pinolith

Pinolith is an unusual variety of marble consisting of dolomite, magnesite, and graphite. Formed when limestone transformed due to the intrusion of superheated fluids, this gemstone is found only in Austria and Spain. Its unusual pattern of dolomite and magnesite crystals is thought to resemble pine nuts, which gave rise to its name, *pinolith*, meaning "pine stone." It has been used as an ornamental and architectural stone since at least the seventeenth century, and today it is celebrated by crystal healers as an effective tool for stress relief, creativity, clarity, and optimism, as well as sometimes worn for overall protection.

Pinolith is an effective detoxifier of stagnant, disruptive, and harmful energies. It offers a clarifying and soothing force that shuts down the effects of psychic attack and helps overcome feelings of confusion, loneliness, and fear that can result from malefic magick and psychic harm. This gentle gemstone opens the heart chakra to promote better self-love, foster loving relationships, and maintain healthy boundaries. It can also be helpful if you are faced with activity from spirits, including hauntings, as it helps trapped souls move on to a more appropriate place.[35]

Preseli Bluestone

A carved spiral of
Preseli bluestone

Preseli bluestone is the name of a variety of igneous rock known as *dolerite* (or *diabase*), which is found in the Preseli Hills in Pembrokeshire, Wales. Preseli bluestone was revered in antiquity and has been used in the construction of many sacred sites and stone circles, including Stonehenge. When spotted with oikocrysts of white quartz (pockets of crystals formed during metamorphic events), Preseli bluestone resembles the night sky. Indeed, its energy has been linked to both the earth and the heavens, thus working with Preseli bluestone allows you to become a vessel through which earth energies and the light of the stars can flow, helping you achieve balance and peace. According to crystal healing experts Sue and Simon Lilly, Preseli bluestone represents the steady, complex interaction of different elements of perception and awareness, and strengthens the internal flows of energies, especially those held deep within the body.[36]

As a protection stone, Preseli bluestone is a steadfast ally that nourishes and strengthens you with earth energies. It helps you reclaim your personal power and can be used to break draining emotional ties. Preseli bluestone fosters a sense of stewardship for the planet, making it ideal for gridding your personal place and for healing the planet. It is especially protective of sacred sites. Bluestone has a shamanic energy that neutralizes geopathic stress and reveals the interconnectedness of all life. This stone helps you recognize friends, allies, and teachers who will assist you on your path—and keep you safe—whether they are living people or spiritual beings.

Author and crystal healer Ethan Lazzerini affirms that Preseli bluestone erects a wall of energy around the body and aura that halts harmful energies and directs them into the earth for purification and transmutation.[37] The shamanic, dreamlike qualities of this stone shield us from intruders during our dreams and will thwart any efforts on the part of remote viewers and psychic stalkers. Bluestone invites peace, justice, and vigilance. This stone protects us during periods of naïveté, innocence, or inexperience by offering insight and discernment. Apart from being generally protective, the understandings gleaned via Preseli bluestone confer additional support and defense.

Psilomelane

Polished psilomelane
from Mexico

Psilomelane is the name given to masses of ore consisting of oxides of manganese and barium. It is usually black and metallic or submetallic in appearance and frequently forms banded, botryoidal masses. Psilomelane can be found in Brazil, England, France, Germany, Greece, Mexico, Morocco, the United States, and several other locations around the world. Its name is derived from the Greek words *psilos*, meaning "bald," and *melas*, meaning "black," a reference to its smooth texture and dark color. Deeply grounding and protective, psilomelane instills clarity, enhances psychic development, and encourages you to remain present in all of life's circumstances.

A deeply cleansing stone, psilomelane draws out and removes intrusive energies accumulated through everyday life. Psilomelane helps you maintain your composure during times of stress and crisis, thereby enabling you to think clearly whether you are dealing with mundane concerns or psychic harm. Psilomelane reflects negativity back to its source with the intention that it will help the source examine why and from where it arises. This stone offers support for general protection and aftercare following psychic attack, and is helpful in binding and reversal magick, too. Sweep it through your aura or spray an elixir around your energy field and home to clear away energies that have not yet rooted themselves, thereby preventing harmful energies from creating long-term concerns. However, take note that due to the presence of barium, which is toxic, a psilomelane elixir should only be made via the indirect method as described in chapter 1.

Raw purpurite
from Brazil

Purpurite

Purpurite is a manganese phosphate with variable amounts of iron. It is found in shades of purple—hence its name—and typically forms in masses rather than as discrete crystals. Rich, purplish masses of gem-quality purpurite are available from Brazil, Namibia, and the United States, and this mineral can be found in other countries, including Argentina, Australia, Canada, China, France, Russia, and more. Purpurite forms as a byproduct of the alteration of another mineral, triphylite, and most specimens on the market have been acid-washed to encourage this transformation from one mineral to another. Purpurite is thought by crystal healers today to embody themes associated with the violet ray, including alchemy, transformation, compassion, freedom, and mercy.

One of purpurite's key messages is that of freedom. This mineral reveals the constraints that hold us in place, particularly those we place on ourselves and inherit from our family or community. It liberates the mind from old patterns and conditions that have held us back and erodes the barriers placed on us by others' thoughts, emotions, and magick. Judy Hall calls this stone the "curse protector" for its ability to defend against and dissolve curses, hexes, and other harmful workings.[38] This gentle yet potent gemstone provides psychic protection of all kinds, as it diminishes the external influences in one's aura and environment. It provides the impetus needed to break free from toxic persons, groups, jobs, and more.

Purpurite helps you overcome feelings of fear, despondency, victimhood, and other negative experiences that may have arisen as a result of psychic attack, and it is an excellent choice for reversal magick, as it restores your vitality, luck, money, and other resources that have been targeted by harmful magick or disruptive energy.

Pyrite

A nodule of pyrite
from Colombia

Pyrite, also called *iron pyrite* and *fool's gold*, is an iron sulfide mineral that belongs to the cubic crystal system. It is typically seen as a golden cube, octahedron, dodecahedron, sunlike disc, glittering mass, or rounded concretion. One of the most common sulfide minerals, pyrite is common throughout the world, and it has a long history of use by humans. It was employed as an apotropaic in China, and polished mirrors of pyrite are well-attested to among indigenous peoples of Central America. The power of pyrite is often harnessed for protection, wealth, and grounding.

Pyrite's iron and sulfur content make it a formidable protection ally. It bolsters strength and stamina and helps clear away harmful energies in your environment. It builds feelings of self-worth and enhances willpower, thus protecting against criticism, gaslighting, and manipulation, whether mundane or magickal in nature. Placed on your desk at work,

Directory of Protection Crystals

pyrite deflects anger, jealousy, and other workplace unpleasantries from dampening your spirit. Set a shiny piece of pyrite near the front door of your home to draw in wealth and turn away harmful energies. When psychic vampirism, oversensitivity, or oppressive environments have sapped your energy, carry pyrite in your pocket to jump-start your vitality and spark your creativity.

Pyrolusite

Acicular (needlelike) pyrolusite from Germany

Pyrolusite is an oxide of manganese, frequently mined as an ore of this metal. It is a member of the tetragonal crystal system, and it usually crystallizes as botryoidal masses or needlelike sprays of crystals. It can be black or dark gray in color and matte or metallic in luster. This mineral is found in many regions worldwide, including some historically important finds in Austria, Czech Republic, Germany, Mexico, Portugal, Romania, and parts of the United States. Deeply grounding, pyrolusite is noted for its warriorlike energy that provides strength, resilience, ambition, and drive. It dispels energetic interference on all planes, so it is useful for general protection as well as when added to rituals where psychic secrecy is needed. Judy Hall recommends working with pyrolusite to thwart outside influences coming from strong-minded people, to dissolve emotional manipulation, and to create a barrier against inhabitants of the lower astral planes.[39]

Pyrolusite not only grounds and protects, it is also helpful in identifying and addressing the underlying causes of life's problems. You can meditate with a piece when trying to identify sources of psychic harm or place some on your altar when performing reversal or banishing spells when the source is unknown. This uncommon mineral is an excellent ally for magickal defense that can help you eliminate inner sources of harm and feel more secure wherever you go.

Quantum Quattro

Tumbled quantum quattro
from Namibia

Quantum quattro, also known as *quantum quattro silica* and *quantum quattro stone*, is the trade name given to massive quartz (i.e., silica) with inclusions of mostly chrysocolla and shattuckite, and occasionally with small amounts of malachite, dioptase, and ajoite. Originally found in Namibia, similar materials (with similar properties) have been found elsewhere that are sold under the name *phoenix stone*. First discovered in the mid to late 1990s, quantum quattro was thereafter marketed as "the millennium stone," as it was felt by many to embody the principles of hope, equanimity, and transformation desired in the coming Age of Aquarius.

Quantum quattro, with its rich copper content and brilliant shades of blue and green, is a gem that invites a positive attitude and instills inner clarity. Its purifying energy promotes detoxification on every level, and it is especially helpful for encouraging negative energies to gently drop away.[40] The visionary combination of minerals in quantum quattro confers protection during spiritual pursuits, as it keeps outside forces at bay when you are relaxed and receptive during meditation, trance, ritual, and channeling. It can be used to eliminate psychic debris and karmic cords, as well as for breaking hypnotic, coercive, or other ties resulting from psychic attack or malefic magick. This "new millennium" gemstone alleviates geopathic stress by restoring equilibrium to environmental energies, and it absorbs and transmutes heavy, uncomfortable, and displaced emotional energies, too.

Quartz

Clear quartz
from Colombia

Quartz is one of the most common minerals on Earth. It is found worldwide in a wide range of geologic environments. Quartz comes in every color of the rainbow and in a diverse array of crystal habits. The classic clear quartz point, shown above, has been universally regarded as a sacred tool throughout the world in all eras of human history, used for protection, healing, luck, divination, and many other purposes.

Clear quartz is considered to be an amplifier of energies, thus it naturally expands and strengthens the human energy field, making it more resistant to outside influences. Quartz can be worn or carried for a simple, passive form of energy protection, as it bolsters your aura even without your conscious direction. Quartz brings light, clarity, and balance to the aura and chakras, thereby ensuring overall healing and harmony. You can work with quartz for preventing psychic attack by outside forces by gridding your home with it. Quartz is also quite effective for ameliorating geopathic stress and restoring health and vitality following any kind of psychic harm, attack, or curse. This versatile crystal provides clarity and discipline to help you follow your spiritual path, lighting the way to balance, peace, and wholeness.

Faden Quartz

Faden quartz forms in Alpine-type fissures in metamorphic rocks, and this unique environment contributes to this stone's unusual appearance, which is marked by an inclusion resembling white twine or yarn (hence *faden*, meaning "twine" in German). Its characteristic inclusions are created by a geological process of repeatedly breaking followed by healing and growth. Some of the best-known sources of faden quartz include Colombia, Germany, Pakistan, Russia, Switzerland, and Arkansas in the United States.

Faden quartz has a pronounced milky inclusion resembling twine or yarn.

Faden crystals are remarkably versatile tools for healing. Given that they have broken and healed many times over, they are masters of self-healing, and they can stitch together broken, damaged, or torn parts of the energy field. Faden quartz cleanses and purifies all the bodies of the aura and removes blockages and attachments to the chakras themselves. When used in meditation and ritual, faden quartz enhances astral travel and shamanic journeying, protecting the integrity of the energy field along the way. It can also be gridded to treat geopathic stress and to help eliminate electromagnetic pollution.

Hematite phantom quartz from Tamil Nadu, India

Phantom Quartz

Phantom crystals occur when changes in a crystal's environment cause a change in color or appearance, which are recorded as a ghostly imprint within the crystal's form. Most often phantoms are created when a foreign mineral is deposited on the surface of a still-growing crystal, capturing the outline of the crystal's former self as it continues to grow. Phantom crystals vary in color, texture, and appearance depending on the nature of the minerals comprising the phantom, and they will exhibit the properties of those minerals in addition to the general properties of phantom quartz.

Phantom quartz preserves the spirit when we are faced with change and transformation. It identifies the forces in your life that might inhibit personal growth, and works to encapsulate them so they can no longer cause harm. Most varieties of phantom quartz will assist you in returning to a state of innocence, purity, and peace such as that experienced by the soul between incarnations; this makes them useful in clearing away psychic debris and the influence of harmful magick, ill-wishing, and other forms of psychic harm. One of the more innovative ways I've employed phantom quartz in my practice is to repurpose it as a spirit trap. Just as the crystal freezes a ghostly impression of its former self within, phantom quartz can be a powerful tool for holding, neutralizing, or otherwise trapping errant spirits that wander too close. Do take note that this crystal requires programming or charging if you have this specific task in mind, as an unprogrammed phantom quartz sitting on a shelf or altar generally won't absorb entities that are just passing through. Even programmed, a phantom quartz may require the additional assistance of a grid or ritual to make it effective against invasive harmful energies.

Tumbled quartz replete with golden needles of rutile

Rutilated Quartz

Rutilated quartz occurs when two minerals, quartz and rutile, combine. Rutile is titanium dioxide, and it usually appears as golden, silvery, or even reddish fibers or needles inside clear or smoky quartz. This natural crystal combination goes by a variety of folk names, including *fleches d'amour* ("arrows of love"), *hair of Venus*, and *angel hair*. Traditionally worn for love, health, and protection, this beautifully included form of quartz augments personal power and promotes meaningful connection to improve relationships and communication. Rutilated quartz is found worldwide.

Quartz and rutile come together to create a dynamic and protective gemstone. Rutilated quartz boosts the natural flow of energy within your body, mind, and spirit as well as in the environment around you. This gem assuages fears and helps you tackle problems head-on. It has also been thought to enhance communion with the Divine, granting the favor of the gods for protection, healing, and manifestation. It confers strength and optimism while offering a warriorlike, fiery shield that defends your aura. World folklore tells us that entities such as ghosts, vampires, and other malevolent, nocturnal beings will stop to count scattered grain, holes in a sieve, and other near-innumerable items; the sun inevitably rises and sends them into retreat, thus preventing their entry into your home. You can achieve the same kind of protection by hanging a piece of densely packed rutilated quartz by a door or window, thereby averting wayward spirits and other hostile entities who will need to count every fiber of rutile.

Bright yellow plumes of sulfur are trapped in this clear quartz crystal.

Sulfur Quartz

Sulfur quartz, as its name implies, is quartz filled with yellow clouds of sulfur inclusions. It is a bit of a geological oddity, as quartz and native sulfur rarely occur in similar geological environments, and most of what is found today comes from Brazil. Sulfur quartz occurs in cloudy masses, small prismatic crystals, and occasionally as clusters.

This brilliant stone is a dynamic tool for ridding the aura of astral parasites, energetic cords, and psychic debris. It works like an etheric antiseptic to clear out wounds, leaks, and tears in the aura to prevent intrusions from entering. It also knits together holes and tears in the etheric body, thereby making it less susceptible to outside influences. Some healers and crystal mystics work with sulfur quartz to protect against mind control and visitations by extraterrestrials, harmful spirits, and cryptids.[41] As the quartz magnifies the sulfur content, it creates an energy field that expunges intrusive, disruptive, and malevolent forces; wearing or carrying sulfur quartz can therefore ward off harmful spirits and enhance any rituals related to banishing, binding, and exorcizing unwanted people, spirits, and other forces. Sulfur quartz not only protects and purifies, it also sparks passion, zeal, and joy to help us pursue our purpose.

Tibetan Quartz

Double-terminated
quartz from Tibet

Quartz from the Himalayas is famous for its unusual formations, inclusions, and mineral associations. Tibetan quartz of the type described here* contains inclusions of carbon-rich anthraxolite and other minerals; it also frequently contains fluid- and gas-filled pockets known as *enhydros*. Many specimens are double-terminated, similar in shape to Herkimer diamonds (page 253).

Tibetan quartz is a supremely balancing and cleansing crystal that shields the aura and increases resilience. It protects and purifies all parts of the energy field, including the major and minor chakras, nadis, meridians, and layers of the aura. Tibetan quartz decreases codependence and prevents psychic vampirism. It regenerates and revitalizes the energy field, thereby assisting in recovery from psychic attack, and it helps clear away karmic and ancestral patterns that may be hindering your forward movement. An ideal stone for planetary healing, it instills hope and optimism while sparking a sense of justice, social responsibility, compassion, and equanimity.

---

*It's worth noting that a lot of this material is not actually mined in Tibet, but in the neighboring province of Sichuan, China. The quartz is more or less identical, with the same properties, but it commands a higher value when marketed as Tibetan quartz, irrespective of its origin. It is also sold under the names *black phantom quartz*, *black spot quartz*, and *Himalayan quartz*, but bear in mind that these names are also applied to unrelated crystals from other regions. For the most part, whether these crystals come from Tibet or neighboring regions, they will exhibit the same properties.

A natural Brazilian quartz crystal studded with rods of black tourmaline

Tourmalinated Quartz

When quartz and tourmaline originate at the same time, rods or needles of the latter may permeate quartz crystals to produce tourmalinated quartz. Most often the resulting formation contains black tourmaline in white or clear quartz, but any number of color variations and combinations are possible. Tourmalinated quartz is found in both discrete crystals and anhedral masses of quartz, and it is common in geologic environments where both minerals are found, such as Brazil, Madagascar, Namibia, Pakistan, and several parts of the United States. We'll address black tourmaline in quartz here, since it is the most common combination.

Tourmalinated quartz is one of my favorite tools for aura cleansing and protection. This combination crystal acts like both a spiritual shield and an etheric vacuum cleaner that removes blockages, stagnant energies, attachments, and other sources of energetic harm and imbalance from the aura and chakras. This crystal helps repair damage to the aura, so it can be used as a preventive measure to reduce susceptibility to psychic attack or as aftercare to ameliorate the effects of psychic harm. Tourmalinated quartz also harmonizes complementary or polar forces, thereby inviting balance and serenity on all levels of your being. It clears confusion, purges fear, reduces anguish, and helps you feel more grounded and self-assured every moment of the day.

A teardrop cabochon of rhodonite from Cornwall, England

Rhodonite

Rhodonite is a manganese chain silicate belonging to the triclinic crystal system and is usually found in shades of pink and red marbled with veins of black manganese oxide. Although it is most often found in masses, it can also produce blocky, bladelike, rosette-shaped crystals. Important sources of rhodonite include Australia, Brazil, Canada,

China, England, Japan, Madagascar, Peru, Sweden, Switzerland, Russia, and the United States. Rhodonite is fortifying and soothing to the emotions, offering comfort, stability, and self-assurance, making it something of an everyday protection stone.

It's no secret that I have a soft spot for rhodonite, and it is easily one of my most trusted allies in the mineral kingdom. This mineral usually forms in metamorphic environments, in a process that resembles the way skin heals when wounded. In a similar fashion, rhodonite can be used to soothe emotional wounds and seal the emotional body when it is damaged by psychic harm. Rhodonite is adept at helping us navigate any strong emotion, including the fear, confusion, and hopelessness that can arise when we are confronted with potential danger. This rose-colored gem offers an emotional anchor and gentle, loving nourishment whenever we are faced with the things that terrify us. This makes it particularly useful when confronted with psychic attack, injustice, or other situations where we feel threatened and vulnerable.

Rose Quartz

Polished rose quartz

Rose quartz is found in two distinct forms: massive quartz without crystal forms that is colored by tiny fibers of dumortierite; and gemmy, etched crystals whose rosy hues are owed to traces of aluminum and phosphorus. The massive variety is known worldwide, but the gemmy, crystalline variety is found only in Minas Gerais, Brazil; Oxnard County, Maine, United States; and Nuristan, Afghanistan. Most rose quartz is pink, but some occurrences may be grayish, red, lavender, and bluish. Rose quartz is a gemstone of love, self-worth, and emotional healing, and it is an excellent choice for general well-being.

Meditating with and carrying rose quartz helps you exude an aura of peace and love that naturally deters disruptive energy; use it to make a sweet, loving psychic shield to keep harm at bay. It is also useful when recuperating from psychic attack, as it addresses the emotional effects of psychic harm and helps restore balance inside and out. Rose quartz can be employed in binding spells, especially those geared to halting gossip, spite, or noisy animals; to do so, press a piece of rose quartz into the mouth of a clay figure representing the offender.[42] Alternatively, you can add a small piece of rose quartz to a pouch or charm bag or place one atop an image of the offender or on a piece of paper with their name written on it.

Ruby

Natural ruby crystal

Ruby is a variety of corundum whose characteristic red color comes from minute amounts of chromium. This gemstone is mined in various locations, including Afghanistan, Brazil, Cambodia, India, Macedonia, Namibia, Nepal, Pakistan, Tanzania, and Vietnam. Rubies are durable, rare, and beautiful, and accordingly have been assigned great power and value throughout the ages.

The crimson ruby is strongly grounding and strengthening, symbolizing power and vitality. This gem is often likened to the color of blood, and it therefore has symbolized safety from physical (and spiritual) harm, particularly in battle. Ruby is a gem of emotional fortitude, enabling us to lean into discomfort along the path to wholeness. As a stone of protection, ruby is associated with victory and power. It has long been worn to conquer enemies both on and off the battlefield, and wearing a ruby can lend additional strength to spells aimed at banishing, binding, reversals, and justice. Carry this gem to deflect negativity, envy, and fear, and to draw out your charisma and joy.

Sardonyx

Tumbled sardonyx typically reveals visible bands or layers.

Sardonyx, whose name is a portmanteau of *sard* (the old name for carnelian) and *onyx*, is a banded or patchy form of chalcedony whose color ranges from white, gray, black, brown, red, orange, and occasionally green. Fine examples of sardonyx are mined in Brazil, Czech Republic, Germany,

India, Madagascar, Slovakia, and Uruguay. Exhibiting the properties of both carnelian and onyx, it is a highly protective and grounding stone that improves willpower and enhances the strength of your character. It was once engraved with images of protective deities such as Mars and Hercules to enhance its apotropaic uses.

Sardonyx promotes feelings of safety even in the face of adversity. This gemstone is recommended to ward against theft and other criminal activities.[43] Grid it around the home or carry it with you if you find yourself in unsafe environs. Sardonyx is thought to lift heavy and somber moods, yielding joy and happiness in its place. This stone strengthens the voice and improves our relationships (romantic or platonic, personal or professional) so that we can seek the help of others when necessary. It promotes positive thinking, decisive action, and a strong, resilient aura.

Sarsen Stone

Sarsen stone from
Wiltshire, England

Sarsen stones are a variety of sandstone originally formed upward of forty million years ago and subsequently deposited atop the chalk downs of southern Britain. These massive rocks may weigh many tons. The word *sarsen* is believed to be taken from *saracen*, originally meaning "Muslim" and later carrying the connotation of "stranger" or "foreigner," as the stone's geology is foreign to the land where it is now found. Sarsen stones are famously found in megalithic structures like West Kennet Long Barrow and the stone circles of Stonehenge and Avebury.

A byproduct of the breakdown of extant rocks, sarsen has an affinity for the past and symbolizes death and rebirth. It's durable enough to withstand the ages, as attested to by its use in megalithic structures. This makes for a potent protective stone, as it generates a safe and secure field that deters harmful and discordant energies while simultaneously eroding the influence of generational curses and ancestral patterns that hold you back. I've noted that sarsen has a filtering effect on one's energy field, and so wearing it filters out unhelpful psychic information, erratic environmental energies, and sources of psychic harm.

The somewhat porous nature of sarsen necessitates somewhat frequent cleansing, so be sure to cleanse after every time you wear or carry it. Sarsen's energy is thought to help you weather the storms in life, and it lends the requisite courage, hope, and persistence to make it through the most challenging of times while simultaneously protecting your light to help you stay grounded and shine your brightest.

Schalenblende

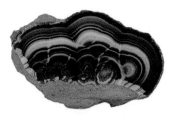

A polished cross-section of schalenblende

Schalenblende is an unusual formation composed mostly of sulfide minerals. Its name derives from German *schale*, for "shell," and *blende*, meaning "ore," an allusion to this stone's round, concentric bands that resemble a seashell. Schalenblende is predominantly composed of sphalerite, and it also contains marcasite, pyrite, galena, and small amounts of wurtzite. It was historically used as a source of lead ore, and it may have been used as an apotropaic device in parts of pre-Christian Germany. Most schalenblende is mined in Belgium, Germany, and Poland, though it may be found in several more places worldwide.

This beautifully patterned sulfide rock scrubs the aura of foreign and harmful energies. Traditionally connected to protection during travel, schalenblende draws down a solar influence to bolster your personal power and maintain an aura of safety during physical and spiritual journeys alike. This stone is deeply protective, as it averts, discharges, and transforms a wide spectrum of harmful and destabilizing energies. Schalenblende counteracts many of the effects of psychic attack, including exhaustion, confusion, insomnia, nightmares, bad luck, breakdowns in communication, and a sense of foreboding or despair. It is the best stone to turn to when it feels as if you've no options left, as its deeply regenerative power draws from heaven and earth to restore vitality and help you move forward. Schalenblende also facilitates easy communication, thereby clearing confusion and miscommunication. Try working with this stone when you feel as if your relationships are strained from harmful magick or when crossed conditions make it difficult for your voice to be heard. A peaceful gem, schalenblende protects and soothes at every level to help you feel more confident, centered, and balanced.

Double-terminated crystal of selenite from Bedford, England

Selenite

Selenite is a transparent, crystalline variety of gypsum, a hydrous calcium phosphate mineral. It usually forms in arid regions as water evaporates. Selenite may be transparent and colorless as well as golden, brown, green, blue, and sometimes black. This mineral is common worldwide, with important deposits in Australia, Canada, Germany, Mexico, Morocco, Russia, the United Kingdom, and the United States, among many other countries. It is an ever-popular crystal, as it is purifying, uplifting, and protective, while simultaneously opening your awareness of the higher realms.

Selenite is effective as a guardian at the threshold of your home. It creates a barrier of light that filters out negative and disruptive energies while simultaneously cleansing and uplifting the vibes in your home. It can be swept through the aura to cleanse psychic debris, and gridding a space with it creates a safe, inviting atmosphere. Despite the sentiments of love and light surrounding selenite nowadays, archaeological evidence suggests that this mineral was sometimes associated with the darker energies and defensive magick in antiquity. There are a handful of ancient Roman and Greek curse tablets carved from selenite inscribed with binding spells to avert harm or attack foes. Modern-day practitioners can use flat pieces of selenite and satin spar for similar purposes by scratching or engraving them with protective symbols, sigils, or messages and hanging them in the home.

Septarian Nodule

This Moroccan septarian nodule has been cut open and polished to reveal a beautiful pattern within that inspires one of this stone's common names, *turtle stone.*

Septarian nodules are silt or clay concretions with fissures lined with crystals (usually calcite and aragonite, but sometimes barite). The cracks initially form as a result of weathering; moisture works its way into the concretions and expands and contracts with changes in temperature. Later stages of crystallization fill in those cracks and seemingly heal the separate fragments of rock. Septarian nodules are most commonly found in Madagascar, Morocco, and Utah, but can also be found in France, Mozambique, New Zealand, Poland, and the United Kingdom. The mineral content of this stone varies by location. They are sometimes known as *septarium* (plural, *septaria*), or borrowing from its appearance, as *beetle stones* and *turtle stones.*

Folklore surrounding septarian nodules is frequently connected to themes of healing, connection, and protection. The word *septarian* is derived from the Latin *septum*, meaning "wall" or "partition," alluding to the angular cracks that separate the angular fragments inside the concretions. These crystal-filled fissures are both insulative and connective. On one hand, these cracks represent the aura's ability to protect and defend itself; on the other they signify the psyche's skills to rebuild lost or broken connections that may have been severed from trauma. Working with these rocks enhances one's personal power and helps repair cracks, tears, or holes in the aura. This stone can also be used as a talisman of invisibility, helping you go unnoticed by astral parasites or would-be psychic attackers. Its deeply regenerative power supports all processes of healing, physical and spiritual alike, and it is excellent for removing ancestral or generational curses.

Polished serpentine egg from the Lizard Peninsula, Cornwall, England

Serpentine

Serpentine is a group of closely related minerals that usually form as components of certain kinds of metamorphic rocks. Never found as single crystals, serpentine instead forms as microcrystalline or fibrous masses in a wide range of patterns and colors, usually ranging from green and brown, to yellow, white, or black. Serpentine is found worldwide and has been carved as an ornamental stone for millennia. Named for its resemblance to serpents' scales, this gem has a long history of protecting against venomous animals, harmful magick, and sickness.

Serpentine is used by modern-day healers to confer protection, awaken ancient wisdom, break up stagnant energy, bring clarity, and attune to the natural world. In the medieval period, grotesque faces called "fright stones" were carved from this gem to scare away danger in an act of sympathetic magick.[44] Once used to draw venom from bites and stings, serpentine is effective at drawing negative or malicious energies out of psychic wounds. Place a polished piece on the affected area or wear a strand of serpentine beads around the neck if the psychic influence is widespread. Serpentine is deeply regenerative, grounding, and soothing; it dissolves fear, helps us draw strength from the earth, and helps maintain a level head in stressful situations. This makes it a versatile stone of protection in the modern era.

Raw shungite

Shungite

The name *shungite* refers to two substances: a mineraloid of almost pure, noncrystalline carbon, and an impure carbon-rich oil shale derived from algae that once lived in the primordial sea. Both varieties are jet black in appearance, sometimes marbled, and with traces of other minerals.

This stone is named for Shun'ga Village in the Karelia region of northwest Russia. Shungite contains trace amounts of fullerenes (carbon molecules that form geometric, meshlike spheres and tubes), and in addition to Russia deposits have been reported in Austria, China, Colombia, the Democratic Republic of the Congo, India, Kazakhstan, and the United States. As a component of Karelian folk medicine, shungite has been used for healing for generations.

Shungite has become one of the world's most popular crystals for grounding and protection. Touted as the premier stone for ameliorating the harmful effects of electromagnetic pollution, shungite filters out harmful energy patterns that influence body, mind, and spirit. It siphons off negative thoughts and disruptive emotions while gently grounding and enlivening the body to ameliorate the effects of stress, overwhelm, and harmful environmental factors. Shungite catalyzes the energy field's natural purification processes and provides a safe outlet for any energies released during healing. This stone can be worn daily as a helpful ally in a changing world, as it provides continuous energetic purification, grounding, and protection in the face of any and all of life's circumstances.

Siderite

A cluster of bladelike siderite crystals from China

Siderite is an iron carbonate often found in rhombohedral, tabular, or bladelike crystals, as well as botryoidal masses. It is usually brown, but may also crystallize in shades of yellow, gold, green, red, or black, and rarely as near-colorless, transparent crystals. Siderite is named after the Greek word *sideros*, meaning "iron," which hints at its protective qualities. Siderite was only identified in the nineteenth century, and it should be noted that earlier uses of the term *siderite* mostly refer to magnetite. Siderite is abundant in many parts of the world. English folklore suggests it may have been carried to ward against mischievous fairies and spirits, and it is still believed by some to avert bad luck.

As a protective stone, siderite is a bit softer and gentler than most iron ores. It has an uplifting, calming, brightening effect on one's disposition. Coupled with its ability to align the chakras and subtle bodies of the aura, this makes siderite a wonderful stone for aftercare following psychic attack. This gemstone draws forth a quiet, gentle courage that helps you navigate difficult times with greater ease. Try wearing or carrying siderite to diffuse feelings of isolation, confinement, and brooding; it softens the effects of psychic harm and helps you draw on the support systems available to you.

Slate

Welsh slate

Slate is a common metamorphic rock composed chiefly of quartz, clay, mica, and chlorite. It is extremely fine-grained and fairly homogeneous in composition. This rock's best known trait is its fissility, an ability to be split in sheets or layers along its foliated structure. Slate is created when shale, marl, claystone, volcanic ash, or other rocks are subjected to low-grade regional metamorphism. It is commonly used as a building material, an insulator, as chalkboards or tablets, as gravestones, and occasionally as a whetstone for sharpening blades. Found worldwide, slate has been used for mundane and magickal uses since antiquity.

Slate's platy form, caused by its inner planes of cleavage, has lent this common rock a number of protective applications over the ages. As a building material, slate produces sturdy roofing, walls, and fences that defend against the natural elements. It is thus associated with protection of hearth and home against all manner of disruptive forces such as storms, imps, sickness, and magick. Slate defends and repairs the aura as well; a small piece can be carried as a psychic shield that deflects envy, hate, and hostility. Thanks to its flat surfaces, slate is an excellent medium for marking with protective signs and sigils. Use chalk for temporary spells and paint or ink for long-term magick; carry your slate sigil or place it in the home to avert harm and ensure a peaceful atmosphere.

Smoky Quartz

Smoky quartz from Antarctica

Smoky quartz, which occurs in shades of brown, gray, and black, owes its color to trace elements such as aluminum that are activated by the decay of radioactive isotopes in nearby rocks. The slow outpouring of energy gradually darkens the crystals from white or transparent to shades of brown, gray, and black. Smoky quartz is found on every continent in a variety of crystal forms, including singly and doubly terminated crystals, clusters, druze, masses, veins, and other formations. A wonderful healing stone, smoky quartz provides grounding, strength, and overall balance.

As a stone of protection, smoky quartz is one of the most versatile and universally helpful. Like other varieties of quartz, it strengthens the bodies of the aura, lending additional fortitude compared to clear quartz. Smoky quartz offers support for grounding, thus helping you feel calm, cool, and centered all day long. It improves the survival instinct and keeps you levelheaded during crisis. This earthy gemstone is ideal for highly sensitive folks and empaths, as it helps filter out unwanted or unnecessary energies and thought forms. It's also a wonderful ally for oversensitivity derived from disproportionately developed higher and lower chakras, as it anchors higher consciousness into the body. Smoky quartz is strongly purifying, drawing out intrusive, disruptive, and foreign energies from the aura and chakras; it initiates the body, mind, and spirit's natural processes of elimination to help break down more persistent sources of psychic harm.

Smoky elestial quartz from Brazil

Smoky Elestial Quartz

Elestial crystals are complex formations exhibiting terminations all over the body of a crystal. They usually form as a confluence of several formation processes and crystal habits, including skeletal growth, scepters, and parallel growth. Most are smoky (brownish or grayish) in color, but elestial crystals can also be found in virtually every kind and color of quartz. This powerful crystal configuration was deemed one of the master quartz formations by crystal healing pioneer and author Katrina Raphaell. She tells us that the elestial purges the darkness of the mind, enabling the revelation of truth and attunement with the celestial sphere.[45]

Smoky elestial quartz is often regarded as the master healer of the psyche, capable of releasing deeply-seeded emotions and mental patterns. It grants strength and support to every layer of the psyche and to every body of the aura while combing through every nook and cranny of the nonphysical self to remove the limitations hidden within. Crystal expert Judy Hall reports that smoky elestial quartz releases karmic entanglements and magick rituals that are no longer helpful.[46] If our own magick backfires or fizzles out, this crystal formation can prevent blowback and help clear out the energetic debris left behind. It is equally effective at expunging magick aimed at you by others.

Reflective crystals of specular hematite adorn this smoky quartz from El Paso County, Colorado.

Smoky Quartz with Hematite

Smoky quartz and hematite converge to make one of the most dynamic protection allies available. This bold combination can occur with a light dusting of reflective hematite on the surface of smoky quartz or as metallic or reddish inclusions inside the crystal. Smoky quartz with hematite is found in many locations worldwide, including Brazil, China, Germany, Madagascar, Namibia, the United Kingdom, the United States, and Zimbabwe.

Smoky quartz with hematite couples the apotropaic powers of iron-rich hematite (page 252) with the deeply grounding and purifying qualities of smoky quartz (page 300). The resulting synergy exudes an aura of strength, protection, and purification that can eliminate attachments from the aura and repel intrusive and malevolent forces from your home. Placed near the front door, it turns away wandering spirits, ill wishes, and harmful magick. This crystal acts like a sentinel watching over your space, tending to its energetic needs to keep the energy stable, lofty, and clear. When worn or carried, smoky quartz with hematite is a dynamic ally that shields the aura from harmful thoughts and intentions while simultaneously connecting you to the earth to replenish and rejuvenate your body, mind, and spirit.

Tumbled sodalite

Sodalite

Sodalite is named for its sodium content, and it often forms as masses that are colored from dark blue to indigo streaked with white. Less commonly, it can also be found in shades of green, gray, pink, violet, and yellow. Commercially important sources of sodalite include Afghanistan, Brazil, Canada, Greenland, Namibia, and Russia, though it is common in many parts of the planet. This azure-colored gemstone is not too distantly related to the feldspar family, and fine specimens often show a faint schiller, or sheen. Sodalite is prized for its purifying and protective qualities, being especially effective for clearing psychic and mental energies from the aura and shielding against electromagnetic pollution. As a cubic mineral it invites calm, order, and peace to the mind, thereby enabling you to make constructive decisions under pressure, such as when your well-being is compromised by deleterious environmental energies or harmful intentions.

Sodalite is among the best stones for purifying the aura, as it absorbs and neutralizes patterns of mental disharmony that weigh down the energy field.[47] It can be worn to cleanse and clear your aura or placed around the home to promote purification and harmony in your environment. Sodalite also addresses many of the signs and symptoms of psychic attack, such as fatigue, mental fog, sense of overwhelm, fear, dread, poor sleep, and persistent bad luck.

Sphalerite

Lustrous sphalerite from Joplin Field, Missouri

Sphalerite is a zinc sulfide mineral that serves as the world's most commercially important ore of zinc. Some important sources of sphalerite include Austria, Canada, England, France, Germany, Kosovo, Peru, Poland, Switzerland, and the United States. This is a supremely balancing stone that helps maintain balance between the upper and lower chakras, between the mind and body, and between the feminine and masculine energies within each of us. This combination makes for a stone that helps us to be less susceptible to harmful energies, especially those coming from our own surroundings, including harmful electromagnetic frequencies, geopathic stress, and intrusive energies from other people in our environs.

Sphalerite also teaches discernment. It separates fact from fiction, and it can therefore protect against deceit and treachery. Sphalerite can also help us become more honest with ourselves, thereby eliminating some of the internal sources of psychic harm. It offers protection while dealing with the public at large, too, and it is especially well-suited to protecting your business or source of income. This stone can upgrade our physical and spiritual anatomy to integrate higher consciousness, thereby making us more resilient and resistant to psychic harm. Sphalerite was the go-to stone for my late friend Gretchen when she was faced with paranormal phenomena. I've had success when working with sphalerite in cases of poltergeist activity and spirit attachment. Used as an elixir, sphalerite has the potential to assist in exorcism and curse-breaking.

Staurolite

Russian staurolite in a matrix of schist

Staurolite is a silicate of aluminum and iron belonging to the monoclinic crystal system. Its name derives from the Greek *stauros*, for "cross," and *lithos*, for "stone," a reference to its frequently twinned crystal habit. Staurolite is commonly brown, red, or black, and is found in many regions of the world, including Austria, Brazil, Russia, Sweden, Switzerland, the United States, and Vietnam. This mineral is an important indicator of regional metamorphism, and geologists study its occurrence to determine what kinds of events transformed the landscape. Staurolite is often associated with luck, protection, and healing in folklore.

Staurolite is frequently known by its folk name, *fairy cross*, as it was once believed to be the crystallized tears of the fairy folk; such a stone would thus protect its bearer from all kinds of harm and trickery. In parts of continental Europe, staurolite is known as *baseler taufstein*, or "christening stone of Basel." It was used to adorn baptismal fonts, as it was believed to confer a purifying and protective influence from the heavens. This mineral is a powerful protection ally, as it signifies the confluence of the elemental forces of earth, air, fire, water, and spirit, thereby bolstering your energy field and enhancing magickal prowess. Work with staurolite in uncrossing rituals and for breaking curses. This earthy gemstone also brings comfort, strength, and patience to help you in times of conflict, danger, and loss. Try placing some in your car to ensure safe travel.

Stibnite

Metallic crystals of toxic stibnite

Stibnite is composed of antimony sulfide and is toxic if not handled appropriately.* It is strongly activating to the flow of the life force within the body, and it stimulates detoxification. Stibnite has a centering effect, and it liberates us from fear and doubt. This mineral is ideal for reclaiming a sense of sovereignty, as it is greatly empowering. Work with stibnite to protect against energy drains from friends, family, and other people in close contact with you. It can shift the dynamics of codependent relationships

---

*Stibnite is safe for normal handling, provided you wash your hands to prevent cross-contamination if any particles should come off your specimen. **Never** make an elixir of stibnite via direct methods.

and cut harmful cords, especially those generated by one's family.

Stibnite is one of the most effective minerals for protecting against harmful spirits, as it severs spirit attachments and can drive out harmful entities from your energy field and home. Carrying or meditating with stibnite helps form a barrier around your energy field that is impenetrable to harmful spirits, while facilitating contact with helpful beings such as your personal spirit allies and guides. It is a valuable stone in cases of psychic attack, psychological abuse, and spirit possession. In Chinese medicine, stibnite (and its principal component, antimony) are sometimes prescribed as a means of protecting your wealth and good fortune from being drained by evil spirits or other entities.[48]

Sugilite

Manganese-rich sugilite from South Africa on the left and green sugilite in matrix from Japan on the right

Sugilite is a relatively rare cyclosilicate mineral rich in lithium. Initially described by the Japanese mineralogist Ken'ichi Sugi in 1944, it was named in his honor when it was approved as a new mineral species in the 1970s. Sugilite is best known from its occurrence in South Africa, where trace manganese brings shades of violet, pink, and magenta to this gem; in other locations, such as Australia, Canada, India, Italy, Japan, and Tajikistan, it can also be green, brown, yellow, or colorless. Since it was discovered in the twentieth century, sugilite has risen in popularity among crystal healers, who praise it for its soothing, relaxing energies and its ability to clear the energy field of unhealthy vibrations.

Sugilite's energy sweeps away accumulations of density, toxicity, and stagnancy in the aura and chakras. It boosts your defenses by filling the energy field with light, all the while transmuting harmful thoughts, difficult emotions, and disruptive environmental energies. Sugilite can be worn to repel negativity and to neutralize harm caused by psychic vampirism and psychic attack. This gem is also a palliative that reduces feelings of oppression, hopelessness, paranoia, and fear resulting from psychic attack. This soothing gem bolsters your confidence and nerves, helping you to stand up for yourself in challenging situations. Work with it to navigate conflict and find ways to neutralize dangers without incurring harm on anyone, victim and oppressor alike.

Sulfur

Natural stalactitic sulfur from Louisiana

Sulfur is a native element that is found worldwide in yellow masses and lustrous crystals, and on rare occasion it can be found as an inclusion in quartz (see page 285). Its energies are strongly purifying, and it can be used in crystal grids or burned (with caution, as the smoke can be harmful if inhaled) to break up persistent negativity. Sulfur scrubs away negative energies, cords, and foreign attachments in the energy field. This mineral is also restorative to the aura, as it prevents and repairs leaks and tears in the human energy field. Working with sulfur will protect and empower, and it helps us face our fears.

As an ingredient in magick and spellcraft, sulfur has been employed in both protective and baneful workings. Powdered sulfur (often mixed with salt) is added to spells used to break hexes and curses, as well as for workings to drive out harmful people and transform enemies into friends.[49] Brimstone, a synonym for *sulfur*, is traditionally associated with infernal energies, and so it can be used based on the principle of "fighting fire with fire" to drive away evil spirits and reflect negative spells back to their sender.

Sunstone

Polished sunstone from Tanzania

Sunstone is aventurescent feldspar with tiny platelets of minerals like hematite, ilmenite, or native copper that create a twinkling effect when moved in the light. Most sunstone is orange, golden, or red in color, though it can occasionally be silver, black, brown, green, or bluish. Some of the finest sunstones can be found in Tanzania, with other deposits found in Australia, India, Madagascar, Norway, Russia, and several parts of the United States.

Sunstone is named for its solar countenance. Its brilliant, fiery color and dazzling inclusions inspire warmth, hope, and optimism. A stone of good cheer, sunstone effaces pessimism, lethargy, and hopelessness, making it a good choice for recovery from psychic attack. Sunstone restores lost willpower and helps you take life by the helm, thereby overcoming harmful, coercive magick. Work with this gem to confer a sense of safety and comfort to the home, either by gridding the four corners of your space with it, or by placing it in a central location. As sunstone is also associated with success and wealth, it can ward against both magickal and mundane drains on your finances and personal energies to protect your resources and livelihood.

Tantalite

Lustrous tantalite
in matrix

Tantalite is a rare mineral, one of the most important ores of the metal tantalum, a rare-earth mineral that is found in mobile phones and other electronic devices as well as in surgical implements and implants. It is an extremely dense mineral that forms in pegmatites enriched with rare-earth elements. Most tantalite is a brown to black and opaque in color, though manganese-rich specimens may be transparent in thin sections. Tantalite is primarily found in Afghanistan, Australia, Brazil, China, the Democratic Republic of the Congo, Mozambique, Rwanda, and occurs in smaller quantities in dozens of other locations worldwide. Tantalite and its constituent metal, tantalum, are named for Tantalus, a figure in Greek mythology. The metal tantalum is extremely resistant to corrosion by heat and acid, thus enabling tantalite to confer the same resistance to corrosive energetic influences. Tantalite is sometimes used by crystal healers to promote insight, reduce worry, increase inner strength, and provide deep, transformative grounding.

Tantalite may be one of the most powerful protection stones I've encountered. Its stabilizing influence keeps us rooted and offers a safe channel for immediately discharging and transmuting harmful energies. This rare mineral curbs psychic attack, deflects negativity, and transmutes harmful energies all around us with ease. Judy Hall notes that it blocks invasion by adverse forces while simultaneously repelling and removing attachments, cords, and other foreign patterns.[50] Melody reports that tantalite was known to nomadic peoples of Russia, where it was highly regarded as a prophylactic against harmful magick, simultaneously promoting the well-being and vigor of the target of such magick.[51] Tantalite creates a protective bubble around you and your possessions to thwart aggressors, and it ameliorates the effects of psychic attack, malefic magick, and the evil eye. Furthermore, this crystal eliminates internal sources of psychic harm and helps dissolve the attitudes, beliefs, and behaviors that leave you vulnerable to fresh attacks.[52] This rare crystal packs a powerful punch for all kinds of protective endeavors.

Tektite

Billitonite tektite from Belitung, Indonesia

Tektites are impactites—natural glasses made by the impact of meteorites. The most abundant variety, which is black to brown in color, is found in Mainland Southeast Asia (formerly known as Indochina) and southern China and is called *indochinite*. Tektites from other parts of the world are known as *billitonite* (Indonesia), *australite* (Australia), *thailandite* (Thailand), and *irghizite* (Kazakhstan). Moldavite is a gemmy, green tektite mostly found in the Czech Republic, and Libyan desert glass is a transparent, golden glass from northern Africa usually classified as a tektite. Tektites are sometimes referred to in myth and legend as *agni mani* ("fire pearl" in Sanskrit); they have been revered as protective amulets and talismans of good fortune since ancient times. In crystal healing today they are considered stones of higher consciousness, alchemy, and transformation.

Tektites are formed by extraordinary forces; they have survived impacts the likes of which we can scarcely imagine. As a result, these cosmic gemstones lend support, strength, and tenacity when life feels overwhelming. Because tektites are formed when foreign matter impacts Earth, they are adept at eliminating intrusive energies, deleterious cords, astral parasites, entities, and other foreign patterns that may attach to the energy field and body. When coupled with gems like jet, stibnite, ilvaite, astrophyllite, and aegirine, tektites help exorcize harmful spirits and neutralize errant magickal forces. Bear in mind that tektites are accelerators of energies and may require additional grounding stones if you choose to wear or work with them long-term.

Tiger's Eye

Tumbled tiger's eye

Tiger's eye is a variety of quartz bearing fibrous, chatoyant inclusions of crocidolite. It is found in Australia, China, Namibia, South Africa, and the United States, most often in shades of gold and brown, although it may also be blue (falcon's eye) or red (dragon's eye). Its cat's-eye phenomenon has led to this stone being used for protection, divination, and vision. This gemstone bestows the gift of discernment, as it cuts through illusion and deception. Tiger's eye is a stone of truth, justice, and balance. It boosts self-confidence, too, enabling you to take action to maintain balance and safety.

Tiger's eye has long been used to dispel negative energies from one's environment, and like many other stones sporting ocular imagery, it wards against envy, harmful magick, and psychic attack. Placing it in the bathwater or around the edge of your tub is a wonderful way to employ this stone in a regenerative and protective bath. Tiger's eye is also helpful when protecting against bullying, and it improves self-esteem.[53] It is a wonderful stone for empaths and young people who may be struggling to find their voice and place in the world.

Tiger Iron

Polished slab of tiger iron showing evidence of metamorphism in its wavy strata

Tiger iron is a combination of golden tiger's eye, red jasper, and hematite—all three containing iron. It is formed by metamorphic activity and found in Australia. Tiger iron is extremely grounding and strengthening, as it is composed of a triumvirate of stones with earthy vibes. This metamorphic rock helps break up stagnant energies and alleviate geopathic stress. Often recommended for counteracting psychic attack, tiger iron is generally protective and is a versatile stone for healing, too.

Work with tiger iron when your aura needs additional strength and resiliency. This gemstone heals tears and holes in the outer layers of the aura, such as those resulting from stress, transition, and psychic attack. Crystal maven Judy Hall writes that this stone "creates a place of refuge when danger threatens," and she recommends it for periods of burnout, stress, and exhaustion.[54] Tiger iron will protect and replenish your vital energy, especially when you feel as though you are spread thin, and it is the perfect ally for adapting to change.

Topaz

Brazilian specimens of golden topaz on the left and blue topaz on the right

Topaz is a popular gemstone found worldwide in a range of colors. In medieval lore, topaz was believed to protect against envy, illness, injury, harmful magick, and death. It was worn to confer invisibility as well. Topaz is an important stone because it assists in manifestation and magick, as it aligns our will with Creator, allowing us to act from the space of divine will. This joyful gem grants inspiration, creativity, motivation, and happiness. It promotes alignment and communication with all parts of the self.

Additionally, topaz has a clearing effect on the aura. It releases blockages, stagnant energies, and attachments in the aura and chakras. The uplifting, joyful energies of this stone overcome many harmful energies and shift harmful patterns into healthy ones. Topaz also teaches the importance of self-care and putting yourself first. According to Naisha Ahsian, coauthor of *The Book of Stones*, golden or imperial topaz in particular is a wonderful stone for sensitive people, as it helps us delineate and honor emotional boundaries, both our own and those of other people,[55] making golden topaz among the best stones for empaths and highly sensitive people.

Multicolored tourmaline from Afghanistan

Tourmaline

Tourmaline refers to a diverse group of related mineral species with varying compositions and similar structures, found worldwide. The tourmaline group varies in color and appearance, and gem-quality specimens command a high price. As a whole, tourmalines are tonifying and healing on many levels. They support the movement of energy in the aura, chakras, and meridians, thus alleviating blockages and removing negative attachments. While all tourmalines are at least mildly protective, the black, brown, and pink varieties are excellent protection stones.

Tourmaline-group minerals can also harmonize and detoxify body and spirit. They eliminate harmful accumulations, both physical and energetic, thereby counteracting environmental pollution and toxic energies. These stones return movement to stagnant energies and transmute densities in the aura and environment. Scientists have discovered that when heated many varieties of tourmaline emit negative ions that support our well-being and help clear harmful substances from our environs; this may underscore tourmaline's ability to do the same at the spiritual level. Use tourmaline to protect and uplift your home or office. Three varieties of tourmaline—black, brown, and pink—are especially effective and are described in detail below.

Madagascan black
tourmaline

Black Tourmaline

Black tourmaline, also called *schorl*, is the most abundant member of the tourmaline group, commonly found around the globe. It is rich in iron, making it a fortifying stone. Black tourmaline may be one of the most popular crystals for protection and purifying negative energy today. This stone draws out hidden influences in the subconscious and discharges harmful energies from your energy field. Because it is so grounding, black tourmaline strengthens the connection between your energy field and that of Earth. It acts like an etheric drain with a garbage disposal to break down and transmute disharmonious energies, thereby keeping your entire energy field free and clear of negative vibrations.

Black tourmaline is great for gridding around the home or office. Additionally, black tourmaline is a helpful companion when traveling. Besides protecting and purifying, this stone invites greater connection and communication throughout your entire being—body, mind, and spirit—thereby instilling coherence among all levels of your makeup.[56] This effect allows for greater resilience when exposed to harmful sources of electromagnetic pollution and other deleterious vibrations such as psychic attack. This stone reduces stress, promotes self-discovery, and encourages restful sleep.

Gemmy double-
terminated crystal of
brown tourmaline

Brown Tourmaline

Brown tourmaline, also called *dravite*, is one of the more common members of the tourmaline group, occurring in places such as Australia, Austria, Brazil, China, India, Italy, Japan, Madagascar, Mali, Norway, Spain, Tanzania, and the United States. It is a stone of regeneration and profound healing, and it initiates feelings of love and self-acceptance, making it a helpful adjunct for self-care, especially fol-

lowing trauma. Brown tourmaline facilitates profound healing and reconciliation of the shadow self, thereby eliminating self-generated sources
of psychic harm. In a way this gemstone protects you from yourself. It
offers strength and stamina and bolsters the etheric body, the layer of
the aura closest to the physical body, thus empowering the etheric body
to serve as a shield against harmful energies in the environment.

Brown tourmaline is especially helpful in group settings as it fosters a
greater sense of community by harmonizing the energy of the individuals in the group. Brown tourmaline can gently shield sensitive people
and empaths from the emotions, thoughts, and energies of other people. Use brown tourmaline in crystal grids or rituals designed to protect
families, tribes, and large groups of people.

Rough pink tourmaline
from Brazil

Pink Tourmaline

Pink tourmaline, also called *rubellite*, is a red
to pink variety of elbaite that can be found in
Afghanistan, Brazil, Canada, the Democratic
Republic of the Congo, Italy, Madagascar,
Myanmar, the United States, and Zimbabwe
among many other locations. Its lithium
content makes for a nurturing gemstone ally
that invites emotional healing and feelings of
love and peace. This gemstone ameliorates
anxiety and is restorative on many levels. It invites a sense of safety and
emotional security as it circumvents the wounds of the past by bringing
your awareness to the present moment, which is where all true healing
takes place. Rubellite's nurturing and balancing effects extend to the
home by promoting harmony and protecting one's family.

Pink tourmaline is superb at protecting against harmful energies,
subtle and measurable frequencies alike. This gemstone guards against
harmful electromagnetic fields, (including microwaves and radio waves)
and from negative emotions and projections from other people. Note
that while it does not protect against internal sources of harm outright,
pink tourmaline does help to resolve the imbalances that create them.
Pink tourmaline also offers an energetic shield that supports the body's

natural healing process, as it prevents foreign energies from disrupting recovery. This gemstone is a good companion while traveling, as it guards against the disharmonious, scattered, and unhealthy patterns encountered in places such as airports; as well it protects you from the stress of travel.[57]

Two examples of tumbled tugtupite from Greenland

Tugtupite

Tugtupite is a rare mineral belonging to the tetragonal crystal system. It is closely related to the sodalite group, and it can be strongly fluorescent (glowing under ultraviolet light) and/ or tenebrescent (darkening in sunlight). Most tugtupite is commercially mined in Greenland. This gem resonates strongly with the heart and pericardium, the membrane around the heart that protects this precious organ. In Chinese medicine the pericardium and its corresponding meridian are known as the "heart opener" and the "heart protector," implying that it works to selectively shield or allow entry to the heart space. Tugtupite enhances this function, allowing in only those energies that are kind, compassionate, loving, and trustworthy.

Tugtupite is also a potent ally for recuperation from psychic attack and other forms of energetic harm. Carrying this gem protects against emotional manipulation, codependency, and emotional vampirism. It works to draw out harmful energy from the heart chakra, dissolve the pain and disturbance caused by psychic attack, and restore an overall state of well-being.[58] It is also adept at connecting with spirit guides and allies who can be called on to assist with protection, cleansing, and overcoming psychic harm. Since it is so intimately linked to the energy of the heart and with higher consciousness, it can shift our awareness almost instantly into a loving state, thereby transcending fear and other limiting patterns created by psychic attack.

Turquoise

High-quality turquoise from Sleeping Beauty Mine in Globe, Arizona

Turquoise, a phosphate mineral that owes its color to its copper content, has been regarded as a sacred stone since prehistory. Found in many places worldwide, including Chile, China, Egypt, England (Cornwall), Mexico, Tibet, Turkey, and the United States, it has long been considered an all-around protective stone, having been employed as an apotropaic against accident, injury, illness, insanity, storms, venomous creatures, poisoning, and death. Turquoise was once thought to change color to warn its bearer of imminent danger. In Tibetan lore, turquoise is associated with *nagas* and *naginis*, the race of half-serpent beings who guard the waters and unseen realms of Earth. Wearing this gem facilitates requests for assistance from spirit guides and guardians.

Turquoise has a pacifying effect and promotes resilience of the heart and lightness of the spirit. It raises the vibrations of the body and aura, thereby helping to neutralize and eliminate unwanted or unhealthy patterns. Turquoise is often worn to protect against psychic attack and the evil eye. It purifies the mind and spirit. This gemstone is a powerful ally for mediums, spiritualists, and psychics, as it enhances psychic ability by enabling you to be a clear channel while simultaneously filtering out negative, disruptive, or harmful energies and spirits.

Unakite

Tumbled unakite

Unakite is a lightly metamorphosed rock composed chiefly of pinkish feldspar, green epidote, and grains of quartz. It is named for its discovery in the Unaka Range, mountains that border Tennessee and North Carolina. Unakite is also found in Brazil, China, Mexico, Sierra Leone, and South Africa. Since it has only been known since the nineteenth century, no ancient traditions regarding its magickal or curative virtues exist, however, it is widely celebrated today as a gem of deep healing, renewal, grounding, and protection.

Unakite is often employed to protect the home, as its soothing energy dissipates the harmful effects of electromagnetic pollution and other sources of environmental harm while instilling a sense of peace and calm. Unakite facilitates recuperation after illness, injury, and depletion by regenerating the aura and restoring it to its original, luminous state.[59] Demonstrating qualities like one of its constituents, epidote (page 243), unakite restores your personal power and throws off the mantle of oppression and victimhood. It resolves conflict through loving compromise and helps you take charge of your own fate, making it a great stone for recovery after psychic attack.

Vivianite

Dark blue–green crystals of vivianite in matrix from Amazonas, Brazil

Vivianite is a hydrous iron phosphate with the unusual property of darkening after it has been mined. Newly unearthed specimens are often transparent shades of blue-green, which slowly darken to nearly blue-black upon exposure to light. This has inspired crystal healers to believe that vivianite absorbs negative energies from the environment, changing color as it becomes more saturated. While this gemstone does offer purifying effects, the change in color is the result of more mundane influences— simply exposure to light. Vivianite is commonly found in Australia, Bolivia, Brazil, France, Germany, Italy, Poland, Russia, the United Kingdom, and many parts of the United States, among many other countries worldwide.

Vivianite invites a sense of inner clarity, an essential quality for psychic development, shamanic journeying, and reaching transcendent states of consciousness. This gemstone ally also works to protect and cloak the energy field, making you less conspicuous to spirits and other entities (including people) who may seek to harm you. As a truth-seeking stone it can reveal the sources of psychic harm in your life, often highlighting the mental and emotional patterns that dwell within your own mind. Vivianite is also helpful for remaining hopeful and optimistic despite these challenging times. It reduces pessimism and hopelessness, helping you feel more connected to the nourishing energies of the planet all around you.

Zircon

Zircon is a silicate of zirconium, usually crystallizing as double-terminated and bipyramidal crystals in shades of yellow, gold, brown, red, orange, green, blue, black, and colorless. Among the oldest minerals on Earth, zircon often contains traces of radioactive isotopes, thereby allowing geologists to use this mineral to date the rocks in which it is found. Zircon is found worldwide, and a few important sources include Australia, Cambodia, Canada, France, Myanmar, and Sri Lanka. Its name is taken from the Persian *zargun*, meaning "gold-colored," a reference to one of its more popular colors in the ancient world. Traditional lore records many uses for zircons, from preserving against pestilence, to drawing wealth, success, and favor.

Several specimens of zircon demonstrating a variety of crystal forms

The density and crystal forms of zircon represent its ability to ground and consolidate energies. This mineral is nourishing when we feel depleted, and it encourages us to release painful ties to the past. As a protective gemstone, zircon is said to ward off illness, poisoning, storms, and injury. It was also used as a remedy against bewitchment and evil magick. Wearing or carrying this gemstone will work prophylactically against all forms of harm, and it can be added to ritual baths to remove the effects of maleficia after the magick has been cast. Zircon is traditionally worn as a traveler's gem, preventing injury and misfortune on your journeys; kept at home it is said to prevent theft and storm damage. This protective gem offers a stabilizing, empowering influence to help you through your life's journey each day.

CONCLUSION

Safe and Sound

Despite our best intentions, psychic harm happens every day. It's true that most people will never be the victim of a curse or attacked by a vengeful spirit, but the world we live in is replete with other kinds of psychic attacks. Social media, corporate advertising, politics, and groupthink subject every person on the planet to psychic attacks of a different nature. Plus we cannot discredit the role we play in our own psychic well-being; the more we buy into the narratives pushed on us by oppressive systems and imbalanced voices all around us, the more we contribute to our own harm.

Twenty-first-century harm requires twenty-first-century protection. The techniques in this book may be inspired by some of the most ancient forms of protection available, but they are presented in a way that works equally well against the psychic undercurrents of the digital world as they do against ancient curses. Remember to revisit the basics often and rotate the shields, wards, and other protections you use to keep your psychic self-defense primed for the scenario each new day brings.

I also urge you to remember that psychic self-defense is *never* a substitute for practical safety. No crystal grid or gemstone amulet will stop oncoming traffic if you fail to look both ways when you cross the street, and there isn't a spell in existence that will stop humanity from its machinations, both harmful and helpful. Don't rely on magick or meditation to the exclusion of common-sense measures and emergency care. Remember to call first responders and other emergency personnel if needed, and use magickal care only as a reinforcement in critical scenarios.

Also, bear in mind that you don't have to do it all alone. When things feel challenging, uncertain, or hopeless, look for support. Your spiritual community and chosen family may be able to join you in your psychic self-defense practices, and you can often find talented witches, magicians, and healers whose services include mitigating the effects of psychic harm. Never attempt to banish a curse, exorcise a person or place, or confront a malevolent force without preparation, assistance, and the right tools.

Finally, although this book presents some pretty heavy topics and confronts the very real nature of harm, evil, and attack, I hope that you will feel empowered to choose love and healing over vengeance and malice. The beauty and power of crystals inspires us to bring more order and merit into the world. Always prioritize the best and most effective route for the health and safety of your loved ones; whenever possible let that choice be informed by love and hope rather than fear. Remember that every choice has its repercussions, a set of karmic tides that ripple outward. Together we can create ripples of healing through our crystal magick to help the world become a safer, more loving place for all.

Notes

Chapter 2. Clear as Crystal

1. Miller, *Protection and Reversal Magick*, 46.

Chapter 3. Personal Protection

1. Penczak, *Witch's Shield,* 90–92; and Penczak, *Inner Temple of Witchcraft,* 176–77.
2. Hall, *Ultimate Guide to Crystal Grids*, 114–15.

Chapter 4. Warding Your Space

1. Penczak, *Temple of Shamanic Witchcraft*, 179–80.

Chapter 5. Protection from Geopathic Stress and Electromagnetic Pollution

1. Martino, *Shungite*, 54–55.
2. Newerla, *Protect Yourself from Electromagnetic Pollution*, 14–16.
3. Newerla, *Protect Yourself from Electromagnetic Pollution*, 12.
4. Martino, *Shungite*, 85.
5. Martino, *Shungite*, 85.

Chapter 6. Combatting Psychic Attack

1 Fortune, *Psychic Self-Defense*, 184.

Chapter 7. Banishing, Binding, and Reversal Magick

1. Penczak, *Witch's Shield*, 173.
2. Conway, *Crystal Enchantments*, 276.
3. Gager, *Curse Tablets and Binding Spells*, 13.

4. Hall, *Crystals for Energy Protection*, 181.

5. Penczak, *Living Temple of Witchcraft*, 127.

Chapter 8. Dealing with Spirits

1. Miller, *Protection and Reversal Magick*, 111.

2. Melody, *Love Is in the Earth*, 185.

3. Hall, *Crystal Prescriptions, Vol. 5*, 223.

Chapter 9. Directory of Protection Crystals

1. Melody, *Love Is in the Earth*, 583.

2. Eason, *Everyday Psychic Defense*, 208.

3. Hall, *Encyclopedia of Crystals*, 171.

4. Simmons and Ahsian, *Book of Stones*, 54.

5. Hall, *Crystals for Energy Protection*, 48.

6. Hall, *Crystal Bible 3*, 72.

7. Barralet, *Crystal Connections*, 65–66.

8. Hall, *Crystal Companion*, 275.

9. Raphaell, *Crystalline Transmission*, 214.

10. Eason, *Complete Crystal Handbook*, 245.

11. Hall, *Crystals for Energy Protection*, 171.

12. Kunz, *Curious Lore of Precious Stones*, 270.

13. Melody, *Love Is in the Earth*, 201.

14. Hall, *Crystal Companion*, 269.

15. Raphaell, *Crystalline Transmission*, 257.

16. Hall, *Crystal Bible 3*, 148.

17. Hall, *Crystal Bible 2*, 150.

18. Melody, *Love Is in the Earth*, 351.

19. Lazzerini, *Psychic Protection Crystals*, 144.

20. Permutt, *Crystal Healer*, 110.

21. Hall, *Crystal Companion*, 251.

22. Cunningham, *Cunningham's Encyclopedia*, 103.

23. Kynes, *Crystal Magic*, 140.

24. Hall, *Crystal Companion*, 82.

25. Hall, *Crystal Companion*, 117.

26. Eason, *Complete Crystal Handbook*, 66.

27. Lazzerini, *Psychic Protection Crystals*, 149.

28. Norman, *Faerie Stones*, 60.

29. Lecouteux, *Lapidary of Sacred Stones*, 228.

30. Eason, *Everyday Psychic Defense*, 219.

31. Hall, *Crystal Companion*, 185.

32. Melody, *Love Is in the Earth*, 508.

33. Hall, *Crystal Bible 3*, 210.

34. Mayor, *Fossil Legends of the First Americans*, 156, 161.

35. Hall, *Crystals for Energy Protection*, 181.

36. Lilly, *Preseli Bluestone*, 76.

37. Lazzerini, *Psychic Protection Crystals*, 153.

38. Hall, *Crystal Companion*, 283.

39. Hall, *Crystal Bible: Definitive Guide*, 223.

40. Hall, *Crystal Bible: Definitive Guide*, 219.

41. Melody, *Love Is in the Earth*, 671.

42. Eason, *Everyday Psychic Defense*, 29.

43. Hall, *Crystal Companion*, 299.

44. Barralet, *Crystal Connections*, 259.

45. Raphaell, *Crystal Healing*, 98.

46. Hall, *Encyclopedia of Crystals*, 187.

47. Katz, *Gemstone Energy Medicine*, 194.

48. Franks, *Stone Medicine*, 437.

49. yronwode, *Hoodoo Herb and Root Magic*, 194.

50. Hall, *Crystal Bible 3*, 335.

51. Melody, *Love Is in the Earth*, 781.

52. Hall, *Crystal Bible 3*, 336.

53. Hall, *Crystal Companion*, 199.

54. Hall, *Crystal Companion*, 274.

55. Simmons and Ahsian, *Book of Stones*, 404.

56. Newerla, *Protect Yourself from Electromagnetic Pollution,* 27.

57. Katz, *Gemstone Energy Medicine*, 292.

58. Hall, *Crystals for Energy Protection*, 11.

59. Hall, *Crystal Companion*, 303.

Bibliography

Auryn, Mat. *Psychic Witch: A Metaphysical Guide to Meditation, Magick, and Manifestation*. Woodbury, MN: Llewellyn Publications, 2020.

Barralet, Adam. *Crystal Connections: A Guide to Crystals and How to Use Them*. East Lismore, New South Wales, Australia: Animal Dreaming Publishing, 2017.

Blackthorn, Amy. *Blackthorn's Protection Magic: A Witch's Guide to Mental and Physical Self-Defense*. Newburyport, MA: Weiser Books, 2022.

Conway, D. J. *Crystal Enchantments: A Complete Guide to Stones and Their Magical Properties*. Berkeley, CA: Crossing Press, 2011.

Cunningham, Scott. *Cunningham's Encyclopedia of Crystal, Gem, and Metal Magic*. St. Paul, MN: Llewellyn Publications, 1998.

Eason, Cassandra. *1001 Crystals: The Complete Book of Crystals for Every Purpose*. New York: Sterling Ethos, 2023.

———. *The Complete Crystal Handbook: Your Guide to More Than 500 Crystals*. New York: Union Square and Co., 2010.

———. *Everyday Psychic Defense: White Magic for Dark Moments*. Woodbury, MN: Llewellyn Publications, 2017.

Fortune, Dion. *Psychic Self-Defense: The Classic Instruction Manual for Protecting Yourself Against Paranormal Attack*. San Francisco, CA: Weiser Books, 2001.

Franks, Leslie. *Stone Medicine: A Chinese Medical Guide to Healing with Gems and Minerals*. Rochester, VT: Healing Arts Press, 2016.

Gager, John G. *Curse Tablets and Binding Spells from the Ancient World*. Oxford, UK: Oxford University Press, 1992.

Hall, Judy. *The Crystal Bible: A Definitive Guide to Crystals*. Cincinnati, OH: Walking Stick Press, 2004.

———. *The Crystal Bible 2*. Cincinnati, OH: Walking Stick Press, 2009.

———. *The Crystal Bible 3*. Cincinnati, OH: Walking Stick Press, 2013.

———. *The Crystal Companion: Enhance Your Life with Crystals*. Blue Ash, OH: Walking Stick Press, 2018.

———. *Crystal Prescriptions, Vol. 5: Space Clearing, Feng Shui, and Psychic Protection, an A-Z Guide*. Winchester, UK: O-Books, 2016.

———. *Crystal Prescriptions, Vol. 6: Crystals for Ancestral Clearing, Soul Retrieval, Spirit Release, and Karmic Healing, an A-Z Guide*. Winchester, UK: O-Books, 2017.

———. *Crystals for Energy Protection*. Carlsbad, CA: Hay House, 2020.

———. *The Encyclopedia of Crystals*. Gloucester, MA: Fair Winds Press, 2006.

———. *The Ultimate Guide to Crystal Grids: Transform Your Life Using the Power of Crystals and Layouts*. Beverly, MA: Fair Winds Press, 2018.

Hoggard, Brian. *Magical House Protection: The Archaeology of Counter-Witchcraft*. Oxford, UK: Berghan Books, 2021.

Hunter, Devin. *Crystal Magic for the Modern Witch*. Woodbury, MN: Llewellyn Publications, 2022.

Katz, Michael. *Gemstone Energy Medicine: Healing Body, Mind, and Spirit*. Portland, OR: Natural Healing Press, 2005.

Kunz, George Frederick. *The Curious Lore of Precious Stones*. New York, NY: Dover Publications, 1941.

Kynes, Sandra. *Crystal Magic: Mineral Wisdom for Pagans and Wiccans*. Woodbury, MN: Llewellyn Publications, 2017.

Lazzerini, Ethan. *Psychic Protection Crystals: The Modern Guide to Psychic Self-Defense with Crystals for Empaths and Highly Sensitive People*. N.p.: self-published, 2018.

Leavy, Ashley. *Crystals for Energy Healing: A Practical Sourcebook of 100 Crystals*. Beverly, MA: Fair Winds Press, 2017.

Lecouteux, Claude. *A Lapidary of Sacred Stones: Their Magical and Medical Powers Based on the Earliest Sources*. Trans. Jon E. Graham. Rochester, VT: Inner Traditions, 2012.

Lilly, Simon, and Sue Lilly. *Crystal Doorways*. Freshfields, UK: Capall Bann Publishing, 1997.

———. *The Crystal Healing Guide: A Step-by-Step Guide to Using Crystals for Health and Healing*. London: HarperCollins, 2016.

———. *Preseli Bluestone: Healing Stone of the Ancestors*. Exminster, Devon, UK: Tree Seer Publications, 2011.

Martino, Regina. *Shungite: Protection, Healing, and Detoxification.* Trans. Jack Cain. Rochester, VT: Healing Arts Press, 2014.

Mayor, Adrienne. *Fossil Legends of the First Americans.* Princeton, NJ: Princeton University Press, 2005.

McCarthy, Josephine. *The Exorcist's Handbook.* Berkeley, CA: Golem Media, 2010.

Melody. *Love Is in the Earth.* Wheat Ridge, CO: Earth-Love Publishing, 2007.

Miller, Jason. *Protection and Reversal Magic: A Witch's Defense Manual.* Wayne, NJ: New Page Books, 2006.

Newerla, Barbara. *Protect Yourself from Electromagnetic Pollution by Using Crystals.* Trans. Astrid Mick. Forres, Scotland: Earthdancer, 2010.

Norman, Ceri. *Faerie Stones: An Exploration of the Folklore and Faeries Associated with Stones and Crystals.* Winchester, UK: Moon Books, 2018.

Pearson, Nicholas. *Crystal Basics: The Energetic, Healing, and Spiritual Power of 200 Gemstones.* Rochester, VT: Destiny Books, 2020.

———. *Crystal Basics Pocket Encyclopedia: The Energetic, Healing, and Spiritual Power of 450 Gemstones.* Rochester, VT: Destiny Books, 2022.

———. *Crystal Healing for the Heart: Gemstone Therapy for Physical, Emotional, and Spiritual Well-Being.* Rochester, VT: Destiny Books, 2017.

———. *Crystals for Karmic Healing: Transform Your Future by Releasing Your Past.* Rochester, VT: Destiny Books, 2017.

———. *The Seven Archetypal Stones: Their Spiritual Powers and Teachings.* Rochester, VT: Destiny Books, 2016.

———. *Stones of the Goddess: Crystals for the Divine Feminine.* Rochester, VT: Destiny Books, 2019.

Penczak, Christopher. *The Inner Temple of Witchcraft: Magick, Meditation, and Psychic Development.* Woodbury, MN: Llewellyn Publications, 2002.

———. *The Living Temple of Witchcraft, Vol. 1: The Descent of the Goddess.* Woodbury, MN: Llewellyn Publications, 2008.

———. *The Temple of Shamanic Witchcraft: Shadows, Spirits, and the Healing Journey.* Woodbury, MN: Llewellyn Publications, 2005.

———. *The Witch's Shield: Protection Magick and Psychic Self-Defense.* Woodbury, MN: Llewellyn Publications, 2004.

Permutt, Philip. *The Crystal Healer, Vol. 2: Harness the Power of Crystal Energy.* New York: CICO Books, 2018.

Raphaell, Katrina. *Crystal Healing: The Therapeutic Application of Crystals and Stones.* Santa Fe, NM: Aurora Press, 1987.

———. *The Crystalline Transmission: A Synthesis of Light.* Santa Fe, NM: Aurora Press, 1990.

Salisbury, David. *A Mystic Guide to Cleansing and Clearing.* Winchester, UK: Moon Books, 2016.

Sebastiani, Althaea. *By Rust of Nail and Prick of Thorn: The Theory and Practice of Effective Home Warding.* N.p.: self-published, 2020.

Simmons, Robert, and Naisha Ahsian. *The Book of Stones: Who They Are and What They Teach.* Berkeley, CA: North Atlantic Books, 2007.

Spencer, Craig. *Witchcraft Unchained: Exploring the History & Traditions of British Craft.* Chicago, IL: Crossed Crow Books, LLC, 2023.

Stein, Diane. *Gemstones A to Z: A Handy Reference to Healing Crystals.* Berkeley, CA: Crossing Press, 2008.

yronwode, catherine. *Hoodoo Herb and Root Magic: A Materia Magica of African-American Conjure.* Forestville, CA: Lucky Mojo Curio Company, 2002.

Index

About the Author

Nicholas Pearson has been immersed in all aspects of rocks and minerals for more than thirty years. As one of the leading voices in crystal healing today, Nicholas offers a unique perspective that blends science and spirituality alongside a grounded and practical approach to crystals. His love of rocks and minerals began in childhood, and he started teaching workshops on crystal healing in high school, later studying mineral science at Stetson University's Gillespie Museum in DeLand, Florida.

Nicholas is also an avid Reiki practitioner and *shihan*, or teacher. He began his Reiki journey in 2006, and in 2009 he undertook a pilgrimage to several sacred sites in Japan, including the founder's memorial at Saihōji in Tokyo and the birthplace of Reiki at Mount Kurama. He offers intensive training that offers deep insight into the roots of the system of Reiki while synthesizing the best practices of traditional and modern approaches alike.

Offering online and in-person classes around the world, Nicholas strives to foster inspiration, understanding, and sincere healing to his students in every situation. His curriculum includes unique and in-depth training on crystals, flower essence therapy, Reiki, and more. You'll also find him sharing his passion for education at conferences and as a guest on radio, podcasts, and other media. He is the award-winning author of several books, including *Crystal Basics*, *Flower Essences from the Witch's Garden*, and *Foundations of Reiki Ryōhō*.

Nicholas makes his home in central Florida with his husband, Steven, and their cat, Cheddar. When he isn't writing or teaching, you're likely to find him enjoying the garden or studying historically informed performance on the French horn.

Visit Nicholas at **TheLuminousPearl.com.**

BOOKS ABOUT CRYSTALS
BY NICHOLAS PEARSON

Crystal Basics Pocket Encyclopedia: The Energetic, Healing, and Spiritual Power of 450 Gemstones (2023)

Crystal Basics: The Energetic, Healing, and Spiritual Power of 200 Gemstones (2020)

Stones of the Goddess: 104 Crystals for the Divine Feminine (2019)

Crystal Healing for the Heart: Gemstone Therapy for Physical, Emotional, and Spiritual Well-Being (2017)

Crystals for Karmic Healing: Transform Your Future by Releasing Your Past (2017)

The Seven Archetypal Stones: Their Spiritual Powers and Teachings (2016)

MORE BOOKS
BY NICHOLAS PEARSON

Flower Essences from the Witch's Garden: Plant Spirits in Magickal Herbalism (2022)

Foundations of Reiki Ryōhō: A Manual of Shoden and Okuden (2018)